W9-ADH-353

Trust and Betrayal in Educational Administration and Leadership

Routledge Research in Education

For a full list of title in this series, please visit www.routledge.com

Trust and Betrayal in Educational Administration and Leadership

Edited by Eugenie A. Samier
and Michèle Schmidt

Routledge
Taylor & Francis Group
New York   London

First published 2010
by Routledge
270 Madison Avenue, New York, NY 10016

Simultaneously published in the UK
by Routledge
2 Park Square, Milton Park, Abingdon, Oxon OX14 4RN

Routledge is an imprint of the Taylor & Francis Group, an informa business

Typeset in Sabon by IBT Global.
Printed and bound in the United States of America on acid-free paper by IBT Global.

Library of Congress Cataloging in Publication Data
    Trust and betrayal in educational administration and leadership / edited by Eugenie
A. Samier and Michèle Schmidt.
        p. cm.—(Routledge research in education ; v. 36)
    Includes bibliographical references and index.
    1. School management and organization—Moral and ethical aspects.   2. Educational
leadership—Moral and ethical aspects.   3. Trust.   4. Organizational behavior.   I. Samier,
Eugénie Angèle, 1954-   II. Schmidt, Michèle.
    LB2806.T777 2010
    371.2—dc22
    2009044221

ISBN13: 978-0-415-87340-6 (hbk)
ISBN13: 978-0-203-85241-5 (ebk)

Contents

PART II:
Research Approaches

PART III:
Critical and Current Issues

Figures

Tables

Editors' Introductions

The Interdisciplinary Foundation of Trust

From Trustworthiness to Betrayal

Eugenie A. Samier

> In modern society, particularly in organizations, we have to trust the
> decision makers to act rightly because we cannot monitor everything
> they do. We trust them in part because we trust the people charged
> with overseeing them. When both the decision makers and their over-
> seers betray our trust, the violation is more than just a double failure
> of individual responsibility. It points to a systematic problem of insti-
> tutional responsibility.
>
> (Thompson 2005: 245)

Trust is part of all relationships in education. Parents and students trust, or
at least hope to trust, in teachers and administrators to foster environments
in which teacher–pupil and teacher–parent trust can form and professional
development and learning can take place. In universities, students, faculty,
staff, and research subjects trust in each other and the senior administration, senate, and boards of governors to maintain standards, provide adequate facilities, and follow principles of administrative law, natural justice,
international codes on academic freedom, labour codes, research policies,
and the policies of the organization. And those in the educational system
trust in government to provide adequate funding and regulatory regimes to
protect their interests.

Trust is expected, but of what does it consist? How does one gain trust,
how does one lose it, and how is it regained? Trust in what, for what purpose?
Under what circumstances? What are the legally required trusts, and what
are the legal and institutional constraints? How do organizational culture and
politics affect it? How does it change under demographic shifts, multiculturalism, civil rights, and codes of tolerance? What is the public trust, and what
relationship does it have to these? How much of one's role is bound to it? How
does one's character and personality play in it? And what trust in society generally is placed on the educational institution to fulfill its role and responsibilities? These, of course, vary considerably depending upon a number of factors,
such as social and cultural values, economic factors, and political regime.

The recent decline in trust in government, professions, and the private sector noted by Thompson (2005: 248) equally affects education
(see Groundwater-Smith and Sachs 2002). Suspicion and mistrust extend

to government officials and departments of education, regional and local administrative agencies, and the management of schools themselves. And it is not only distrust of administrators, but their overseers, the superintendents, university boards of governors, regulatory officials, and politicians who have the added challenge of restoring trust in an era already fraught with financial constraint and mastering the market model that has come to dominate education. A number of organizational failures have eroded public trust in public and private sector organizations, some with educational responsibilities, such as the failure of financial institutions and Catholic Church scandals (see Kramer and Cook 2004: 2).

The failure of administrators and leaders to live up to moral standards has played a strong role in the recent focus on ethics in public and educational administration that documents the many abuses such as Adams and Balfour's *Unmasking Administrative Evil* (1998) in public administration, Ackerman and Maslin-Ostrowski's *The Wounded Leader* (2002), analysing the damaging effects that the principalship can have on its incumbents, and Blase and Blase's *Breaking the Silence: Overcoming the Problem of Principal Mistreatment of Teachers* (2003), examining insensitivity, harassment, and abuse that teachers can suffer at the hands of their administrators. At the university level, bullying and mobbing have been the subject of an increasingly international literature.

Clearly trust and the related concepts of distrust and betrayal are complex phenomena composed of moral, emotional, social, cultural, and political factors, stretching from the individual, through interpersonal relations, organizational structures, and the macrostructures of society, and articulated through various statutory and regulatory mechanisms among societal sectors. It is clearly a phenomenon that requires an inter- and multidisciplinary approach: since the mid-1980s, the problem of trust has experienced a 'dramatic resurgence', led primarily by economics, organization theory, political science, and sociology (see Kramer and Isen 1994), followed by psychology and philosophy (primarily in ethics). Trust is often referred to in discussions of educational leadership ethics, appearing in a list of core values, related at least implicitly to team-work and collegiality, indicating that people should have a moral disposition to trust and be trusted; however, the concept has received little conceptual and contextualized development in education compared to its treatment in primary disciplines. This volume attempts to explore many of these facets as they apply to educational settings internationally; contributing to theory development in educational administration, management, and leadership; to the models and standards of roles, identity, and practices; and to research agendas.

The trust literature is now so large that no chapter can do justice to outlining the range of definitions, approaches, and conceptions involved. This chapter has been designed to provide some overview of many of the more prominent authors and features of the trust discussion that have relevance for educational administration and leadership.

THE NATURE AND STRUCTURE OF TRUST

Conceptually, the nature and structure of trust are complex in a number of ways. First, it is not a unitary concept, but is necessarily related to mistrust or distrust and betrayal. These collectively connote a range of related concepts having to do with confidence in others and one's self, suspicion, risk, affect, calculative decision-making, faith, belief, and interaction rituals. It is important to note in these discussions that it is not just a matter of trusting and not trusting, but distinguishing those one can trust about particular matters under particular conditions from those one can't. For a number of authors, such as Hardin (2002), trust is a complex concept consisting of a three-part relationship among the truster, the trustee, and the setting or transactional domain in which they are embedded, where the context facilitates determining whether the truster can be trustworthy in the context, that is, have ongoing commitment.

As an inter- and multidisciplinary topic, it is related to many concepts in other disciplines. For example, from a political point of view it is related to conceptions of authority, power (e.g., Cook, Hardin, and Levi 2005; Luhmann 1979), hierarchy, and ideologies. Farrell, commenting on the lack of discussion on trust and power, offers two criteria that need to be met in a theory of the relationship between trust and power: 'it should account for the difficulties of maintaining trust in a situation of extreme disparities of power' as well as 'accommodate trust in relationships in which disparities of power exist . . . but are less marked', and 'be able to distinguish between those social situations in which power drives out trust', leading to distrust, and those 'in which power and trust are not mutually exclusive' (2004: 86). Some book collections aim at a complex approach, reflecting the necessity for a multidisciplinary treatment such as Kramer and Cook's intentionally including contributions from social psychology, sociology, political science, and economics, as well as representing a diversity of professional settings and both quantitative and qualitative research methodologies (2004: 3).

The philosophical literature on trust is extensive; much of it lays a groundwork for direct extension to administration and leadership. Baier is one of the most notable in the field, the most influential of her writings being 'Trust and Antitrust' (1986), where she argues against a rational and contractarian approach, and *Moral Prejudices* (1995), where she explains how trust necessarily involves vulnerability, including not only the trust that others will act where appropriate, but that they will refrain from acting out of 'ill will'. There are many problems in relying upon another's good will; there are many reasons for this not being sufficient for trustworthiness: manipulation (Baier 1986; Holton 1994), unwelcome trust (Jones 1996), and benevolence motivated by factors other than trust such as social norms (Jones 1996; McLeod 2002).

Holton views trust as an attitude, 'a distinctive state of mind', that interacts with belief and will in trusting, rather than simply relying upon, a person to do something. It involves holding a participant stance towards another that carries the possibility of betrayal (1994: 63, 67). Hardin (2002) has contributed an important distinction between trust and trustworthiness, demonstrating that most discussions are actually about the latter concept. The philosophical literature also raises many questions about what one trusts others for, when one trusts (under what circumstances that are possible and appropriate or justified), and trusting those one does not personally know. This latter is most important in organizations or social institutions where most individuals will never personally know those in senior authority positions. And does one trust on the basis of their formal obligations, on their personality, character, assumed motivations, and intentions? Potter argues that those who comply with behavioural norms in order to avoid legal sanctions, such as suppressing sexism in the workplace, are not genuinely trustworthy (2002: 5).

An important strand in the philosophical literature is the epistemology of trust: what knowledge one must have in order to justifiably trust, and trusting whether the other knows that they are a trustee or not. This field includes important questions about how much one can believe another's 'testimony' (Hardwig 1991; Jones 1999). Trusting is not simply a rational process because it inherently involves risk and creates a resistance to evidence that could compromise one's optimism about a trustee (Jones 1996). We are also limited in how much of one's daily life can be subjected to a rational reflection on evidence (Webb 1993). The evidentiary approach is fraught with problems: bias, partiality, unconscious motivations, selective perception, self-deception, lack of sufficient evidence.

From a psychological perspective, Becker advances a non-cognitive theory of trust to complement the dominant cognitive approach, that is, 'a sense of security about other people's benevolence, conscientiousness, and reciprocity' based on 'trustful attitudes, affects, emotions, or motivational structures that are not focused on specific people, institutions, or groups'. In contrast, cognitive trust is based on 'beliefs or expectations about others' trustworthiness . . . in some or all situations'—that is, strategic choices (1996: 43, 44, 45) or 'calculative trust' (see Gambetta 1988). Three forms of trust Becker uses for his discussion, which have non-cognitive and cognitive forms and are particularly relevant for organization studies, are: credulity, 'a disposition to believe what another person says and to banish skeptical thoughts'; reliance, 'a disposition to depend upon other people in some respect' and 'banish fear of such dependence'; and security, 'a disposition to have confidence about other people's motives [and] to banish suspicious thoughts about them' (1996: 45–46). Frowe points out that both have limitations in professional trust: cognitive trust is aimed at acquiring enough information to reduce risk, the logical conclusion of which is that trust is no longer required (and virtually impossible to achieve); non-cognitive trust can lead to naivety and a very high level of risk. In practical terms, we cannot avoid trusting many individuals and social institutions, and, therefore, are always at risk of betrayal (2005: 39; Becker 1996).

Jones argues that a theory of trust based in affect covers a broader range of trusting and is freed of evidentialism for justification (1996: 5); however, affect and emotion are highly unreliable ways of establishing trust due to emotional complexity, unknown factors, and their unconscious nature. Some interesting aspects of expectations of trust are raised in Jones's argument, which include the coercive and unwelcome form of trust others can impose, possibly one causal factor in group-think and the manipulative aspects of team-work or where followers attach a 'saviour' role to a new leadership incumbent. At times, professionals have to reject clients on the basis of their unreasonable trust expectations. Another limitation lies in persistent trusting in strong affective relationships, such as friendship, where one is repeatedly let down: administrators or leaders who create affective bonds in subordinates motivated emotionally to continue to trust despite evidence of untrustworthiness are situations seen in the psychoanalytic critique of neurotic leadership.

Trust is necessary to the very fabric of society, and its social institutions. As Flores and Solomon (1998) note, it is the establishment of trust that is a basic requirement in transition societies, like the former Soviet bloc, that accompanies the building of a new polity and economy, as well as established democracies. As they also note, managers are not comfortable talking about trust due partly to the lack of control inherent to trust and its risks, yet it is frequently incurred in discussions about organizational renewal. Trust is also assumed in the current leadership fad in public sector administration, yet inadequately addressed in the sense that Flores and Solomon understand it: a quality of interaction and relationship that requires initiation, maintenance, and restoration rather than the more common understanding of trust as a 'medium', 'ground', 'atmosphere', or climate' that operates on different levels—simple trust, basic trust, authentic trust, and blind trust, which is 'trust without warrant, foolish trust' (1998: 206).

The context within which institutions and organizations operate has a strong influence. Papadakis examines the social, political, and cultural factors that shape trust in Australian institutions in the form of confidence and those practices that 'sustain trust in government', such as changing cultural attitudes and economic transformations (1999: 75, 77). His findings indicate that some factors one would assume increase trust levels, such as economic influence, in fact, do not, whereas 'perceptions of inefficiency and wastefulness, spending money on the wrong things, concessions to special interests, and politicians' lack of integrity' create distrust (1999: 77). In economic theory, trust plays a role in fiduciary relationships, coping with risk, and uncertainty in exchange relationships, game theory, calculating transaction costs, and rational decision-making (Lane 1998: 3–4), as well as characterizing 'transactional' leadership styles.

In sociology, trust is examined as values, norms, and fiduciary responsibilities, in the social exchange theory of Simmel (1900/1978) and Blau (1967), the ethnomethodology of Garfinkel (1984), systems theory of Luhmann (1979), structuration theory of Giddens (1984), and neo-institutionalism of Zucker (1986) (see Lane 1998: 8–12). Luhmann's work has been particularly influential recently, arguing that the 'internal' dimension of trust is not simply an analogy with cognition (see 1979: 79), and in maintaining a distinction between trust and confidence (see 1988: 94–107). Multicultural factors also heavily affect the way trust is conceptualized, expressed, and institutionalized (e.g., Markova and Gillespie 2008). An example of comparative studies in trust are Yamagishi and Yamagishi (1994), who demonstrate that Americans are generally more trusting than Japanese in business relations, place a higher value on reputation, consider themselves more honest and fair, and note that public trust also varies by social location, that is, by age-group, gender, and educational level.

From a political perspective, trust has appeared in a number of discussions ranging from interpersonal politics in organizations (e.g. Potter 2002) to the politics of suspicion (Webb 1992), the importance of trust in democratic systems (Warren 1999), including the role of education in creating democratic relationships (Macedo 2003), problems of distrust in eroding democratic institutions (Ely 1980; Rosanvallon 2008), and trusting relationships necessary in international relations for overcoming conflict and establishing international agencies (Child 1998; Hoffman 2006), not a small consideration in an era of university internationalization. Nye and Zelikow (1997) examine how the loss of public trust in one area usually transfers to loss in other interrelated areas—pride and belief in nation, democracy, institution, electoral process, and political leaders' authority—demonstrating that not all loss of trust in education originates with this institution, but also that loss of trust in educators can transfer to other important social institutions. In the political discussion is located social contract theory of trust in which one carries out 'risk-assessment' based on calculating another's self-interest in being trustworthy (Jones 1999: 68), however, this assumes that people behave only out of self-interest rather than having a complex psychology of motivation that includes contradiction and unconscious motivation.

An important political dimension is the feminist perspective, represented in Baier (1995), Govier (1992), Potter (2002), and Orbell, Dawes, and Schwartz-Shea (1994). The last demonstrated in their study of participation rates in the prisoner's dilemma game through social categories that women are expected to be more trusted to co-operate than men in general, suggesting that gender differences play a strong role in people's judgments about contracts, promises, and agreements in social life. However, they also found that judging another to be co-operative in an anticipated activity was higher for particular male and female individuals than for a gender category, in other words, on a case-by-case basis. Their review of the empirical literature on gender and co-operation reveals inconclusivity: some studies do find a higher level of co-operation among women, which is what most of the leadership literature assumes, yet there are many studies that show no difference between genders, or that men are more co-operative. Given the range of experimental designs, though, the object of the trust and its context may produce average or general gender differences.

Distrust has received some recent attention in management studies. In popular literature, two of the more notable are Ciulla's *The Working Life: The Promise and Betrayal of Modern Work* (2000) and Reina and Reina's *Trust and Betrayal in the Workplace* (2006). Ciulla's, though, is a much more thoughtful discussion, grounded in philosophy, the empirical record of history, and management practice, as well as contextual considerations, focused on the development of character in creating and sustaining trust relationships and the changed nature of work that no longer provides the meaningful experience and values necessary to healthy employment or professional life. One of the key concerns is central to educational administration and leadership under current neo-liberal conditions: 'problems arise when professionals act or are made to act like business people', driven by self-interest that erodes an 'implicit "public vow to society"', and loyalty to one's colleagues and organization (Ciulla 2000: 68, 99). Administrative features of this transformation are the replacement of work ethic by personnel departments and morality by morale or the motivation to work, the myth that people think and create well in groups, and managerial control masquerading as empowerment programmes or team-work (2000: 109, 112, 136, 139). These effects can have a magnified effect on universities, where intrinsic motivation is important, and individual thought and creativity to scholarship are both important in sustaining academic freedom.

Distrust, like trust, is a function of culture, understood and expressed in different ways, due to history, societal conflict and complexities, belief systems, ideologies, patterns of social interaction, and the institutional structures of a society including its laws and customs. Form contributed to the international comparison of trust quite early in a 1974 article that outlines many differences that are now equally recognized within multicultural states, including some cases of inter- and intracommunity and organizational conflict where a researcher may very well be taken as a spy for competitors for influence or enemy organizations. Form singles out bureaucratic distrust for extensive discussion. Given the power at the top of bureaucratic hierarchies, if a single highly placed individual is resistant to research, then there will be no co-operation at any level of the organization (1974: 42–43).

Betrayal is the opposite of trust: in relationships in which trust is required, the possibility of betrayal always coexists. It also has many motivations, as do most things, given, as Turnaturi explains, the complexity and ambiguity in every individual, interaction, and relationship: 'passions and interests, opposing representations of oneself and of others, contradictory but simultaneous needs for membership and separation, and a desire for collectivity and singularity, for protection and emancipation, for trust and for distance—are interwoven in a thousand ways, and they can give rise to infinite types of betrayal' (2007: 1). Some are probably more common in administration and leadership, such as ambition, vengeance, jealousy, and insecurity. They are part and parcel of organizational micropolitics, toxic cultures, and environments in which competition is a cardinal value. It is also likely in organizations that require many to be dependent upon others for the processing of important documents or information, approvals, and support, trusting that they will be competent, vigilant, fair, and motivated by good will.

Turnaturi describes betrayal as an act of deluding others by behaviour contrary to expectations and accepted standards and failing to: fulfill duties or moral or juridical obligations; be faithful and loyal; keep secrets or confidences; or keep a pact (2007: 7–8). While the impact of betrayal on a targeted individual can be much greater than that of mistrust, mistrust is perhaps more pernicious organizationally than betrayal—it can pervade the atmosphere, leading to a condition of uncertainty and ambiguity. When one is betrayed, specific individuals and events allow one to know with greater certainty who is responsible. Mistrust impairs the general organizational culture, interpersonal relationships, and all aspects of work.

CONCLUSION

Trust, as many of the commentators on this topic note, takes a long time to form authentically, and once lost is almost impossible to recover. Bottery identifies may of the conditions required at the governmental level: a change in policies or even legislation and the ideology from which they issue, as well as the organizational structures, such as agencies or branches of departments; job design through evaluative positions; personnel turnover or reassignments; and the standards or criteria by which practice is judged, in particular a shift away from calculative trust (2003: 256–57).

On an institutional level, Thompson proposes a position that initially seems counterintuitive, and certainly runs against the general flow of trust discussion, yet is a crucial consideration for those in positions of power and authority, whether in a senior administrative, leadership, or governance role. He claims that the restoration of distrust is required in practical ethics for the 'organization-dominated public life in which we now live and work'. This requires replacing individual-level trust with an institutional form based on distrust for which monitoring positions or agencies are created, drawing on principles of government established by Hume, and reflected by Madison in the US in the Federalist Papers (2005: 249). In cases Thompson examines—Enron, the Catholic Church, and the FBI—the overseers are not culpable in the same sense as the offenders. The latter were condemned in the language of individualist ethics, evidencing character flaws and vices, and who acted 'deliberately and with full knowledge of what they were doing' (2005: 250). The overseers, on the other hand, did not have the same bad character, did not do wrong deliberately or with 'full knowledge of the consequences' (2005: 250). Yet it is at the overseer levels that ultimate governance, leadership, and administrative responsibility lies.

REFERENCES

Ackerman, R., and Maslin-Ostrowski, P. (2002) *The Wounded Leader.* San Francisco: Jossey-Bass.
Adams, G., and Balfour, D. (1998) *Unmasking Administrative Evil.* Thousand Oaks, CA: Sage.
Baier, A. (1986) 'Trust and antitrust'. *Ethics* 96 (2): 231–60.
———. (1995) *Moral Prejudices: Essays on Ethics.* Cambridge, MA: Harvard University Press.
Becker, L. (1996) 'Trust as noncognitive security about motives'. *Ethics* 107 (1): 43–61.
Blase, J., and Blase, J. (2003) *Breaking the Silence: Overcoming the Problem of Principal Mistreatment of Teachers.* Thousand Oaks, CA: Corwin.
Blau, P. (1967) *Exchange and Power in Social Life.* London: John Wiley.
Bottery, M. (2003) 'The management and mismanagement of trust'. *Educational Management, Administration & Leadership* 31 (3): 245–61.
Child, J. (1998) 'Trust and international strategic alliances: The case of Sino-foreign joint ventures'. In *Trust Within and Between Organizations*, ed. C. Lane and R. Bachmann. Oxford: Oxford University Press.
Ciulla, J. (2000) *The Working Life: The Promise and Betrayal of Modern Work.* New York: Three Rivers Press.
Cook, K., Hardin, R., and Levi, M. (2005) *Cooperation without Trust?* New York: Russell Sage Foundation.
Ely, J. (1980) *Democracy and Distrust: A Theory of Judicial Review.* Cambridge, MA: Harvard University Press.
Farrell, H. (2004) 'Trust, distrust, and power'. In *Distrust*, ed. R. Hardin. New York: Russell Sage Foundation.
Flores, F., and Solomon, R. (1998) 'Creating trust'. *Business Ethics Quarterly* 8 (2): 205–32.
Form, W. (1974) 'The politics of distrust: Field problems in comparative research'. *Studies in Comparative International Development* 9 (1): 20–48.
Frowe, I. (2005) 'Professional trust'. *British Journal of Educational Studies* 53 (1): 34–53.
Gambetta, D. (1988) 'Can we trust trust?' In *Trust: Making and Breaking Cooperative Relations*, ed. D. Gambetta. Oxford: Basil Blackwell.
Garfinkel, H. (1984) *Studies in Ethnomethodology.* Cambridge: Polity Press.
Giddens, A. (1984) *The Constitution of Society.* Cambridge: Polity Press.
Govier, T. (1992) 'Trust, distrust, and feminist theory'. *Hypatia* 7 (1): 16–33.
Groundwater-Smith, S., and Sachs, J. (2002) 'The activist professional and the reinstatement of trust'. *Cambridge Journal of Education* 32 (3): 341–58.
Hardin, R. (2002) *Trust and Trustworthiness.* New York: Russell Sage Foundation.
Hardwig, J. (1991) 'The role of trust in knowledge'. *Journal of Philosophy* 88 (12): 693–708.
Hoffman, A. (2006) *Building Trust: Overcoming Suspicion in International Conflict.* Albany: SUNY.
Holton, R. (1994) 'Deciding to trust, coming to believe'. *Australasian Journal of Philosophy* 72 (1): 63–76.
Jones, K. (1996) 'Trust as an affective attitude'. *Ethics* 107 (1): 4–25.
———. (1999) 'Second-hand moral knowledge'. *Journal of Philosophy* 96 (2): 55–78.

12   *Eugenie A. Samier*

Kramer, R., and Cook, K. (2004) 'Trust and distrust in organizations: Dilemmas and approaches'. In *Trust and Distrust in Organizations: Dilemmas and Approaches*, ed. R. Kramer and K. Cook. New York: Russell Sage Foundation.

Kramer, R., and Isen, A. (1994) 'Trust and distrust: Its psychological and social dimensions'. *Motivation and Emotion* 18 (2): 105–7.

Lane, C. (1998) 'Introduction: Theories and issues in the study of trust'. In *Trust within and between Organizations*, ed. C. Lane and R. Bachmann. Oxford: Oxford University Press.

Luhmann, N. (1979) *Trust and Power*. Chichester: John Wiley and Sons.

———. (1988) 'Familiarity, confidence, trust: Problems and alternatives'. In *Trust: Making and Breaking Cooperative Relations*, ed. D. Gambetta. New York: Blackwell.

Macedo, S. (2003) *Diversity and Distrust: Civic Education in a Multicultural Democracy*. Cambridge: Harvard University Press.

Markova, I., and Gillespie, A. (eds.) (2008) *Trust and Distrust: Sociocultural Perspectives*. Charlotte, NC: Information Age.

McLeod, C. (2002) *Self-Trust and Reproductive Autonomy*. Cambridge: MIT Press.

Nye, J., and Zelikow, P. (1997) 'Conclusion: Reflections, conjectures, and puzzles'. In *Why People Don't Trust Government*, ed. J. Nye and P. Zelikow. Cambridge, MA: Harvard University Press.

Orbell, J., Dawes, R., and Schwartz-Shea, P. (1994) 'Trust, social categories, and individuals: The case of gender'. *Motivation and Emotion* 18 (2): 109–28.

Papadakis, E. (1999) 'Constituents of confidence and mistrust in Australian institutions'. *Australian Journal of Political Science* 34 (1): 75–93.

Potter, N.N. (2002) *How Can I be Trusted? A Virtue Theory of Trustworthiness*. Lanham: Rowman & Littlefield.

Reina, D., and Reina, M. (2006) *Trust and Betrayal in the Workplace*. 2nd ed. San Francisco: Berrett—Koehler.

Rosanvallon, P. (2008) *Counter-Democracy: Politics in an Age of Distrust*. Trans. A. Goldhammer. Cambridge: Cambridge University Press.

Simmel, G. (1900/1978) *The Philosophy of Money*. London: Routledge & Kegan Paul.

Thompson, D.F. (2005) *Restoring Responsibility: Ethics in Government, Business, and Healthcare*. Cambridge: Cambridge University Press.

Turnaturi, G. (2007) *Betrayals: The Unpredictability of Human Relations*. Trans. L. Cochrane. Chicago: University of Chicago Press.

Warren, M. (ed.) (1999) *Democracy and Trust*. Cambridge: Cambridge University Press.

Webb, M. (1992) 'The epistemology of trust and the politics of suspicion'. *Pacific Philosophical Quarterly* 73:390–400.

———. (1993) 'Why I know about as much as you: A reply to Hardwig'. *Journal of Philosophy* 90 (5): 260–70.

Yamagishi, T., and Yamagishi, M. (1994) 'Trust and commitment in the United States and Japan'. *Motivation and Emotion* 18 (2): 129–66.

Zucker, L. (1986) 'Production of trust: Institutional sources of economic structure, 1840–1920'. *Research in Organizational Behavior* 8 (1): 53–111.

Theoretical, Practical, and Research Perspectives of Trust in Educational Administration and Leadership

Michèle Schmidt

The purpose of this introduction is to present some background on the topic of trust in educational administration. While the scope of this topic is far too broad to be definitively discussed here, this introduction will provide a brief overview of key themes emerging on this topic at the school and higher education level as well as some of the challenges encountered not only by educators and leaders but also researchers. The chapter is intended to demonstrate the relevance of trust in the theory and practice of the field, that is, the successes and challenges as documented so far in the literature. As such, the focus is on the application of trust as it affects our understanding of, and practice in, educational organizations.

THE STUDY OF TRUST IN EDUCATIONAL ADMINISTRATION AND LEADERSHIP

One of the first challenges, then, is definitional. Even identifying the quality of trust is challenging. Neither of these conceptual tasks is straightforward. In fact, trust involves many disciplines and traditions as well as conceptual challenges beyond the scope of this volume. Nevertheless, the authors make an important contribution to theorizing and practically applying trust in educational administration. Each of the authors has explicitly or implicitly selected some definitional construct within which to base their discussion. While Samier's introduction focused primarily on the foundational theories of trust, this second introduction focuses more on the conceptualization and applicability of trust within the educational administration arena. Needless to say, the study of trust in educational administration and leadership covers a range of approaches and is mired in many theoretical, practical, and research problems.

One of the most common examinations of trust is that between head teachers or principals and their teaching staff. More emergent literature revolves around trust throughout the entire district level and in higher education itself, where it is seen primarily in emotional and moral terms. In addition, the notion of trust typically remains a relatively unambiguous attribute with which to build capacity, implement reforms, increase student achievement, et cetera. We maintain, however, that such a view is myopic. In fact, while there is no doubt a plethora of literature on the topic of trust and education, there is little discussion of the economic, sociological, or legal forms of trust. The extant literature also tends to treat trust as a binary rather than gradient value, that is, one either trusts or does not trust, instead of giving a more accurate depiction of trust which differs from situation to situation, or variable as to the object of trust. Issues such as mistrust and betrayal are also frequently not addressed; the socio-cultural, psychological, economic, and micropolitical impediments to trust such as vested political and social interests, or contextual patterns and structures that obstruct trust, remain downplayed; and the implications of trust related to government policy and external societal and global conditions are under-theorized. This volume intends to ameliorate this gap in the literature by bringing together thoughtful empirical and theoretical chapters that conceptualize trust using a number of theoretical lenses, some including empirical research and doing so at all levels of educational administration, that is, public school, public district, and higher education.

TRUST IN EDUCATIONAL ADMINISTRATION AND LEADERSHIP

There are many claims which assert that trust is a key factor in school effectiveness. The problem in constructing a theory or model of administrative and leadership practice in enhancing trust, however, is that its effectiveness has been measured in so many ways: operational success by Beeson and Matthews (1993); productivity by Bruhn (2001); student achievement by Bryk and Schneider (2002); positive climate by Goddard, Tschannen-Moran, and Hoy (2001); productive communication by Henkin and Dee (2001); teacher–principal relationship by Tschannen-Moran and Hoy (1998); teacher commitment and team-work (for governance, instructional, and planning teams) by Park, Henkin, and Egley (2005) and Dee and Henkin (2001); and collaboration by Tschannen-Moran (2004), to name only a few examples.

Overall, however, the discussion of trust remains limited in the field of educational administration compared to the general management literature. In addition, long-standing topics dealing with very current problems such as narcissism and other personality issues, toxic culture, and micropolitical disorders, are virtually absent from the educational administration literature. Furthermore, as the theoretical gap widens, robustness in the research methods employed seems to diminish since much of the research conducted is positivistic and experimental—empirical with a reliance on bureaucratic organizational theory rather than hermeneutic or phenomenological empirical (see Mintzberg 1989). What seems to be missing is a discussion distinguishing between structures and roles in different organizations that have a high proportion of professionals and opportunities to account for the many dimensions of trust.

For the most part, it is not clear in the literature on educational administration how the term 'trust' has been conceptualized or defined. For example, it is often associated with empowerment, as in Blase and Blase (2001), necessary in providing the co-operation, effective communion, shared governance, and openness that empowerment requires. Their main source for a definition of trust is Covey's *Seven Habits of Highly Effective People* (1989), which hails from the management spectrum of organizations, is grounded in limited empirical evidence, and is not easily replicable or conceptually developed in the education organizational arena. Further to this, Bryk and Schneider (2002) propose a theory of 'relational trust', a concept that has become highly influential in the field, emanating from social exchanges that involve high levels of respect, integrity, competence, and empathy. Alternatively, there exists 'organic trust', a concept that evolves from unquestioning acceptance of the moral authority of an institution. This perspective of trust, Bryk and Schneider (2002) argue, requires a consensus about beliefs, including moral values, that often is not effective in diverse and inclusive settings. They also criticize 'contractual trust' for being instrumental, thereby being too narrow for the complexity of a school environment and its educational goals.

Of all of the aforementioned definitions of trust, relational trust to have enough breadth in possibilities to encompass teachers, administrators, and parents, and to provide 'a set of organizational conditions, some structural and others social—psychological, that make it more conducive for individuals to initiate and sustain' activities and which 'undergirds a highly efficient system of social control where extensive supervision of individuals' work is not required, and shirking behavior remains minimal' (Bryk and Schneider 2002: 35, 116). While limited in its reliance on conformity, control, and consensus, it has thus far proven successful as an educational administration tool. For example, Forsyth, Barnes, and Adams's (2006) quantitative study of parent–teacher trust, based on Bryk and Schneider's (2002) relational model in enhancing school effectiveness, provides a detailed study of trust-effectiveness patterns. They adopt Hoy and Tschannen-Moran's definition of trust as the 'willingness to be vulnerable to another party based on the confidence that the latter party is benevolent, reliable, competent, honest, and open' (1999, cited in Bryk and Schneider 2002: 130). While their main focus in examining the effects of trust on formalized and centralized structures was on parent trust in schools, they also examined teacher trust of the principal and other teachers. Forsyth, Barnes, and Adams stressed the dependence teachers have on colleagues and administrators for relations that allow them to develop effective professionalism and empowerment that work in tandem or might replace a reliance on 'bureaucratic mechanisms of control . . . and check[s] the proliferation of rules and close supervision' (2006: 127).

Varying types, levels, or degrees of trust exist which this volume discusses in detail. Yet, for the sake of illustration, Moye, Henkin, and Egley (2005) surveyed an American urban school district's elementary schoolteachers using measures of psychological empowerment and affect and cognition-based trust. The findings revealed that teachers who felt trusted and empowered found their work personally meaningful, exercised significant professional autonomy, and had significantly higher levels of trust in their school principals than other teachers. Park, Henkin, and Egley (2005) used a survey instrument with school-teachers to examine the relationship between trust and commitment for team-work: the results suggested the importance of trust. San Antonio and Gamage (2007) examined the empirical relationship between Participatory School Administration, Leadership and Management (PSALM) and trust levels among stakeholders in the Philippines within a democratic framework from Dewey, drawing on an increasing body of literature that has argued for the importance of trust in creating productive participation of membership in school communities (e.g., Blase and Blase 2001; Bryk and Rollow 1992; Tschannen-Moran 2001). While school achievement levels did not improve, participants did report improved communication and working relationships.

The aforementioned examples are not exhaustive, yet they do reveal the importance of trust and also some of the challenges in researching it. One of the limitations of these studies, as with many others, is that trust is taken to be a distinctive element rather than a dimension of relationships. In other words, there is little investigation into the varying conceptions of trust that participants hold, and types or levels of trust are not distinguished. Another problem that emerges from a review of the literature is that trust in education seems to be often valued only in terms of effectiveness measured in output terms, rather than in terms of ethics, quality of life, personality development, et cetera. And it is not clear whether trust is a causal factor in all of these studies or the result of other causal factors. Finally, trust is frequently treated as a panacea for all kinds of administrative and organizational ills.

Despite these conceptual problems, however, there is clear evidence in the literature that trust has numerous positive effects. For example, Blase and Blase (2001) have claimed that a trusting environment allows people to deal better with organizational problems that result in increased levels of school performance. The good news is that despite the dearth of studies that supercede the effects of trust, research is currently emerging that provides a step in the right direction in our study of trust in education. For example, in terms of the positive effect of trust, Siegall and Worth (2001) report on increased faculty productivity when the faculty is able to trust the administration. Groundwater-Smith and Sachs see the creation of trust among school professionals for community building as an alternative reaction to the market model of schooling or a model of education as an industry or an entrepreneurial business in compliance with bureaucratic surveillance used in the recent private sector–style accountability regimes that are predicated upon inherent distrust. The bureaucratic domination of professional expertise and practice are an effect of the 'audit society' in which 'the more intense the gaze of the audit, the less the trust invested in the moral competence of the practitioners to respond to the needs of those they serve' (2002: 341). Goddard (2003) maintains that where there is evidence of teacher trust and student achievement as a form of social capital, education can rise above the market model just depicted. Other studies that have found a positive correlation between teacher trust and academic achievement in students include Bandura (1993); Bryk and Schneider (2002); Goddard, Hoy, and Woolfolk (2000); Goddard, Tschannen-Moran, and Hoy (2001); Goddard, Hoy, and LoGerfo (2003); Ross, Hogaboam-Gray, and Gray (2004); and Tartar, Sabo, and Hoy (1995). In their study of Catholic schools, Bryk, Lee, and Holland (1993) found that a trusting environment allows teachers to feel affirmed and empowered in their work, to believe in a 'collective efficaciousness', and be able to dispel fears and vulnerabilities. Furthermore, trust allows for engaged teaching and positive school outcomes. Seashore (2003: 29) found in a case analysis that low trust in administrators was 'associated with lower cohesion'. Tarter, Sabo, and Hoy found that 'trust in the principal and trust in colleagues independently move the organization toward effectiveness' (1995: 47).

Similar to problematic issues of conceptualization at the school level, trust has emerged as a problematic in the higher education literature. For example, Aasen and Stensaker (2007) report on participants' perspectives on leadership training programmes for academics from a number of Western European countries. The main desire on their part was a new collegial form of governance integrated into university culture. This might allow for a 'trustful' mediation process between external demands on the organization and its internal values and potential. This is particularly true within the context of the new public management, globalization, and the market model for education to overcome the internal hierarchical power divisions. Gasman et al. (2004) found, in their study of African American graduate students and non–African American faculty members who attempt to provide support through shared values of inclusivity, that race, gender, and status (professor, student) can create difficult professional environments. During the course of the study, the importance of trust arose in several forms: trust had to develop among teaching and student members in overcoming some initial resistance to the study due to negative past experience, in engaging in a personally risky form of sensitive reporting, and overcoming the barriers of status for students and professors in full collaboration engagement. Most importantly, trust was required to establish new relationships 'based on honesty, equity, reciprocity, respect, and integrity' (2004: 708). A related body of literature examines cultural mistrust, particularly along racial differences, such as Phelps, Taylor, and Gerard (2001) who found that Black students (in contrast to African and West Indian/

Caribbean) scored high on mistrust of Whites in education, training, and interpersonal relations, inhibiting their willingness to engage.

In conclusion, it becomes evident that trust is multilayered and remains elusive within the field of education. The positive impact of trust is clearer, yet the challenges of understanding, defining, and researching trust are numerous. While the research seems to yield primarily quantitative empirical work exploring the effects of trust, casting a wider net in the exploration of the dynamic of trust to include dimensions of varied meanings and types according to individual, situation, and context is needed.

CHAPTER OVERVIEWS

The first part, 'Theoretical Foundations', includes discussion of various definitions of trust that emerge primarily from a sociological perspective. A differentiation is made between familial and the social trust found in organizations. For example, Bolton and English's chapter argues that trust emerges from emotions and is intertwined with cognition in educational leaders' decision-making. A second focus in this part draws from social theorists such as Bourdieu (1986), Coleman (1987), and Putnam (1995) who are necessary to a discussion of trust as a critical component of social capital in Schmidt's chapter in this volume. Finally, Samier provides the conceptual frameworks of trust employed in organizational, leadership, and management studies.

Cheryl Bolton and Fenwick English base their chapter, 'Exploring the Dynamics of Work-Place Trust, Personal Agency, and Administrative Heuristics', on the exploration of the nature of administrative heuristics in the management of educational organizations in the UK and the US. Over a five-month period the authors came upon the presence of trust as a variable in explaining the nature of heuristics and also found a connection to personal agency. The research that triggered the linkage to trust was originally initiated to examine the nature and content of heuristics that educators employed within educational agencies and institutions. This study was conducted without assuming that such approaches had to be rational or had to conform to the dictates of any particular ideological perspective. This is an important point because of the role of emotionality in decision-making that many models either factor out or minimize. It was the awareness of emotion in decision-making that revealed the linkage to trust.

Michèle Schmidt explores the impact of districts' information dissemination and knowledge-sharing capacities as an effort to (de)cultivate social capital within the families of their students. Her chapter, 'Educational Trust: A Critical Component in the (De)Cultivation of Social Capital in School Districts' argues the importance of examining the influence of social capital on districts' ability to disseminate (or not) information to and share knowledge with the community, the cumulative effect of which often generates disadvantages among students leading to variations in resources/ climate and class/race segregation. Such findings show how social capital, and in particular trust, is central to understanding the patterning of group inequality and suggest that stratification pertaining to race and educational outcomes may be reproduced through institutions and their expenditures. Theorists like Bourdieu, Coleman, and Putnam play a prominent role in understanding the responsibility trust plays as a critical component of social capital in the lives of children and schooling. This chapter, therefore, theorizes the element of trust from a social capital perspective in its exploration of institutional mechanisms in the (de)cultivation of capital for children. These then translate into cultural capital, resources, and information about the education system and educational routes to socio-economic mobility.

Finally, Eugenie Samier, in her chapter 'Trust in Organizational, Leadership, and Management Studies: Theories, Approaches, and Conceptions', provides an overview of the organizational, leadership, and management studies literature, the scope of its approaches and conceptual frameworks, the forms of trust, mistrust, and betrayal it has examined, and the causal factors attributed to the formation and deformation of trust that seem most relevant to the contemporary university, including trust issues in professionalism and trust (or lack thereof) in the market economy.

The second part of this book, 'Research Approaches', highlights various research approaches employed to the study of trust. As we know, one of the key challenges, and a gap in the extant literature, regarding trust in educational administration proves to be the limitations in research approaches used, making it difficult to explore the dynamic, multilayered aspects of trust. This part, then, brings to the forefront varied research approaches that draw upon hermeneutic philosophy, psychoanalysis, cultural analysis, and collaborative narrative research.

To start, Stephanie Mackler and Séamus Mulryan, in their chapter 'Reconceptualizing Educational Administration as a Hermeneutics of Trust', draw upon hermeneutic philosophy in order to show how hermeneutic work relies upon trust and, as such, offers a corrective to the predominantly suspicious modes of scholarly and social interaction in the academy and beyond. The chapter begins with a critique of what Ricouer (1974) calls the 'hermeneutics of suspicion', showing how modernist approaches to knowledge are inherently and dangerously based upon doubt, scepticism, and mistrust. As the chapter advances it offers a critique of this approach on both epistemological and ethical grounds, showing its implications not only for scholarship, but also for human relationships. It then considers Ricouer's alternative to suspicion, the 'hermeneutics of retrieval' and draws upon Gadamer's (1975) normative account of the hermeneutic encounter to show how hermeneutic scholarship can and should be grounded in belief, anticipation of meaning, and trust. By looking at Gadamer's account not only of how we can relate hermeneutically to texts but also to other human beings, the authors maintain that we are able to gain a sense of the manners in which a radical shift in academic research methodology could also have great influence on human relationships.

Eugenie Samier, in her chapter 'Studying the Psychological and Cultural Wages of Mistrust: An Essay on Organizational Torment under a Suspicious Regime', discusses the use of psychoanalysis and cultural analysis. In explaining the loss of trust in the increasingly difficult work environment of education institutions, she focuses primarily on the work of Manfred Kets de Vries, who regards trust as an important value for organizational success, requiring a number of administrative skills in building a culture that supports the requisite honesty, respect, fairness, and integrity for trusting relationships to form. The predominant neurotic organizational type produced mainly by a lack of trust is the persecutory suspicious attitude, leading to the micropolitics of secretiveness, envy, and hostility. Furthermore, senior administrators, who selectively and distortionally read the actions of others as deception, find themselves exercising intense control and harsh punishment, reacting aggressively to honesty by producing a flight–fight culture and academic bullying and mobbing. Narcissists in particular create a toxic culture of distrust through paranoia, distortion of reality, and incapacity for strategic and effective spontaneous action, making subordinates insecure and disenchanted. Samier stresses that trust is antecedent to most administrative and leadership practices, contributing to individual well-being, achievement, and the overall positive conditions within which to teach and research. It is argued, therefore, that mistrust, exacerbated by the entrepreneurial characteristics of the market model in education, has placed undue stresses on professional roles and relationships, potentially compromising academic integrity, standards, freedom, and collegial governance.

Finally, Cynthia Gerstl-Pepin and Marybeth Gasman's chapter, entitled 'Developing Trust through Collaborative Research: Mentoring Graduate Students of Colour', explores the potential for creating trust in collaborative narrative research relationships, particularly when faculty mentor graduate students of colour. Drawing on hooks's (1994) work, the authors share hooks's own experience in graduate school to explain how faculty teaching styles can harm students of colour and hooks's own heuristic of the academy as a site of political and personal struggle over knowledge. The authors believe that how we mentor can lead students to feel silenced, excluded, and as if their personal narrative of racial and ethnic identity is of little consequence, and challenge those working within the academy to create supportive learning environments by transgressing boundaries. Specifically, the authors examine how power differentials in terms of faculty/student status can be intertwined with inequities in race, ethnicity, socioeconomics, and gender. They posit that it is possible to overcome these differences by developing trust through the creation of collaborative research projects in which students are mentored and valued as co-researchers. What is particularly interesting in this chapter is the narrative writing style that is used to draw the reader into the experiences of the authors' themselves and of the students they mentor through the use of collaborative research.

The final part of this volume, 'Critical and Current Issues', discusses current issues with trust: work-place aggression and violence in higher education contexts through leadership practices known as toxic or destructive leadership; bullying and harassment in schools and the safety and trust implications between schools and students; a 'crisis of trust' in an environment of accountability; the (im)possibility of restoring trust between policymakers and stakeholders; and a conceptualization of how trust operates in the personalization of official policy texts.

In her chapter, 'Toxic Leadership and the Erosion of Trust in Higher Education', Sheri Klein examines evidence from current research on the topic of work-place aggression that acknowledges the existence of violence in higher education contexts through leadership practices known as 'toxic' or 'destructive leadership', or more commonly known as 'bullying' and 'mobbing'. The tactics, influence, and consequences of these leaders on organizational members are discussed, drawing upon narrative accounts as well as research in leadership and organizational studies. Klein argues that leadership and educational administration tend to focus on dispositions and personality traits of leaders. She recommends that the field look to social psychology, which may better explain situational power, forces, and factors such as de-individuation, dehumanization, moral disengagement, and evil inaction that allow for toxic leadership to emerge and thrive. She makes a case that Marxist theory may best explain what role toxic and destructive leadership plays in maintaining the status quo by eliminating competent members and critical discourse. Finally, the consequences of toxic leadership, namely the erosion of trust of colleagues, leaders, and institutions, are explored.

Dominique Johnson's chapter, 'In Schools We Trust? Leadership *in loco parentis* and the Failure to Protect Students from Bullying and Harassment', begins by asking if students and families can trust schools to ensure safety from bullying and harassment, particularly in light of a recent group of bullying-related suicides in America. The stories of three such students are discussed in the context of *in loco parentis* and the responsibilities of school leadership. The chapter then turns to a discussion of bullying as a way for youth to police traditional gender roles among peers, placing this in the context of a school student murder case. The tolerance of peer abuse such as bullying and harassment by school administration, either through a lack of prevention or intervention, is argued to constitute a systemic violence in schools. Even though evidence suggests a strong relationship between gender role nonconformity and the increased likelihood of experiencing bullying, research and practice in educational administration have yet to address how schools might better support gender nonconforming students. Acting in the place of the parent, schools and their leadership betray the trust of those students and their families who experience bullying and harassment, particularly when it is based in peer gender role regulation. The chapter concludes with a discussion of possibilities for school leadership to move from (potential) failure to protect students from bullying and harassment toward the promise of regaining the trust of students and families.

Richard Bates asks in his chapter, 'Administration, Education, and the Question of Trust', whether a revolution in accountability can remedy our 'crisis of trust'. Administration and education are both forms of social relationships dependent upon trust for their effectiveness; however, conventionally administration is driven by considerations of efficiency and effectiveness, while education is driven by considerations of learning and the social virtues. One of the consequences of these differences is the difficulty that O'Neill (2002) points to: the administrative adoption of the 'new accountability' that distorts the proper aims of professional practice in many service organizations. In theory, such accountability is due to public demand but in practice it is often due to conflicting requirements of regulators, departments of government, fund-raisers, and legal standards. When accountability is combined with notions of choice and market competition, the professional relationship of trust on which learning depends can be jeopardized, producing problems for both teacher and learner. This chapter explores the consequences of this dilemma.

In his chapter, 'The Politics of Derision, Distrust, and Deficit: The Damaging Consequences for Youth and Communities Put at a Disadvantage', John Smyth traces the policy relay between contemporary educational policies of disparagement and 'policy hatred' (Hattam 2001) and their associated deficit-driven narratives that have been imposed with such devastating consequences upon young people and communities already ravaged by markets, deindustrialization, and globalization. Particular evidence for this argument was drawn from the 'get tough' crackdown policies and populist campaigns on students and young people that commenced in the late 1980s with the emergence of 'zero tolerance' and 'three strikes and you are out' programmes, and the variants of these that have been rolled out ever since. These policy strategies have been directed at discrediting and controlling minorities and students and young people of disadvantage in schools. The chapter examines the way the moral panic has been constructed, how it has done its damaging work in schools through educational policies, and what an alternative 'rising movement' (Mediratta 2006) around youth and student voice might look like as a basis for restoring and reversing the corrosive and corrupting effects of neo-liberal versions of educational leadership.

Uroš Pinterič examines the significant reforms of higher education in many European Union member states, as well as applicant countries, through the Bologna Reform between 2004 and 2009 in '(Non)-Legal Requirements for Trust in Slovenian Higher Education'. In some countries, like Slovenia, this reform process changed not only curricula but also relations in the higher education policy arena. Higher education institutional frameworks became more open, allowing for the establishment of private institutions, and consequently changed long-established relationships within public higher education institutions and state agencies. In addition, pre-reform existing social/policy networks (drawing upon van Waarden 1992) were legally covered as long as the policy arena was more or less stable. After the reform was introduced, the level of trust between state and state-established institutions in the existing network became significantly diminished. The author maintains that this lower level of trust is connected to three main factors: political change, higher environmental uncertainty, and flexibility in the newly established policy actors. The argument advanced in this chapter, therefore, is that if all three factors emerge at the same time, previously informal institutionalized networks would collapse due to the personnel change of decision-making institutions and to some extent also in state executive bodies.

Finally, Helen Gunter, Stephen Rogers, and Charlotte Woods argue, in their chapter 'Personalization: The Individual, Trust, and Education in a Neo-Liberal World', that reform in Western democracies has been based traditionally on neo-liberal ideas located in arguments about the individual in control of their own lives and work. For example, in England trust located in the collective and social practice of post-war public education is being unravelled in different ways and at different paces, and in ways that are presented as logical and seductive. One such approach in the English education system is through 'personalization' where the individual is supposed to be able to exercise choice through the structures, cultures, and customer experience of services. Instead of membership within a school community, the student is conceptualized as a selector of options, and the children's work-force (teachers, social workers, health workers, psychological services) often uses ICT packages, espoused to deliver services meeting individual needs. Trust is located in negotiations about the personal and gambles over choices regarding the risk that the individual carries alone. In this chapter the authors examine the conceptualization of personalization in official policy texts, and how data from people who are working on generating meaning and ensuring implementation in the education system are reported. In particular, they focus on what personalization means for relationships inside and outside schools, and how trust operates in the conceptualization and practice of doing the personal and thinking personally.

REFERENCES

Aasen, P., and Stensaker, B. (2007) 'Balancing trust and technocracy? Leadership training in higher education'. *International Journal of Educational Management* 21 (5): 371–83.

Bandura, A. (1993) 'Perceived self-efficacy in cognitive development and functioning'. *Educational Psychologist* 28 (2): 117–48.

Beeson, G., and Matthews, R. (1993) 'Collaborative decision making between new principals and teachers: Policy and practice'. Paper presented at the annual meeting of the American Educational Research Association, Atlanta.

Blase, J., and Blase, J. (2001) *Empowering Teachers: What Successful Principals Do*. 2nd ed. Thousand Oaks, CA: Corwin Press.

Bourdieu, P. (1986) 'The forms of capital'. In *Handbook of Theory and Research for the Sociology of Education*, ed. J.G. Richardson. New York: Greenwood.

Bruhn, J. (2001) *Trust and the Health of Organizations*. New York: Kluwer Academic/Plenum.

Bryk, A., Lee, V., and Holland, P. (1993) *Catholic Schools and the Common Good*. Cambridge, MA: Harvard University Press.

Bryk, A., and Rollow, S. (1992) 'The Chicago experiment: Enhanced democratic participation as a lever for school improvement'. *Issues in Restructuring Schools* 3:3–8.

Bryk, A., and Schneider, B. (2002) *Trust in Schools: A Core Resource for Improvement*. New York: Russell Sage Foundation.

Coleman, J.S. (1987) 'Families and schools'. *Educational Researcher* 16 (6): 32–38.

Covey, S. (1989) *Seven Habits of Highly Effective People*. New York: Simon & Schuster.

Dee, J., and Henkin, A. (2001) *Smart School Teams: Strengthening Skills for Collaboration*. Lanham, MD: University Press of America.

Forsyth, P., Barnes, L., and Adams, C. (2006) 'Trust-effectiveness patterns in schools'. *Journal of Educational Administration* 44 (2): 122–41.

Gadamer, H.-G. (1975) *Truth and Method*. New York: Continuum.

Gasman, M., et al. (2004) 'Developing trust, negotiating power: Transgressing race and status in the academy'. *Teachers College Record* 106 (4): 689–715.

Goddard, R. (2003) 'Relational networks, social trust, and norms: A social capital perspective on students' changes of academic success'. *Educational Evaluation and Policy Analysis* 25 (1): 59–74.

Goddard, R., Hoy, W., and LoGerfo, L. (2003) 'Collective efficacy and student achievement in public schools: A path analysis'. Paper presented at the Annual Meeting of the American Educational Research Association, Chicago.

Goddard, R., Hoy, W., and Woolfolk, A. (2000) 'Collective teacher efficacy: Its meaning, measure and impact on student achievement'. *American Educational Research Journal* 37 (2): 479–507.

Goddard, R., Tschannen-Moran, M., and Hoy, W. (2001) 'A multilevel examination of the distribution and effects of teacher trust in urban elementary schools'. *Elementary School Journal* 102 (1): 3–17.

Groundwater-Smith, S., and Sachs, J. (2002) 'The activist professional and the reinstatement of trust'. *Cambridge Journal of Education* 32 (3): 341–58.

Hattam, R. (2001) 'Nurturing democratic relationships in schools against policy "hatred"'. Paper presented at the annual meeting of the American Educational Research Association, Seattle.

Henkin, A., and Dee, J. (2001) 'The power of trust: Teams and collective action in self-managed schools'. *Journal of School Leadership* 11 (1): 47–60.

hooks, b. (1994) *Teaching to Transgress: Education as the Practice of Freedom*. New York: Routledge.

Hoy, W., and Tschannen-Moran, M. (1999) 'Five faces of trust: An empirical confirmation in urban elementary schools'. *Journal of School Leadership* 9 (3): 184–208.

Mediratta, K. (2006) 'A rising movement'. *National Civic Review* 95 (1): 15–22.

Mintzberg, H. (1989) *Mintzberg on Management: Inside Our Strange World of Organizations*. New York: Free Press.

Moye, M., Henkin, A., and Egley, R. (2005) 'Teacher–principal relationships: Exploring linkages between empowerment and interpersonal trust'. *Journal of Educational Administration* 43 (3): 260–77.

O'Neill, O. (2002) *Spreading Suspicion*, Lecture 1 of the Reith Lectures, on BBC Radio 4, Online. Available HTTP: http://www.bbc.co.uk/radio4/reith2002/lecture1.shtml (accessed 10 June 2009).

Park, S., Henkin, A., and Egley, R. (2005) 'Teacher team commitment, teamwork and trust: Exploring associations'. *Journal of Educational Administration* 43 (5): 462–79.

Phelps, R., Taylor, J., and Gerard, P. (2001) 'Cultural mistrust, ethnic identity, racial identity, and self-esteem among ethnically diverse black university students'. *Journal of Counseling & Development* 79 (2): 209–16.

Putnam, R.D. (1995) 'Bowling alone: America's declining social capital'. *Journal of Democracy* 6 (1): 65–78.

Ricouer, P. (1974) *The Conflict of Interpretations: Essays in Hermeneutics*. Trans. W. Domingo et al. Evanston, IL: Northwestern University Press.

Ross, J., Hogaboam-Gray, A., and Gray, P. (2004) 'Prior student achievement, collaborative school processes, and collective teacher efficacy'. *Leadership and Policy in Schools* 3 (3): 163–88.

San Antonio, D., and Gamage, D. (2007) 'Building trust among educational stakeholders through participatory school administration, leadership and management'. *Management in Education* 21 (1): 15–22.

Seashore, K. (2003) 'Trust and improvement in schools'. Keynote address presented at the British Educational Leadership and Management Association, Milton Keynes.

Siegall, M., and Worth, C. (2001) 'The impacts of trust and control on faculty reactions to merit pay'. *Personnel Review* 30 (6): 646–56.

Tartar, C., Sabo, D., and Hoy, W. (1995) 'Middle school climate, faculty trust, and effectiveness: A path analysis'. *Journal of Research and Development in Education* 29 (1): 41–49.

Tschannen-Moran, M. (2001) 'Collaboration and the need for trust'. *Journal of Educational Administration* 39 (4): 308–31.

———. (2004) *Trust Matters: Leadership for Successful Schools*. San Francisco: Jossey-Bass.

Tschannen-Moran, M., and Hoy, W. (1998) 'Trust in schools: A conceptual and empirical analysis'. *Journal of Educational Administration* 36 (4): 334–52.

Van Waarden, F. (1992) 'Dimensions and types of policy networks'. *European Journal of Political Research* 21 (1–2): 29–52.

Part I
Theoretical Foundations

1 Exploring the Dynamics of Work-Place Trust, Personal Agency, and Administrative Heuristics

Cheryl L. Bolton and Fenwick W. English

It is a frequent enough situation in conducting research to answer one set of questions and then researchers find something else entirely unanticipated. In his classic work *The Art of Scientific Investigation*, Beveridge explained, 'New knowledge very often has its origin in some quite unexpected observation or chance occurrence arising during an investigation' (1950: 55). This chapter represents such an occurrence. In conducting an exploration of the nature of administrative heuristics in the management of educational organizations in the UK and the US over a five-month period (English and Bolton 2008), we came upon the presence of trust as a variable in explaining the nature of heuristics and also found a connection to Bandura's (2001) concept of personal agency.

The research which triggered the linkage to trust was originally initiated to examine the nature and content of heuristics educators employed within educational agencies and institutions without assuming that such approaches had to be rational or had to conform to the dictates of any particular ideological perspective. This is an important point because of the role of emotionality in decision-making, which many models either factor out or minimize as important (see Bolton and English 2009). It was the awareness of emotion in decision-making that revealed the linkage to trust.

We were reminded by Davis that it is within heuristics 'that the greatest practical potential for becoming a better decision maker lies. It is also here that the elements of real-world decision making are found' (2004: 631). The reason advanced by Davis is that thinking heuristically enabled the decision-maker to cut problems into smaller pieces by 'chunking patterns of information into rules of thumb'. Davis clarified that by 'rules of thumb' he meant that certain information 'is organized mentally via predetermined meta-rules that are category based and whole pattern in structure' (2004: 631).

Such chunking based on experience as a factor in job success had been reported in a study of 44 Ohio school superintendents by Nestor-Baker and Hoy (2001). What they discerned was that as school superintendents acquired experience in their positions, they began to chunk that experience into patterns so that when similar problems arose, they took less time to recognize and deal with them.

THE ORIGINAL LINE OF RESEARCH

Three rounds of interviews occurred in a five-month period, two in the UK and one in the US. The group interviewed was a convenience sample consisting of 13 middle-level managers, nine women and four men, who were working in higher and further education settings in both countries. They were contacted by the researchers because of their known roles as middle-level managers in US or UK programmes and institutions. Some were teachers and part-time administrators and others were full-time administrators.

In selecting an appropriate methodology to determine if educational leaders engaged in heuristics or rules of thumb, it became clear that with as few preconceptions as possible, an approach utilizing a normative sampling model was inappropriate. We were not going to 'sample' representative types of decisions because even the concept of 'type' was problematic. The co-investigators therefore employed a sampling strategy that Mason has termed, 'theoretical' or 'purposive' (1996: 93). Creswell has called a study in which the investigators are examining 'a phenomenon, as described by participants in a study' phenomenological research (2003: 15), and Mason indicates that theoretical sampling must be flexible because within the process of data gathering itself, the researchers may engage in manipulating 'their analysis, theory, and sampling activities *interactively* during the research process, to a much greater extent than in statistical sampling' (1996: 100). This certainly proved to be the case in the three sets of interviews.

A grounded theory began to unfold during the second set of interviews. First, the focus shifted to include not only the individual administrator, but the larger decision-making context which included other decision-makers. Whilst Davis commented that heuristic decision-making may seem 'automatic', it is 'actually a phenomenon activated through conscious effort' (2004: 632). Leaders interviewed typically did not envision their work at a level where they were conscious of rules of thumb as far as decision-making heuristics were concerned. This may be related to the notion that where decisions are related to the affective domain, 'responses occur rapidly and automatically' (Slovic et al. 2000: 3). Our respondents did, however, view some decisions as being 'pre-cast' in the form of institutional relations or regulations and referred to these if not explicitly as heuristics at least as triggers to either make or defer a decision when they served as barriers or when potential decisions became risky to them personally.

An intriguing notion in the literature on trust is that of 'institutional scripts' (Hanson 2001). Such scripts are solidified forms of institutional memories involving past interactions of individuals and the organizations in which they work. The idea of individual scripts as forms of ideologies was proffered by Goertzel, who said that 'a script is a set of guidelines that people develop and use to understand their role in the world around them' (1992: 38). Tomkins identified scripts as 'an organized set of ideas about which human beings are at once both articulate and passionate and about which they are least certain' (1978: 202).

Tomkins did not specify whether individuals were consciously aware of their scripts. We found that our respondents became more aware of their own thinking patterns when a decision was kicked back for them to reconsider for some reason. When that occurred, they expressed an awareness of their role or part within the larger organization hierarchy. The respondents were co-ordinators or chairs, deans or provosts, and these were socially constructed sets of behaviours or expectations in which they engaged in certain actions, that is, they 'enacted' or did things in accordance with their role and known procedures.

During interviews, participants were asked to describe their emotions before, during, and after specific decisions. From these more focused queries we perceived that emotion influences decision-making—it runs prior to and follows a decision. This insight did not represent an unexpected finding, but it was of potential importance because whilst emotion was clearly identified and illustrated by respondents, no one interviewed recognized emotion as a factor in triggering any heuristics in their decision-making. Similarly, the data also suggested to us that trust formed an important element in decision-making and was bound up with emotion.

The interviews also demonstrated that trust was relational within organizations and appeared to be a critical factor regarding the impact on an individual's decision-making process—that is, knowing that a decision will be supported or that there is some room for error encourages confidence in decision-making. This recognition supports existing studies relating to organizational trust where it is defined as 'one's willingness to participate in a relationship that involves being vulnerable to another person' (Chhuon at al. 2008: 228; Daly 2004). What was evident from these interviews was an indication that there was a reduced incidence of heuristics where the persons interviewed were less likely to 'pass the buck' or to 'delay' decisions if there was 'trust'.

EMOTION AND THE LINKAGE TO MANAGERIAL TRUST

Our investigation of heuristics in decision-making led us to the central role of emotion in decision-making and then to the linkage of emotion to contextualized situations of risk and uncertainty in organizational life. This triumvirate of variables became the hinge for managerial or work-place trust as shown in Figure 1.1.

We took note of definitional differentiations of trust as proffered by Fukuyama (1995), who separated familial trust which exits within families and social trust which is external to families and exists in human organizations. This is echoed by Cosner, who writes that 'many scholars who study trust within organisations suggest that trust formation in work relationships and settings is somewhat different than the development of trust in either close personal or romantic relationships, or between relative strangers' (2009: 254). General social trust might be likened to climate measures in schools (see Tschannen-Moran and Hoy 1998).

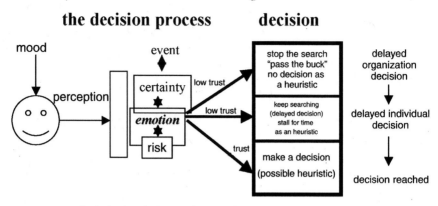

Figure 1.1   The linkage of trust to decision heuristics.

The research reported in this chapter was more narrowly focused. It did not begin with an exploration of trust, but rather took the perspective that trust was an element in the kinds of decision heuristics employed by managers in educational institutions. Trust was therefore not an end in itself or a desirable condition to be obtained irrespective of a specific work context. In other words, work organizations represent a specific type of human organization in which decisions are rendered by individual leaders at their level of functioning within the organizational structure (see Wang and Clegg 2002).

We show three types of decision heuristics in Figure 1.1 connected to trust. In turn, trust is connected to risk and uncertainty. For instance, where there is uncertainty and risk involved (and emotion elevated), trust was indicated as being low and as a result an administrator may decide not to make a decision, preferring instead to 'kick the problem upstairs', which is a kind of non-decision and a heuristic. Or the administrator may delay making a decision by stalling for time. The complex set of interactions in which administrators function revolves around how they perceive events, unpack the risks, deal with knowns and unknowns (certainty/uncertainty), and continually juxtapose emotion, which is in part connected to trust levels hierarchically (vertical trust) and laterally (work-team trust) by shuffling the problem off to a committee.

For us, what our respondents were discussing about trust concerned confidence that their superiors and colleagues would back them if they made a difficult decision. It also included material and moral support in their work and a measure of autonomy in going about their jobs, something Bandura has called personal agency. He defined it as: 'the power to originate actions for given purposes'. Personal agency is the most fundamental measure of autonomy that 'people believe they can produce desired results and forestall detrimental ones by their actions' (2001: 6, 10). He called this belief 'self-efficacy' and we found it in the comments of many of our respondents.

Table 1.1 Interview Data Showing Two Dimensions of Managerial Trust and Personal Agency

Respondent Comment	Lateral Trust	Vertical Trust	Personal Agency
1. It's an emotional reaction. A tension you feel between what you want to do and what somebody else wants you to do. It's the tension. I find it hard to deal with.			X
2. How much of your weaknesses can you reveal? Every time you pass a decision over, you are exposing yourself to various forms of risk.	X	X	
3. It's important to be quiet and really listen and pay attention to people. I trust myself to make the decisions.			X
4. Humility begins the steps towards building trust.			X
5. The key to effective delegation is trust. Trust . . . is key to making a manager's role manageable and to reduce risk.	X		
6. No apprehension about making decisions. The part that I am most concerned about is making sure I understand more fully all sides of the question.			X
7. The decision is better consulting with a couple of colleagues.	X		
8. Almost all the operational decisions are delegated—I deal with the exceptions.	X		X
9. The faculty have academic freedom. Officials have a different world.		X	
10. I'm constantly weighing and navigating how much I make suggestions of how strong, sometimes with passion and ideas. In this role I must be restrained. I'm not here to redo the politics of the college.			X
11. I do have options. . . . I do not have to bow.			X
12. Trust that is built up over time. . . . highly skilled and professional staff.		X	
13. I do take into consideration the orientation of senior management. I would be careful not to act out of protocol. I look for negotiation strategies.		X	
14. If you do this all by yourself you will die quickly. The strength of a leader is to recognize when you need help. If you don't ask, people feel it is a sign of stupidity.		X	X
15. My boss won't give me funds. He doesn't want to hear any bad news. He wants to sanction a decision already made.		X	X
16. I do talk to people. I have an internal network. A big part of my week is networking.	X		X

(continued)

Table 1.1 (continued)

Respondent Comment	Lateral Trust	Vertical Trust	Personal Agency
17. I know I need another person to read the situation. I'm a quick read. When an issue happens I have not experienced before, I don't know the power players then I see someone.	X		
18. You can't operate without trust. Trust in the sense of having common values. You have to trust them and their values.	X	X	
19. Relationship building is very important. You can't get a lot done if you don't. You are a human being.	X	X	
20. I've learned over the years to trust my instincts. I self-question. I look for the good in people. The common good.			X
21. Perhaps I work now for an organization that listens to you. That allows them to make mistakes. That filters down to all levels.		X	
22. I do find it difficult to trust people. If it was something that was delicate and I wouldn't want it to get around I would be very limited who I would talk to.	X	X	
23. It's important to be quiet and really listen and pay attention to people. I trust myself to make the decisions.			X
24. I do weigh up and consult people beforehand. I'm a passionate person and a person of conviction. I'm consistent. I'm not seen as an indecisive person. I believe in shared decision-making.	X	X	X
25. I've always worked with a little management team. Take it to others. I learned to do that. It takes a big onus off you because you are not working alone. Far easier to implement than if you do it alone.	X		
26. You can't change overnight. You have to hire enough new faculty and hope they don't get sucked into the old culture. You can see the culture change. You give them a chance. If they don't make the move than I have to do something which is good for the college.			X
27. The students are my incentive to keep going. It's self-preservation. If we get them through and they pass, our achievement rates look good. That will please management. You do it to keep the hassle off our backs. These students can be discouraged. They only have themselves. I'm doing their negotiating for them. I want them to stay in school. I want the numbers.		X	X
28. The nature of my personality. I couldn't work in any organization that suppressed my personality. There is a real good balance at work. This is the job. Get on with it.		X	
29. Did that for 10 years before I came here. The job got progressively more managerial. As the job gets bigger there's more management to it. At the end I reached the sort of limits on my management skills. I was beginning not to enjoy it.		X	

Table 1.1 shows some of the comments given to us in our interviews in which work-place or managerial trust was present. 'Lateral trust' was work-team or collegial trust and 'vertical trust' was superior–subordinate trust revolving around how an administrator related to his/her superior, in other words, 'the boss'. In their study of school system trust between school sites and central office, Chhuon et al. (2008) defined lateral or work-team trust as 'relational trust' and managerial trust or vertical trust as 'leadership trust'.

We show comments categorized by one or more of the elements. These comments illustrate the interaction between two dimensions of work-place trust and the presence of personal agency. What these comments show is that trust is more than a generic atmospheric or climatic condition. Rather, trust is relational and contextual and is codependent on elements of personal agency (see Russell 2003: 152).

THE DIMENSION OF PERSONAL AGENCY AND SELF-EFFICACY

The data in Table 1.1 show that in the interviews we conducted, matters of personal agency/self-efficacy were present in the respondents' perceptions in performing their jobs. Personal agency is bound up with matters of self-efficacy. In turn, self-efficacy involves the capability of an administrator in an organizational context to exercise 'control over one's own thought processes, motivation, and action' (Bandura 1989: 1175). The relationship between self-efficacy and decision-making was factored against the risks of having a decision fail. This interactive and highly contextual dilemma was identified as follows:

> When faced with difficulties, people who are beset by self-doubts about their capabilities slacken their efforts or abort their attempts prematurely and quickly settle for mediocre solutions, whereas those who have a strong belief in their capabilities exert greater effort to master the challenge. (Bandura 1989: 1176)

Our interview data suggest a similar set of relationships. The interjection of trust is an important factor. A number of the comments shown in Table 1.1 reflect the factor of self-doubt as an issue with self-efficacy. For example, comments from respondents number 1 and number 29 reflect self-doubt. However, learning to 'trust' oneself can be translated as remaining calm under adverse circumstances with the understanding that you will prevail in the long run. Here trust is confined to an internal conversation a decision-maker has with himself/herself. Its importance is underscored by Bandura:

> people who believe strongly in their problem-solving capabilities remain highly efficient in their analytic thinking in complex decision-making situations, whereas those who are plagued by self-doubts are erratic in their analytic thinking. (1989: 1176)

Our respondents who exhibited personal trust in themselves are numbers 3, 6, 8, 10, 20, 23, and 26. These complex interactions are beginning to be probed by decision-making researchers who are examining so-called 'affective heuristics' (Finucane et al. 2000). 'Affective heuristics' are defined as a 'feeling state' linked to a specific stimulus. What is understood is that an affective reaction to a situation will lead to a decision that does not factor in all of the potential relevant data which could be examined, for as Shafir, Simonson, and Tversky observed, 'People's choices may occasionally stem from affective judgments that preclude a thorough evaluation of the options' (1993: 32).

For example, Sunstein concluded that 'when emotions are intense, calculation is less likely to occur, or at least that form of calculation that involves assessment of risks in terms of not only the magnitude but also the probability of the outcome'. Sunstein called this phenomenon 'probability neglect' (2002a: 67; 2002b: 50). We see emotional overlay in Table 1.1 in the comments from our respondents in numbers 1, 10, 15, 22, and 28. We see aspects of 'probability neglect' in numbers 10, 13, 22, 24, and 27. The fact that some of the comments from the respondents fall into multiple categories is indicative of the complex interaction involving uncertainty, risk, and emotionality that we found in this preliminary foray into managerial heuristics (see English and Bolton 2008). What we are interested in pursuing is not the sequence of these aspects but how they trigger decisions. From this perspective we view the decision as the outcome and are not so much interested in the outcome of the decision.

THE CONCEPT OF PASSION

Based on the interview data, we perceived that the level of emotionality present in work-place administrative contexts is potentially more dynamic than portrayals the climate literature suggest for teacher efficacy (Tschannen-Moran, Hoy, and Hoy 1998). Studies have attempted to explain and to classify emotion, for example Izard (1993) has identified 12 basic emotions: interest, enjoyment, surprise, sadness, anger, disgust, contempt, fear, guilt, shame, shyness, and inward-directed hostility. However, Eckman and Friesen indicate that only six (happiness, sadness, surprise, fear, anger, and disgust) are 'found by every investigator in the last thirty years who sought to determine the vocabulary of emotion' (2003: 22). We proffer that the work of Frijda represents a dynamic portrayal of emotionality in the work-place.

Frijda (2007) maintains that in his opinion there are 'laws' which govern emotion and passion, some of which appear directly relevant to the triggers for decision heuristics as found in the interviews. Emotions arise in response to events that are important to the individual's concerns. 'Every emotion hides a concern, that is, a motive or need, a major goal or value, a more or less enduring disposition to prefer particular states of the world. A concern is what gives a particular event its emotional meaning' (2007: 7).

Perhaps the most salient aspect of what our data reveal is not whether emotions are present, because we found no evidence that they were not always present in some form, but the relationship of emotion to the other two factors, that is, risk and certainty (or uncertainty).

Frijda sees a behaviour as a complex interaction as a person experiences an 'event'. A certain amount of concerns already influence that experience (called 'mood'). Then the person appraises that event within rules and regulations; there is an action repertoire which is an interaction between readiness, affect (impact), arousal, and finally a behaviour which is an action. Frijda has already stipulated that the nature and intensity of emotion depend on the relationship between an event and some frame of reference with which the event is compared. It is not the magnitude of the event that decides the emotion, but its magnitude relative to that frame of reference. The frame of reference is often the prevailing state of affairs.

THE FACTOR OF RISK

The second component in our research is that of risk and the perception of risk to the managerial decision-maker. Risk has been identified as one of the 'subconstructs of trust' (Daly 2004; Tschannen-Moran and Hoy 1998). Importantly, Louis (2003) has suggested that both dimensions of trust, lateral and vertical, are important to obtaining a level of social capital critical to enable co-operative/collective actions to be undertaken by administrators. Drucker notes that to try and eliminate risk from an organization is futile because '[r]isk is inherent in the commitment of present resources to future expectations' (1974: 512). Bryk and Schneider explain that the dependencies in school systems make all members feel vulnerable (2002: 20).

Our approach suggests that personal perception of the risks involved in making decisions does influence a selection of a heuristic. We discerned in our interviews that when some managers began to see more risks than they believed they could handle or would want to be accountable for, they 'kicked the problem upstairs'. This is a kind of heuristic (Slovic et al. 2002) called 'the affect heuristic' in which by 'affect' they mean 'the specific quality of 'goodness' or 'badness' of a 'rule of thumb' as: (a) experienced as a feeling state (with or without consciousness); and (b) demarcating a positive or negative quality of a stimulus.

Pratkanis proposed that attitudes serve as heuristics, 'with positive attitudes invoking a favoring strategy toward an object and negative attitudes creating disfavoring responses'. Pratkanis also indicated that the use of the *attitude heuristic* enabled persons to assign objects to a favourable class or an unfavourable class, 'thus leading to approach or avoidance strategies appropriate to the class' (1989: 72).

A study by Fischhoff et al. (1978) found that 'judgments of risk and benefit are negatively correlated'. This means that for some problems the 'greater the perceived benefit, the lower the perceived risk and vice versa':

That the inverse relationship is generated in people's minds is suggested by the fact that risk and benefits generally tend to be positively (if at all) correlated in the world. Activities that are low in benefit are unlikely to be high in risk (if they were, they would be proscribed). (Fischhoff et al. 1978, as cited in Slovic et al. 2002: 410)

One view of this by Epstein is that individuals perceive reality by 'two interactive, parallel processing systems'. The first system is the rational one, which is logical and analytical. The second is experiential and this system 'encodes reality in images, metaphors, and narratives to which affective feelings have become attached' (1994, as cited in Slovic et al. 2002: 413). It is this second processing system that has drawn a great deal of attention in educational system administration in the trust research and is a fabric comprised of eight facets: risk, competence, reliability, integrity, benevolence, communication, openness, and respect (Waters, Marzano, and McNulty 2003).

Available theory suggests that decision-makers weigh risks and benefits, that they utilize different processing systems to appraise the risks and benefits, and that there is an emotional overlay to the process. When their feelings are connected to a consideration of risks and benefits (and possibly consequences) they may dispose of a problem in repetitive and similar ways. In some sources, 'affect' and 'emotion' are identified as synonyms (see Dai 2004: 452). It is important to differentiate between affect or emotion and mood. Our research is not about moods. We concentrated on the role of emotion coupled with risk and uncertainty. Linnenbrink and Pintrich offer this distinction:

Moods and emotions are distinct in terms of intensity and duration. Moods tend to be longer lasting than emotions, which are characterized by short, intense episodes. However, while emotions tend to be intense or rather short-lived, they may also fade into general mood states over time . . . mood states do not have a particular reference; the source of the mood is unclear. In contrast, emotions tend to be a reaction or response to a particular event or person. (2004: 58)

BOUNDED RATIONALITY AND CERTAINTY/UNCERTAINTY

As we reviewed our data, we also took account of the notion of bounded rationality in which organizational decision-makers engage in decisions when it is impossible to know everything about any situation. So what is certain or uncertain has limitations or boundaries in organizational life.

Furthermore, boundedly rational choice recognises explicitly that search is costly and that heuristic procedures for decision making arise that are based on experience and that economize on information-processing requirements. One decision-making procedure consistent with the boundedly rational view of action is incrementalism defined as 'a pattern of marginal change in final allocation outcome relative to some base'. (Pfeffer 1982: 6–7)

In the preliminary research reported in this chapter we understood that all of our respondents worked in organizational settings which were bounded. It was clear to us that no one ever expressed the notion that they 'knew everything' about any problem or situation, particularly at the middle-management levels where most of our respondents worked and lived. Nearly everyone was aware that their state of knowledge was incomplete. In fact we see the concept of 'bounded rationality' from Table 1.1 in the comments of numbers 6, 7, 14, 16, 17, 23, 24, and 25. However, even with this recognition, there may come a time in a manager's life when there are more unknowns than they are willing to chance on the consequences of a failed decision. So even within the restrictions of organizational life, the perception of risk in less than perfect conditions of certainty is at work. The relationship between certainty and risk is complex and has been the subject of intense scrutiny and debate, especially in economics (see Luce and Raiffa 1957; Ellsberg 2001).

What we learned when we compared our data to the literature on risk is that in many perspectives, especially in economic models, it is related to levels of certainty/uncertainty. An early definition was made by Alexis and Wilson when they described 'certainty' as 'complete and accurate knowledge of the consequences of each choice', in decision-making based on game theory, and 'uncertainty' as 'the consequences of each choice [which] cannot be defined by a correspondence relationship even within a probabilistic framework'. 'Risk' was then seen as an assumption that 'accurate knowledge exists about the probability distribution of the consequences of each alternative' (1967: 151).

Later Taylor spoke of measurable and unmeasurable uncertainty. 'Measurable certainty' exists when 'the probability of an event is objectively known on the basis of historical data or a priori calculations. This type of certainty is called *risk* and figures prominently in gambling. 'Unmeasurable uncertainty' involves 'situations in which probabilities are not known— which includes most decisions in organizations' (1984: 122).

While these distinctions have been criticized because they rarely, if ever, exist in completely pure states (that is, total knowledge or total ignorance), we have found them useful in our research if conceptualized as degrees of information, more or less. We hypothesize that in general, risk increases as uncertainty increases and vice versa. At least one researcher has suggested that as problem complexity increases, human capacity for rational analysis decreases, and the mind searches for heuristic and intuitive ways to reduce cognitive demands (Davis 2004).

NEW EYES: THE DOOR BETWEEN DECISION-MAKING AND TRUST, RATIONALITY, AND EMOTIONALITY

The data reported in this chapter could be positioned within two fields, each with a long trajectory of research (see Figure 1.2). The first is that of rational decision-making as a calculus of economic probability models. This is the standard business and military model but it leaves out the human dimension, the emotional, and feeling aspects of the work which are important, for, as Albert Einstein once observed, 'we have learned that rational thinking does not suffice to solve the problems of social life' (Clark 1971: 596). The second field of research is the emotional and interpersonal work on trust as a general factor in creating organizational social capital to improve the overall quality of work life and organizational performance, however measured. That trajectory in education has taken root and blossomed in the last 20 years (see Louis 2003).

We believe that the work on heuristics, as reported in this chapter, cuts across both of these fields and presents a different repositioning for both rational decision-making and trust. Our preliminary work thus far would point to an intersection of rationality and emotionality that may be more complex and nuanced than the literature of both the fields has so far suggested. Levit similarly observed that emerging thought in the literature of cognitive psychology 'says that people use subconscious habits of decision making that entail biases, behavioural or motivational tilts, mental shortcuts, and predictable patterns of cognitive errors' that 'fail to maximize their expected utility' (2006: 406). This perspective contradicts rational/ mathematical models of decision selection that negate earlier calculations

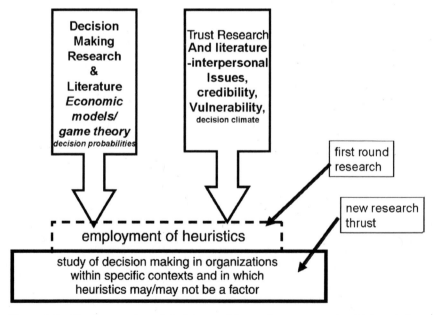

Figure 1.2   The intersection of decision-making and trust research with heuristics.

of the 'expected' or 'rational' decision, purely encapsulated in the concept of 'bounded rationality'.

It is to that very intriguing possibility that our future research is positioned with the addition of affect heuristics which we have briefly explored. We see a different door to open now and we are reminded that Marcel Proust once presciently observed, 'The voyage of discovery lies not in finding new landscapes . . . but in having new eyes' (Conrad and Conrad 2002: 171).

REFERENCES

Alexis, M., and Wilson, C.Z. (1967) *Organizational Decision Making.* Englewood Cliffs, NJ: Prentice Hall.
Bandura, A. (1989) 'Human agency in social cognitive theory'. *American Psychologist* 44 (9): 1175–84.
———. (2001) 'Social cognitive theory: An agentive perspective'. *Annual Review of Psychology* 52 (1): 1–26.
Beveridge, W.I.B. (1950) *The Art of Scientific Investigation.* New York: Vintage Books.
Bolton, C., and English, F. (2009) 'My head and my heart: Deconstructing the historical/hysterical binary that conceals and reveals emotion in educational leadership'. In *Emotional Dimensions of Educational Administration and Leadership*, ed. E.A. Samier and M. Schmidt. London: Routledge.
Bryk, A.S., and Schneider, B. (2002) *Trust in Schools: A Core Resource for Improvement.* New York: Russell Sage.
Chhuon, V., Gilkey, E., Gonzalez, M., Daly, A., and Chrispeels, J. (2008) 'The little district that could: The process of building district-school trust'. *Educational Administrative Quarterly* 44 (2): 227–81.
Clark, R.W. (1971) *Einstein: The Life and Times.* New York: World Publishing.
Conrad, B., and Conrad, J. (2002) *Costa Rica.* Edison, NJ: Hunter Publishing.
Cosner, S. (2009) 'Building organizational capacity through trust', *Educational Administration Quarterly*, 45, 2: 248-91.
Creswell, J. (2003) *Research Design: Qualitative, Quantitative, and Mixed Methods Approaches.* 2nd ed. Thousand Oaks, CA: Sage.
Dai, D. (2004) 'Epilogue: Putting it all together: Some concluding thoughts'. In *Motivation, Emotion, and Cognition: Integrative Perspectives on Intellectual Functioning and Development*, ed. D. Dai and R. Sternberg. Mahwah, NJ: Lawrence Erlbaum Associates.
Daly, A.J. (2004) 'A question of trust: Predictive conditions for adaptive and technical leadership in educational contexts'. Unpublished dissertation, University of California, Santa Barbara.
Davis, S. (2004) 'The myth of the rational decision maker: A framework for applying and enhancing heuristic and intuitive decision making by school leaders'. *Journal of School Leadership* 14 (6): 621–52.
Drucker, P. (1974) *Management: Tasks, Responsibilities, Practices.* New York: Harper and Row.
Eckman, P., and Friesen, W. (2003) *Unmasking the Face: A Guide to Recognizing Emotions from Facial Clues.* Cambridge: Malor Books.
Ellsberg, D. (2001) *Risk, Ambiguity and Decision.* New York: Garland Publishing.
English, F., and Bolton, C. (2008) 'An exploration of administrative heuristics in the United States and the United Kingdom'. *Journal of School Leadership* 18 (1): 96–119.
Epstein, S. (1994) 'Integration of the cognitive and psychodynamic unconscious'. *American Psychologist* 49 (8): 709–24.
Finucane, M., Alhakami, A., Slovic, P., and Johnson, S. (2000) 'The affect heuristic in judgments of risks and benefits'. *Journal of Behavioral Decision Making* 13 (1): 1–17.

Fischhoff, B., et al. (1978) 'How safe is safe enough? A psychometric study of attitudes towards technological risks and benefits'. *Policy Sciences* 9 (2): 127–52.

Frijda, N. (2007) *The Laws of Emotion*. Mahwah, NJ: Lawrence Erlbaum Associates.

Fukuyama, E. (1995) *Trust: The Social Virtues and the Creation of Prosperity*. New York: The Free Press.

Goertzel, T. (1992) *Turncoats & True Believers: The Dynamics of Political Belief and Disillusionment*. Buffalo, NY: Prometheus Books.

Hanson, M. (2001) 'Institutional theory and educational change'. *Education Administration Quarterly* 37 (5): 637–61.

Izard, C. (1993) 'Organizational and motivational functions of discrete emotions'. In *Handbook of Emotion*, ed. M. Lewis and J.M. Haviland. New York: Guilford Press.

Levit, N. (2006) 'Confronting conventional thinking: The heuristics problem in feminist legal theory'. *Cardozo Law Review* 28 (1): 391–440.

Linnenbrink, E.A., and Pintrich, P.R. (2004) 'Role of affect in cognitive processing in academic contexts'. In *Motivation, Emotion, and Cognition: Integrative Perspectives on Intellectual Functioning and Development*, ed. D.Y. Dai and R.J. Sternberg. Mahwah, NJ: Lawrence Erlbaum Associates.

Louis, K.S. (2003). 'School leaders facing real change: Shifting geography, uncertain paths'. *Cambridge Journal of Education* 33 (3): 371–82.

Luce, D., and Raiffa, H. (1957) *Games and Decisions*. New York: John Wiley.

Mason, J. (1996) *Qualitative Researching*. London: Sage.

Nestor-Baker, N., and Hoy, W. (2001) 'Tacit knowledge of school superintendents: Its nature, meaning, and content'. *Educational Administration Quarterly* 37 (1): 86–129.

Pfeffer, J. (1982) *Organizations and Organization Theory*. Boston: Pitman.

Pratkanis, A. (1989) 'The cognitive representation of attitudes'. In *Attitude, Structure and Function*, ed. A.R. Pratkanis, S.J. Breckler, and A.G. Greenwald. Hillsdale: Lawrence Erlbaum and Associates.

Russell, M. (2003) 'Leadership and followership as a relational process'. *Educational Management & Administration* 31 (2): 145–58.

Shafir, E., Simonson, I., and Tversky, A. (1993) 'Reason-based choice'. *Cognition* 49:11–36.

Slovic, P., Finucane, M., Peters, E., and MacGregor, D.G. (2002) 'The affect heuristic'. In *Heuristics and Biases: The Psychology of Intuitive Judgment*, ed. T. Gilovich, D. Griffin, and D. Kahneman. Cambridge: Cambridge University Press.

Sunstein, C. (2002a) 'Probability neglect: Emotions, worst cases, and law'. *Yale Law Journal* 112 (1): 61–107.

———. (2002b) *Risk and Reason: Safety, Law, and the Environment*. Cambridge: Cambridge University Press.

Taylor, R.N. (1984) *Behavioral Decision Making*. Glenview, IL: Scott, Foresman.

Tomkins, S. (1978) 'Script theory: Differential magnification of effects'. Ed. H.E. Howe and R.A. Dienstbier. Special issue, *Nebraska Symposium on Motivation* 26:201–6, 217–23.

Tschannen-Moran, M., and Hoy, W. (1998) 'A conceptual and empirical analysis of trust in schools'. *Journal of Educational Administration* 36 (4): 334–52.

Tschannen—Moran, M., Hoy, A., and Hoy, W. (1998) 'Teacher efficacy: Its meaning and measure'. *Review of Educational Research* 68 (2): 202–48.

Wang, K., and Clegg, S. (2002) 'Trust and decision making: Are managers different in the People's Republic of China and Australia?' *Cross Cultural Management* 9 (1): 30–45.

Waters, J.T., Marzano, R.J., and McNulty, B.A. (2003) *Balanced Leadership: What 30 Years of Research Tells Us about the Effect of Leadership on Student Achievement*. Aurora, CO: Mid-Continent Research for Education and Learning.

2 Educational Trust

A Critical Component in the (De)Cultivation of Social Capital in School Districts

Michèle Schmidt

In an era of democratic learning, it is incumbent upon school districts to create equitable mechanisms for knowledge sharing and information dissemination for *all* within school districts. Sociological perspectives of these networks (e.g. district offices), such as social capital and social accountability, offer theoretical lenses that can be used to determine school districts' potential for innovative knowledge sharing and (de)cultivation of social capital in districts. A critical component of these theoretical perspectives, which serves as the foundation of such networks, is the element of trust. This chapter, therefore, sets the theoretical stage to discuss the (im)possibilities of (de)cultivating social capital—that is, trust—in school districts. For example, the information parents receive from district networks (e.g. via websites, newsletters, parent nights) can provide insights into their children's school experiences, such as their successes and failures. Such information can help parents influence their children to engage with school—it can introduce parents and students to opportunities for educational mobility and resources and it can create potential contacts with teachers and school administrators—all of which have the potential to enhance their social capital (Sandefur and Lauman 1998).

Sociologists (e.g. Putnam 2000) claim that there has been a decline in social capital in society that may be reducing students' academic success. While social capital has received little attention from a policy perspective in the past, this phenomenon has garnered increased interest in educational policy debates (e.g. Goddard 2003). In fact, since the heightened high-stakes nature of the testing and accountability culture that developed in the 1990s, recent education policy has emphasized forms of parental and community involvement that may eventually serve to build social capital (Goddard 2003; National Education Goals Panel 1995). Coleman (1987) suggests the need for public policy in institutions to cultivate more personal interest and intimacy among students and the community in order to increase student achievement. He stresses that such relationships, however, must go beyond after-school and summer programmes by fostering trusting teacher–student and teacher–parent relationships in schools that are academically supportive and nurture social relations in order to better assist students academically.

Aspects of social capital and social accountability perspectives often offer the theoretical tools necessary to examine district networking facilities or resistances. Research, however, reveals that districts have the capacity to play an integral part in informed communication via the website, newsletters, et cetera that transforms such networks into valuable social capital tools for students, parents, teachers, administrators, and the surrounding communities. The success of information dissemination and knowledge sharing, however, is often dependent upon a culture of trust and social accountability ensuring that information is transparent, equitable, accurate, reliable, current, accessible, and efficient. More to the point, research demonstrates that institutional networks' information dissemination and knowledge sharing has the potential of generating (dis)advantages among students leading to variations in access to resources and information. Such findings illustrate how social capital, and, more importantly, a culture of trust, is central to understanding the equitable distribution of financial resources, information about the education system, and educational routes to upward socio-economic mobility. Such patterns often indicate group inequality and stratification pertaining to race and educational outcomes as they are reproduced through institutions, their expenditures, and their mechanisms of information dissemination and knowledge sharing, all leading to a decline in trust and social accountability (Parcel and Dufur 2001).

When information dissemination and knowledge sharing are dependent upon characteristics of clear communication, it becomes critical to take note of the problematic nature of the production and dissemination of information or 'knowledges' via various media (e.g., face-to-face, newsletters, meetings, newspaper, internet, websites). This is particularly true when such knowledge/information may result in (mis)trust. Such an outcome often makes it difficult to extricate the medium from the message. Dissemination of information and knowledge sharing hold the potential to enhance participation or to increase propaganda and obfuscation. To help us unpack these potential dangers, an intersection of social accountability and social capital is used as a theoretical tool to assist in the discussion of district networks and their potential for developing a culture of trust. Therefore, from a sociological perspective, we are able to examine the (un)intended consequences of policy dissemination by using the tools under discussion (i.e. social capital, social accountability, trust). While it is beyond the scope of this chapter to go into greater detail about any of these theories, brief descriptions of each are provided in the sections that follow to enhance the discussion.

While there are many definitions of trust, this chapter conceptualizes the term from a social capital perspective in its exploration of how institutional mechanisms contribute to the (de)cultivation of social capital for children. This often translates into cultural capital, resources, and information about the education system, and into educational routes to socio-economic mobility. And, while the conception of social capital is not very political in isolation, the introduction of social accountability will enable the exploration of the political and civic engagement implications of district policy and information dissemination.

Trust and social accountability, while not synonymous, are conceptually closely intertwined. This chapter, therefore, focuses on school districts as viable social networks that, by virtue of their facility/resistance for social accountability and the implications for trust, become either assets or liabilities in advancing student academic achievement. Sociologists such as Putnam, Woolcock, Bourdieu, Portes, and Coleman play a prominent role in understanding the role of trust as a critical component of social capital in the lives of children and schooling.

SOCIAL CAPITAL

The concept of social capital was popularized by two seminal sociologists, Bourdieu (1986) and Coleman (1988, 1990). Social capital has been a growing theoretical field since Bourdieu reintroduced the idea in 1985, expanded on more recently by Coleman (1988, 1990), Putnam (1995, 2000), and other social theorists. Even though it is a much discussed and critiqued topic in government, bureaucratic, and academic circles, a clear definition of social capital remains elusive. For example, questions remain as to how it is measured, cultivated, accumulated, depleted, and, perhaps most importantly, whether or not it can actually contribute to social change (Falk and Kilpatrick 1999). While these questions will not be answered in this chapter, we can begin to see the difficulty of operationalizing social capital. While there seems to be a plethora of extant empirical research studying the effects of social capital on school children. Parcel and Dufur (2001) maintain that there is a dearth of studies about how social capital is cultivated, in particular, independently of socio-economic status (SES) and family levels of social capital. In fact, much research has been conducted examining family capital and its influence on academic achievement (Bourdieu and Passeron 2000), yet the inclusion of school and district influence has only recently emerged as a new focus of research to determine student outcomes (Parcel and Dufur 2001). Parcel and Dufur (2001) maintain that a sole focus on family disadvantage may overestimate its influence on achievement, and underestimate or ignore influences brought about by educational institutional mechanisms. Researchers have drawn the attention of policymakers to the impact districts, schools, and teachers have in contributing to educational attainment, the probability of dropping out, the risk of expulsion, and the risk of being held back a grade (Parcel and Dufur 2001). School and district capital often generate and reproduce general and race-specific family disadvantages that include racial inequalities in enrolment, school social class composition, instructional expenditure, and crime. This can lead to variations in school resources/climate and degree of class/race segregation at the school level, impacting educational opportunity (e.g. Roscigno 2000; Wenglinsky 1998).

Sociologists have posited theories such as Woolcock's (1998) notion that social capital reflects the norms and networks of collective action and benefit. Woolcock (2001) discusses the notion of 'linking' social capital, which enables individuals with different amounts of power (i.e., senior management/administrators, other staff/lecturers/teachers, students) to leverage resources, ideas, information, and knowledge within a community or a group. This enables individuals with different amounts of power capacities to connect in a mutually beneficial way resulting in reciprocal relationships among individuals, with each viewed as being in a position to exchange equally. Portes (1998) stresses that social capital is an inherent element of relationships. Bourdieu (1986) highlights the invisible nature of social capital mostly acquired as a result of being part of a group or community, yet at the same time is often implicated in the reproduction of inequality. According to Coleman (1988), social capital is not within individuals per se, rather the individual can benefit from it as a resource to individual or collective ends. Coleman (1990) maintains that social capital can actually be an equalizer of disadvantaged individuals and groups. In these cases, he cites disadvantaged students who achieve high test scores as a direct result of parent involvement reducing existing inequalities.

While critics (e.g. Arneil 2006) maintain that there is no more incremental decline of social capital than normal, this chapter will rely heavily on Putnam's theory of social capital, which builds on Coleman and Bourdieu's work and reflects a more contemporary view of social capital and trust. Despite criticism, Putnam has been concerned with the apparent decline in social capital since the 1960s. According to Putnam (2000), communities and individuals benefit from social capital. But if communities typically gain only from co-operation among their members, individuals may only turn uniquely to people in the community they have ties with for support. These two levels of networks—the individual and the community—become important later in the discussion of theorizing how well districts might (or might not) be able to make their network of information accessible to *all* and, in doing so, (de)cultivate social capital in their communities. For networks to function in a healthy way, Putnam (2000) argues that interactions need to be frequent and reciprocal. In this way, districts are able to foster connectedness and *trust* with individuals, the community, and civil society.

The decline in social capital, connectedness, and trust can be, according to Putnam, attributed to the changes in community structures and family relationships. This may result in distanced relationships, unintended privacy or estrangement, and isolation, resulting in the loss of social support from friends and families. In particular, families located in low-income neighborhoods face disadvantages and social network obstacles that become more impermeable in terms of access to 'educational resources, power, and the process of social learning and reproduction of values, knowledge and norms of behaviour' (Bourdieu 1986: 3). Putnam (2000) stresses that the number of connections an individual makes is an indicator of the cultivation of social capital. He further argues that it is the density of these networks and their connections that allow for rich social capital. Bourdieu also emphasizes their quality, all of which require equal consideration. Bourdieu's theory takes on a more critical stance by positing that many individuals or groups are constrained by economic and cultural factors, limiting their range of possibilities, based on their marginalized economic or cultural status, for creating networks or drawing on the resources inherent in them. This perspective, according to Bourdieu, questions the quintessential normative function of social networks and illuminates power relations within these networks.

Research in the UK (e.g. Morrow 1999, 2001) highlights how youth, parents, and the public experience their local community and schools. Their findings show that academic choices are constrained by everyday contexts, and a range of community, environmental, family, and socioeconomic factors. A key aspect, however, of declining social capital, emphasized by Putnam, includes the extent of (or lack thereof) participation in networks, emotional, and instrumental support gained, trust and reciprocity, and shared norms. These, in turn, are linked to child welfare outcomes such as physical health, mental health, cognitive skills, and life skills. Indeed, if any of a student's and/or their family's level of trust with either an individual or institution is low, Goddard (2003) argues that this affects academic engagement.

While the earlier definitions of social capital have an explicit theoretical quality to them, in an attempt to reify this abstraction, contemporary organizations such as the Organization for Economic Co-operation and Development (OECD), UK Office for National Statistics (ONS), and the Australian Bureau of Statistics (ABS) currently rely on an agreed upon definition. There, social capital is defined as the cultivation of networks fostering shared norms, values, and understandings that facilitate co-operation within or among groups (OECD 2001). According to Nieminen et al. (2008), Canada also relies on the aforementioned definition although it is not yet officially endorsed. Statistics New Zealand has its own variation which reflects a focus on fostering relationships among individuals, groups, and/or organizations that provide the capacity to act for mutual benefit or a common goal (Zukewich and Norris 2005).

Therefore, while it seems that no one definition of social capital exists, it is not surprising that several debates concerning the definition that remain unresolved. While it is beyond the scope of this chapter to discuss these definitions exhaustively, one definition seems most suitable for the purpose of this chapter: social capital's potential as a social resource facilitating community between and among individuals and groups. Resources can generate social mobility, educational mobility, and academic success. What is important to note, however, is that the foundation of the concept of social capital has traditionally been community based, although there is some debate among scholars as to the community-based versus individual-based element of social capital. Historically, the focus was community based as theorists such as Fukuyama (1995), Kawachi et al. (1997), Portes (1998), and Putnam (2000) introduced the notion of social capital as the property of individuals who use it to access resources. Further to this, Glaeser (2001) concurs that it is individuals who decide if, when, and how they will access social capital. Currently, therefore, a consensus has emerged that claims social capital can begin from both an individual and from a community level (Nieminen et al. 2008). Subramanian, Kim, and Kawachi (2006) provide an example by explaining that individuals with high levels of trust may be healthier than individuals with low levels of trust regardless of the amount of trust in the community. Poortinga (2006) adds that the benefits of social capital can be the result of an individual's access to social networks and not necessarily from the levels of social capital within the community.

There remains some concern, however, that as a group resource, social capital has the potential to exclude those who are not 'in' the group characterized by productive relational networks, trust, and norms (e.g., social solidarity). Kerbow and Bernhardt (1993) attempt to discredit this myth with their research showing that after controlling for SES, African American and Hispanic families were still contacting schools and participating in school events (e.g. PTO). These findings reveal that social capital was still cultivated among disadvantaged families despite SES. We might conclude then, that social capital refers to individuals' and communities' access to resources, networks, shared values, and trust. Any individual who has access to such tangible and intangible resources and relationships should find that life opportunities are considerably enhanced (Balatti and Falk 2002).

The second debate among scholars (e.g. Coleman 1990; Paxton 1999) questions the notion that social capital is always productive, making possible the achievement of certain ends that would be unattainable in its absence. Often individuals with high levels of social capital are highly educated with high earning potential and good social networks giving them privileged access to knowledge, information, and opportunities (Burt 2000; Inkpen and Tsang 2005). Nevertheless, Paxton (1999) claims that a major problem with this theoretical notion is that researchers have assumed that social capital's effects will always be positive. Acknowledging that social capital can exist at different levels can help us understand that it need not always imply positive effects for all members of a community. That is, within a single group it need not be positively related to that at the community level.

While social capital within a particular group may be expected to have positive effects for the members of that group, this need not necessarily result in positive gains in social capital for the entire community. Paxton (1999) provides an example by explaining that an ethnic group might have high social capital within its endogamous group but a reduced level in the larger, exogamous community by either having no ties with others outside of the group or in reducing the overall level of trust in those outside the group. Granovetter (1983) has found in his research that weaker ties usually link individuals in small groups and expand the network of the groups but also only deliver knowledge that is not too complex while stronger ties may be able to pass along more complex knowledge to fewer individuals and groups. For example, interest groups could potentially decrease trust within the entire community resulting in outcomes that may not benefit the community as a whole or every member of the community.

Given the multifaceted nature of these challenges in attempting to define social capital as a concept, the focus of this chapter, then, is to theorize how districts might enhance or deplete social capital when disseminating information and sharing knowledge. Knowledge possessed by one member (i.e., an individual, a group of individuals or institution, or district) in a network can either be shared easily and efficiently in organizations with sufficient social capital, while in contrast, disseminated and shared inefficiently and inequitably when there is insufficient social capital (Collins and Hitt 2006). Makino and Inkpen (2003) believe that when sufficient social capital exists it can foster a common organizational understanding of knowledge aided by communal resources in cultivating a common culture (e.g. a shared identity, language, artifacts, and norms). Lucas (2005) concludes that trust is the key factor in sharing organizational knowledge yet it can be hindered by structural conditions such as bureaucracy or toxic cultures. In fact, it is believed by many scholars that trust is considered the most important, the most complex, and the most difficult to measure the dimensions of social capital (Zukewich and Norris 2005).

THEORIES OF TRUST

Trust remains a difficult concept to define. A number of psychological definitions describe trust as: 'a generalized expectancy held by an individual that the word, promise, or statement of another individual can be relied upon' (Rotter 1980: 1); 'a confidence that one will find what is desired from another, rather than what is feared' (Deutsch 1973: 148); or 'reflecting confident expectations of positive outcomes' (Holmes and Rempel 1989: 188).

From a sociological perspective, Putnam, Coleman, and Bryk, and Schneider stress the importance of trust, or 'social trust', in its capacity to provide valuable opportunities for the exchange of quality information.

Bryk and Schneider (2003) maintain that social trust instills confidence in the expectation that institutions will act reliably and competently. Furthermore, individuals engaged in relationships characterized by high levels of social trust are more likely to openly exchange and receive information than those in relationships with low levels of trust.

While definitions of trust are often typically outside the realm of educational literature and refer more closely to interpersonal relationships rather than to family–school/district relationships, for the purposes of this chapter, it is necessary to re-examine trust from an educational perspective. Despite a paucity of research examining trust between families, schools, or districts, a few studies are highlighted here. For example, Dunst et al. (1992) discovered in a survey of administrators and parents of children with special needs that trust was a key element in establishing positive parent–professional partnerships. Adams and Christenson's (1999) research examined levels of trust between parents and teachers of middle school students in an urban setting in regular and special education; it indicated that parent trust for teachers was higher than teacher trust for parents, regardless of income, ethnicity, and type of educational service (e.g. for special education or the regular curriculum). There were, however, higher trust levels evident among parents of special education children. The authors speculate that these high trust levels among parents were a direct result of positive school culture which nurtured family–school interaction. The study also concluded that any evidence of mistrust influenced parents' attitudes and behaviours related to participation in their children's education.

In order to gain a better understanding of what we mean by 'educational trust', Barber defines trust as expectations individuals have of each other, of the organization and institutions, and of the moral social values by which they abide. Rempel, Holmes, and Zanna (1985) theorize that trust is based on predictability, dependability, and faith.

The first and lowest level of trust to which they refer, 'predictability', occurs when individuals rely on established or predictable behaviour and emotional responses in a given environment. In terms of information dissemination or the sharing of knowledge, predictability garners trust when it is disseminated regularly and routinely. Holmes and Rempel's (1989) research on 82 couples demonstrated that level of trust often determines the amount of caring and responsiveness to others. Additionally, individuals in low trust relationships typically expected the worst and took control of their interactions with others, or what Holmes and Rempel call security insurance to enhance their own social capital.

'Dependability', a characteristic of medium trust, refers to trust as a personal attribute where individuals or institutions are viewed as trustworthy when their behaviour is predictable and responsive to the needs of others (e.g. parents, students) on a routine basis, instilling a feeling of dependability. Medium trust relationships are characterized in Holmes and Rempel's (1989) research as a type of trustworthiness that remains uncertain and precarious. In other words, individuals wanting to trust others or institutions are typically in a defensive mode, always scrutinizing the others' actions for flaws or deception. Medium trust relationships usually under-recognize positive behaviours while over-emphasizing negative behaviours. In contrast, high trust interactions where interactions are frequent tend to develop a common knowledge that sustains trustworthy relationships (Power and Bartholomew 1987).

The third level, 'faith', the highest developmental stage of trust, reflects an emotional security in others or institutions where there is a belief that individuals or institutions will keep their promises in their efforts to be responsive to the needs of stakeholders. In high-level trust relationships, individuals place less value on negative actions and focus on past and present positive actions. Individuals in high trust relationships, therefore, tend to be able to see the big picture and realize that ultimately, despite setbacks, positive actions will prevail (Holmes and Rempel 1989).

Each of these types of trust can be defined using varied terminology. For example, with higher levels of trust Adams and Christenson (1999) use the term 'confidence' interchangeably with the term 'faith'. Luhmann (1988) points out that often the public does not have any choice but to have confidence or faith in organizations. For example, parents must simply rely on those that they do not know, guided by policies of which they are unaware. In these cases, individuals can only have what Paxton (1999) calls 'institution specific' levels of trust based on generalized estimates of the technical competence and moral obligations of individuals in an institution, as well as estimates of the sanctions inherent in the social structure of that institution. This perspective of trust is similar to Giddens's (1990) notion of trust in what he calls 'expert systems' in which we may not actually know the details of how our car or house was constructed but we believe in the trustworthiness of the system to ensure a quality product.

It becomes evident that not only is trust difficult to define, but the terms used to define it are used interchangeably, contributing to its definitional ambiguity in meaning. For example, a definitional conundrum occurs when terms such as 'confidence' and 'faith' are conflated, particularly when 'faith implicitly embodies pure or unconditional belief in others, [when in actuality] trust implies a reasoned expectation, what some call "enlightened calculation" about outcomes caused by others' (Leveille 2006: 87). Regardless of these definitional discrepancies, however, it seems that when there is limited amount of contact in the family–school relationship, trust usually remains at the lowest level, despite the fact that parents and teachers may continue to seek out evidence of trustworthiness. Once there is a breakdown of trust, the relationship is at risk of failing and even more at risk of ever gaining the public's trust again despite positive trustworthy outcomes in the past (Holmes and Rempel 1989). Swinth (1967) maintains that individuals (e.g. parent–teacher relationships in this case) are less likely to trust others if interactions are infrequent or absent. Developing trusting relationships takes not only time but also transparency and accountability (Leveille 2006).

TRUST AND THE PUBLIC GOOD

As this chapter's main focus is on the (de)cultivation of trust as a critical component of social capital during information dissemination and knowledge sharing by the school district with the community, the discussion moves beyond the school-house to implications of trust between the public and the school district, particularly since little is known about the processes by which trust is constructed between school sites, the community, and the district office (Chhuon et al. 2008). The role of the district central office, until recently, has typically been absent in discussions of educational innovation and school reform and, in fact, has been viewed as a hindrance to innovation (Berends, Bodilly, and Kirby 2002). Recent studies suggest that the district office can indeed serve as an agent of change in significant ways (Firestone et al. 2005). Most relevant here are the findings from empirical studies showing that a prerequisite to profound and sustainable change is the development of trust among district, schools, and the public (Anderson 2003; Bryk and Schneider 2003; Chhuon et al. 2008; Elmore and Burney 1999).

A review of the literature reveals some common elements shared by districts that have been successful in achieving reform. These include the following: a district-wide vision and strategy to improve instruction; data-based inquiry and accountability; a commitment to the development of and investment in teachers and staff; collaboration among and communication between all shareholders (Chhuon et al. 2008). When focusing on trust specifically, Leveille (2006) reminds us that public trust is an important aspect of education in the Western world. A decline of this trust leads to a decrease in public funds and collaboration with policymakers, and an increase in governmental intervention. In recent years, the actions of certain policies (e.g. No Child Left Behind) in the education sector have eroded public trust, making the education system susceptible to public scrutiny in order to maintain confidence in its work (Leveille 2006). In these tenuous times, Leveille (2006) recommends actions on the part of educational leaders that can rebuild trust such as: ethical practices, fair allocation of resources, a leveraging of power, clear goals, and reasonable infrastructures to comply with accountability systems that keep the public interest as a priority.

Corporate consequences of Enron, Global Crossing, Adelphia, and other companies' mishandling of trust have contributed to the dismantling of public confidence (Leveille 2006). In fact, the economic consequences have put the education forum under intense scrutiny along with other public services, creating a call for trust-building processes within organizations. Kochanek (2005) and Chhuon et al. (2008) lament that the organizational literature typically presents a static view of trust, ignoring its dynamic nature and potential for growth. In fact, elements that aid in creating and sustaining public trust in the 'marketplace' include transparency, integrity, interaction between an organization (e.g., school/district) and its community, and the recognition of emotional aspects of change, all of which are needed to begin rebuilding trust (Hargreaves and Fullan 1998; Leveille 2006).

SOCIAL ACCOUNTABILITY

One component in the (de)cultivation of trust in district interactions that remains under-examined is accountability—more precisely social accountability. While knowledge is more easily shared among partners who trust each other, such relationships are often influenced by network structures and institutions leading to either successful or unsuccessful communication (Levin and Cross 2004). An argument might be made that information dissemination and knowledge sharing rely on the (de)cultivation of trust ranging from organizations to families. Their success by an organization can not only be examined using a social capital lens to confirm the importance of trust in such endeavours, but also a social accountability lens to identify the potential obstacles and facilitators. Also, since social capital as a concept does not allow for critical analyses of politics, power, and policies, this secondary theoretical tool is useful when examining the networking potential of school districts and its implications in cultivating a culture of trust.

Social accountability takes many forms, including monitoring government activities, input on policies, action around single issues, media scandals, and legal action (Peruzzotti and Smulovitz 2006). Due to the nature of these types of activity, organizations and individuals who rely on networking are required to do so responsibly within a framework of social accountability (Rivera 2006). For example, journalists rely on contacts in order to reach sources, and resources need to be mobilized to bring about an investigation into government practices (Rivera 2006). Because of this need for social organization and networking, as well as the increased levels of trust created by accountability, it can be argued that social capital and social accountability are necessarily intertwined in any discussion about information dissemination, knowledge sharing, and trust.

Much is being made of e-governance and e-democracy and the potential for citizens to participate in the decision-making of policies. Such a focus illustrates a horizontal or bottom-up decision-making process involving input by public and non-profit organizations instead of relying solely on top-down decision making (Peruzzotti and Smulovitz 2006). Increasingly, attention is being paid to demands placed on institutions by citizens, non-governmental organizations (NGOs), and the media for the development of 'adequate and effective mechanisms of accountability' (Peruzzotti and Smulovitz 2006: 3). This demand moves institutional accountability beyond traditional mechanisms of control, such as elections, and allows for direct citizen action and input (Peruzzotti and Smulovitz 2006[1]).

While determining whether and how social capital is created via school district networks, one is encouraged to consider if connections between and among stakeholders are cultivated. More specifically, examining how districts contribute to social accountability makes one wonder whether *all* stakeholders are empowered. Therefore, some discussion is warranted to unpack the relation of social accountability and social capital when discussing district networking. Often the ability of community members to become actively involved with district issues depends on how willing the district is to share information and involvement. For example, an important characteristic of an effective public organization is its level of openness (Demchak, Friis, and La Porte 2000). Demchak, Friis, and La Porte maintain that 'better governance is achieved by more open public agencies with better citizen access to internal administrative information' (2000: 4). They argue, however, that the definition and achievement of openness has not been standardized, allowing for public agencies to create propaganda with the intent of promulgating an alleged transparency, or, failing to provide enough information or providing too much information, rendering it useless (Wong and Welch 2004).

For the purpose of this chapter, the definition of social accountability supplied by Wong and Welch (2004) will be used, namely, the degree to which an institution answers to the public for its performance. There are two major elements of accountability according to this perspective: (a) citizens need to know what an organization is doing (transparency/openness); and (b) they must be able to interact with the organization (interactivity). Furthermore, it is not just data availability that contributes to accountability and trust, but also the timely delivery of that data and the ability of individuals to use it effectively (Demchak, Friis, and La Porte 2000).

Transparency and social accountability are of the utmost interest in this section as these are values inextricably intertwined with trust. Using Leveille's (2006) definition, transparency involves voluntarily making information available to *all* stakeholders (e.g. public, parents etc.). Districts and educational leaders should ideally be open about their mission statement, goals, resources, budget, student successes and areas needing improvement, special programmes, demographics, et cetera. More importantly, however, this information should be made accessible in an accurate, achievable way. Simply saying that the information is available is not enough to gain the public's trust; accountability and transparency must involve the public (Leveille 2006). This means that educational leaders of schools and district offices are accountable for using the public's money in ways that will benefit *all* stakeholders since their key mandate is to responsibly serve the interests of the public (Leveille 2006). Ultimately, the impact of trustworthy district information dissemination and knowledge sharing is significant since it is dependent upon the district to be vulnerable to the public (Abrams et al. 2003; Inkpen and Tsang 2005; Lucas 2005). Relationships with high levels of trust generally share knowledge easily. It is less costly since individuals are less defensive and apt to protect their own interests; and knowledge tends to be absorbed and retained (Levin and Cross 2004; Lucas 2005). Furthermore, depending on what information districts choose to publish, individuals can more readily monitor performance, access information about the district, and learn how they can be involved and how well the district responds to citizen input. These are important elements in improving transparency (Demchak, Friis, and La Porte 2000; La Porte, Demchak, and de Jong 2002).

By attempting to locate an intersection between social accountability and social capital, therefore, the issues of cultivating citizen trust and reciprocity of an organization bring us full circle to the earlier discussion of the key components of social capital (La Porte, Demchak, and de Jong 2002). For example, individuals who feel they can trust their school district will be able to draw from it more comfortably and feel part of such an information network. La Porte, Demchak, and de Jong (2002) argue that a high level of trust among individuals (communities that already have strong social capital) allows information to move freely, with less hoarding. Social accountability may increase social capital in areas that already have a high amount and serve to compound the lack of social capital in areas with less.

CONCLUSION

In an era of democratic learning, it is incumbent upon districts to contribute to social accountability networks in order to create equitable mechanisms for knowledge sharing and dissemination of information to *all*, both within and beyond the school and district. Sociological perspectives of these networks might rely on social capital and social accountability theoretical lenses to determine their potential for innovative knowledge sharing and a transformation or cultivation of capital within school districts. Research examined in this chapter demonstrates that social capital contributes to academic outcomes. When examining the influence of social capital on student achievement, the cumulative effect of the district often generates (dis)advantages among students leading to variations in resources/climate and class/race segregation. Such findings show how social capital is central to understanding the patterning of group inequality and suggest that stratification pertaining to race and educational outcomes may be reproduced through institutions and their expenditures. Information dissemination and knowledge sharing hold great potential for increasing district accountability *or* creating stratification among stakeholders in its transparency of information.

In summation, this chapter presented a theoretical discussion to examine the (de)cultivation of capital through the use of district information dissemination and knowledge sharing. More specifically, aspects of social accountability and social capital perspectives offered the theoretical tools with which to examine districts' potential to allocate resources, information about the education system and educational routes to socio-economic mobility for *all*. The research examined reveals that districts have the capacity to play an integral part in knowledge sharing and dissemination of their district policies by transforming such viable networks for their surrounding communities. Depending on what, how, and to whom districts choose to publish information, individuals can more readily monitor performance, access information about the district, find out how they can be involved, and how well the district responds to citizen input (Demchak, Friis, and La Porte 2000).

On a micro level, studies show that social capital (or lack thereof) often generates (dis)advantages among students and student achievement as a result of racial inequalities in enrolment, school social class composition, and instructional expenditure, all of which lead to variations in school resources/climate and degree of class/race segregation impacting educational opportunity (Coleman 1988). While this chapter does not specifically examine the micro level of schooling, it focuses on the larger macro findings that inevitably impact the micro-level of schooling. It theorizes how contemporary social organizational networks and institutional processes (i.e. school districts) are central to understanding the patterning of group inequality and stratification pertaining to race and educational outcomes, which may in fact be reproduced through institutions and their expenditures (Bourdieu and Passeron 2000). The critical components under study here are the knowledge sharing, information dissemination, transparency, equity, accuracy, and accessibility that introduce a form of district social accountability and (de)cultivation of social capital, or trust. Essentially, these criteria have the potential to transform or hamper networks that impact social capital at the school level.

With the increasing importance of producing research that meets the demands of the public interest, in an era where there is a decline of social capital and public trust of institutions and organizations, transparency of accountability systems is critical. Communication of these systems, methodological processes, and the process of how they impact students' learning and, ultimately, achievement, is of utmost interest to parents, educators in general, and governing bodies. Along with transparency comes the potential for dialogue and opportunities to adapt jurisdictional mandates to local settings. These issues are central to districts and the schools they govern, as well as concepts and principles that act as a mediating force and support for reform policy implementation through knowledge sharing and information dissemination, and in renewing the superintendent's leadership role at the district level in implementing and transforming the perception of transparent information systems and networks through trust.

NOTES

1. Peruzzotti and Smulovitz (2006) have been credited with adopting the expression 'social accountability' to describe this phenomenon. Although Peruzzotti is the first author to use social accountability in the context of democracy and political control, it has been used previously in sociology literature in relation to interpersonal social interaction.

REFERENCES

Abrams, L., et al. (2003) 'Nurturing interpersonal trust in knowledge-sharing networks'. *Academy of Management Executive* 17 (4): 64–77.

Adams, K.S., and Christenson, S.L. (1999) 'Trust and the family–school relationship examination of parent–teacher differences in elementary and secondary grades'. *Journal of School Psychology* 38 (5): 477–97.

Anderson, S.E. (2003) 'The school district role in educational change: A review of the literature'. ICEC Working Paper No. 2, Toronto: Ontario Institute for Studies in Education. Online. Available HTTP: http://fcis.oise.utoronto.ca/~icec/workpaper2.pdf (accessed 20 September 2005).

Arniel, B. (2006) *Diverse Communities: The Problem with Social Capital*. Cambridge: Cambridge University Press.

Balatti, J., and Falk, I. (2002) 'Socioeconomic contributions of adult learning to community: A social capital perspective'. *Adult Education Quarterly* 52 (4): 281–98.

Berends, M., Bodilly, S., and Kirby, S. (2002) 'Looking back over a decade of whole-school reform: The experience of new American schools'. *Phi Delta Kappan* 84 (2): 168–75.

Bourdieu, P. (1986) 'The forms of capital'. In *Handbook of Theory and Research for the Sociology of Education*, ed. J.G. Richardson. New York: Greenwood.

Bourdieu, P., and Passeron, J. (2000) *Reproduction in Education, Society and Culture*. Thousand Oaks, CA: Sage.

Bryk, A.S., and Schneider, B. (2003) 'Trust in schools: A core resource of school reform'. *Educational Leadership* 60 (6): 40–44.

Burt, R.S. (2000) 'The network structure of social capital'. *Research in Organizational Behavior* 22 (2): 345–423.

Chhuon, V., et al. (2008) 'The little district that could: The process of building district–school trust'. *Educational Administration Quarterly* 44 (2): 227–81.

Coleman, J.S. (1987) 'Families and schools'. *Educational Researcher* 16 (6): 32–38.

———. (1988) 'Social capital in the creation of human capital'. *American Journal of Sociology* 94 (1): 95–120.

———. (1990) *Foundations of Social Theory*. Cambridge, MA: Harvard University Press.

Collins, J.D., and Hitt, M.A. (2006) 'Leveraging tacit knowledge in alliances: The importance of using relational capabilities to build and leverage relational capital'. *Journal of Engineering and Technology Management* 23 (3): 147–67.

Demchak, C., Friis, C., and La Porte, T.M. (2000) *Webbing Governance: National Differences in Constructing the Face of Public Organisations*. Online. Available HTTP: http://www.cyprg.arizona.edu/publications/webbing.rtf (accessed 23 March 2007).

Deutsch, M. (1973) *The Resolution of Conflict: Constructive and Destructive Processes*. New Haven, CT: Yale University Press.

Dunst, C.J., et al. (1992) 'Characteristics of parent and professional partnerships'. In *Home–School Collaboration: Enhancing Children's Academic and Social Competence*, ed. S.L. Christenson and J.C. Conoley. Silver Spring, MD: National Association of School Psychologists

Elmore, R.F., and Burney, D. (1999) 'Investing in teacher learning'. In *Teaching as the Learning Profession*, ed. L. Darling Hammond and G. Sykes. San Francisco: Jossey-Bass.

Falk, I., and Kilpatrick, S. (1999) 'What is social capital? A study of interaction in a rural community'. CRLRA-D5 Discussion Paper Series. Online. Available HTTP: http//:www.crlra.utas.edu.au (accessed 9 November 2008).

Firestone, W.A., et al. (2005) 'Leading coherent professional development: A comparison of three districts'. *Educational Administration Quarterly* 41:413–48.

Fukuyama, F. (1995) *Trust: The Social Virtues and the Creation of Prosperity.* New York: Free Press.

Giddens, A. (1990) *The Consequences of Modernity.* Stanford: Stanford University Press.

Glaeser, E.L. (2001) 'The formation of social capital'. *Canadian Journal of Policy Research* 2 (3): 34–40.

Goddard, R.D. (2003) 'Relational networks, social trust, and norms: A social capital perspective on students' chances of academic success'. *Educational Evaluation and Policy Analysis* 25 (1): 59–74.

Granovetter, M. (1983) 'The strength of weak ties: A network theory revisited'. *Sociological Theory* 1:201–33.

Hargreaves, A., and Fullan, M. (1998) *What's Worth Fighting for Out There?* New York: Teachers College Press.

Holmes, J.G., and Rempel, J.K. (1989) 'Trust in close relationships'. In *Close Relationships*, ed. C. Hendrick. Newbury Park, CA: Sage.

Inkpen, A.C., and Tsang, E.W. (2005) 'Social capital, networks, and knowledge transfer'. *Academy of Management Review* 30 (1): 146–65.

Kawachi, I., et al. (1997) 'Social capital, income inequality and mortality'. *American Journal of Public Health* 87 (9): 1491–98.

Kerbow, D., and Bernhardt, A. (1993) 'Parental intervention in the school: The context of minority involvement'. In *Parents, Their Children, and Schools*, ed. B. Schneider and J.S. Coleman. San Francisco: Westview Press.

Kochanek, J.R. (2005). *Building Trust for Better Schools: Research-Based Practices.* Thousand Oaks, CA: Corwin Press.

La Porte, T.M., Demchak, C.C., and de Jong, M. (2002) 'Democracy and bureaucracy in the age of the Web: Empirical findings and theoretical speculations'. *Administration & Society* 34 (3): 411–46.

Leveille, D.E. (2006) *Accountability in Higher Education: A Public Agenda for Trust and Cultural Change.* Berkeley: University of California Center for Studies in Higher Education.

Levin, D., and Cross, R. (2004) 'The strength of weak ties you can trust: The mediating role of trust in effective knowledge transfer'. *Management Science* 50 (11): 1477–90.

Lucas, L.M. (2005) 'The impact of trust and reputation on the transfer of best practices'. *Journal of Knowledge Management* 9 (4): 87–101.

Luhmann, N. (1988) 'Familiarity, confidence, trust: Problems and alternatives'. In *Trust: Making and Breaking Cooperative Relationships*, ed. D. Gambetta. New York: Basic Blackwell.

Makino, S., and Inkpen, A. (2003) 'Knowledge seeking FDI and learning across borders'. In *Handbook of Organizational Learning and Knowledge Management*, ed. M. Easterby-Smith and M. Lyles. Malden, MA: Blackwell.

Morrow, V. (1999) 'Conceptualizing social capital in relation to the well-being of children and young people: A critical review'. *Sociological Review* 47 (4): 744–65.

———. (2001) 'Young people's explanations and experiences of social exclusion: Retrieving Bourdieu's concept of social capital'. *International Journal of Sociology and Social Policy* 21 (4–6): 37–63.

National Education Goals Panel. (1995) *The National Education Goals Report: Building a Nation of Learners.* Washington, DC: US Government Printing Office.

Nieminen, T., et al. (2008) 'Measurement and socio-demographic variation of social capital in a large population-based survey'. *Sociology Indicators Research* 85 (3): 405–23.

Organization for Economic Co-operation and Development. (2001) *The Well-Being of Nations: The Role of Human and Social Capital.* Paris: Centre for Educational Research and Innovation.

Parcel, T.L., and Dufur, M.J. (2001) 'Capital at home and at school: Effects on student achievement'. *Social Forces* 79 (3): 881–912.

Paxton, P. (1999) 'Is social capital declining in the United States? A multiple indicator assessment'. *American Journal of Sociology* 105 (1): 88–127.

Peruzzotti, E., and Smulovitz, C. (eds.) (2006) *Enforcing the Rule of Law: Social Accountability in the New Latin American Democracies.* Pittsburgh: University of Pittsburgh Press.

Poortinga, W. (2006) 'Social capital: An individual or collective resource for health?' *Social Science & Medicine* 62 (2): 292–302.

Portes, A. (1998) 'Social capital: Its origins and applications in modern sociology'.
Annual Review of Sociology 24 (1): 1–24.

Power, T.S., and Bartholomew, K.L. (1987) 'Family–school relationship patterns: An ecological assessment'. *School Psychology Review* 16 (4): 498–512.

Putnam, R.D. (1995) 'Bowling alone: America's declining social capital'. *Journal of Democracy* 6 (1): 65–78.

———. (2000) *Bowling Alone: The Collapse and Revival of American Community.* New York: Simon & Schuster.

Rempel, J.K., Holmes, J.G., and Zanna, M.P. (1985) 'Trust in close relationships'.
Journal of Personality and Social Psychology 49 (1): 93–112.

Rivera, A.J.O. (2006) 'Social accountability in Mexico: The civic alliance experience'. In *Enforcing the Rule of Law: Social Accountability in the New Latin American Democracies,* ed. E. Peruzzotti and C. Smulovitz. Pittsburgh: University of Pittsburgh Press.

Roscigno, V.J. (2000) 'Family/school inequality and African-American/Hispanic achievement'. *Social Problems* 47 (2): 266–90.

Rotter, J.B. (1980) 'Interpersonal trust, trustworthiness, and gullibility'. *American Psychologist* 35 (1): 1–7.

Sandefur, R.L., and Lauman, E.O. (1998) 'A paradigm for social capital'. *Rationality and Society* 10 (4): 481–501.

Subramanian, S.V., Kim, D.J., and Kawachi, I. (2006) 'Social trust and self-rated health in US communities: A multilevel analysis'. *Journal of Urban Health* 79 (1): 21–34.

Swinth, R.L. (1967) 'The establishment of the trust relationship'. *Journal of Conflict Resolution* 11 (3): 335–44.

Wenglinsky, H. (1998) 'Finance equalization and within-school equity: The relationship between education spending and the social distribution of achievement'. *Educational Evaluation and Policy Analysis* 20 (4): 269–83.

Wong, W., and Welch, E. (2004) 'Does e-government promote accountability? A comparative analysis of website openness and government accountability'. *Governance* 17 (2): 275–97.

Woolcock, M. (1998) 'Social capital and economic development: Toward a theoretical synthesis and policy framework'. *Theory and Society* 27 (2): 151–208.

———. (2001) 'The place of social capital in understanding economic outcomes'.
Isuma 2 (1): 11–17.

Zukewich, N., and Norris, D. (2005) *National Experiences and International Harmonization in Social Capital Measurement: A Beginning.* Online. Available HTTP: http://www.stat.fi/sienagroup2005/douglas1.pdf (accessed 12 February 2008).

3 Trust in Organizational, Leadership, and Management Studies
Theories, Approaches, and Conceptions

Eugenie A. Samier

The examination of trust in organization theory has been well established since the early 1990s. Early authors include Putnam's *Making Democracy Work* (1993), Kramer and Tyler's *Trust in Organizations* (1996), and Lane and Bachmann's *Trust within and between Organizations* (1998), followed by Sztompka's *Trust* (1999), Putnam's *Bowling Alone* (2000), and Bachmann and Zaheer's *Handbook of Trust Research* (2006). The Russell Sage Foundation has played a prominent role by publishing a series of volumes on various aspects of trust and its relationship to society and societal institutions. They range in topic from Braithwaite and Levi's *Trust and Governance* (1998), Cook's *Trust in Society* (2001), Cook, Hardin, and Levi's *Cooperation without Trust?* (2005), Hardin's *Trust and Trustworthiness* (2002) and *Distrust* (2004), and Tyler and Huo's *Trust in the Law* (2002), as well as Kramer and Cook's *Trust and Distrust in Organizations* (2004).

Hardy, Phillips, and Lawrence (1998) provide a comprehensive overview of the literature on organizational trust that developed in the mid-1980s up to the 1998 publication of their survey. The major topics of this period include trust fostering co-operation beyond what contractual relationships can, trust as 'an alternative or supplement to hierarchies and markets' and rational prediction, trust as important for interorganizational co-operation, for collaboration, strategic alliances, reducing uncertainty, and uncovering innovative solutions. Many in organizational, leadership, and management studies connect productive practices to trust, covering virtually every facet of work relations and activities. Warah (2001) argues for trust building being part of risk-management models. Even prior to this period researchers were finding that trust greatly enhanced goal clarification, information exchange, problem-solving, and commitment in implementation (Zand 1972), and enhanced job satisfaction (Driscoll 1978). Trust also promised 'virtues' as a 'social resource', by reducing organizational transaction costs, creating spontaneous interpersonal sociability, and facilitating deference to organizational authorities (Kramer and Cook 2004: 2). Most of this literature rests upon two definitions of trust that Hardy, Phillips, and Lawrence regard as insufficient since they assume functionalism and benefice while ignoring problems of asymmetrical power and interest conflicts: 'one that defines trust as predictability, and one that emphasizes the role of goodwill' (1998: 64–65).

The momentum has not slowed down since 1998. A notable contribution is Nooteboom and Six's collection (2003) that examines the concept of the trust process, as well as many ways in which trust affects different aspects of organizational, administrative, and governance roles and relationships including the problems of norm violations and informal control, trust in work teams, 'epistemic communities', and leadership. The collection was designed to fill two gaps in the literature: the lack of empirical studies, and the trust process on organizational 'micro levels', or interpersonal relationships.

This chapter provides an overview of much of this literature, the scope of its approaches and conceptual frameworks, the forms of trust, mistrust, and betrayal it has examined, and the causal factors attributed to the formation and deformation of trust that seem most relevant to the contemporary university, including trust issues in professionalism and trust under the market economy.

TRUST AND MISTRUST IN MANAGEMENT AND LEADERSHIP

For studies on trust in educational leadership and administration, the implication is clear: a growing volume of research and theory on this concept has accumulated in organizational psychology, social psychology, depth psychologies, management and public administration studies, organizational behaviour, political studies, sociology, and leadership studies, but has not yet incorporated into educational studies. I would argue here, too, that the vast historical and biographical field containing an international repository on actual cases is vital to a comprehensive and sufficiently developed understanding of trust in educational organizations. And just as crucial is international comparison accounting for cultural, political, religious, and social factors.

Hardin (1999) raises an important limitation to the ability to trust, particularly apt in large industrialized societies where trusters cannot acquire adequate information to know whether it is misplaced, that is, in the hands of those who may not act in their best interests. This kind of public trust has been severely damaged by prominent corruption cases, and is stretched by the anonymity and distance they have from senior levels of public administration. This condition can also exist in large bureaucratic organizations, such as major universities where most faculty members have little contact, and receive little information about, what the executive level actually does. Herriot et al. (1998) claim that rapid economic growth and related global changes can damage or destroy the social capital of trust and reciprocity that allows for co-operation and collaboration, particularly when various forms of cost-cutting, like downsizing, flexible contracts, and outsourcing, reduce staff's ability to meet professional responsibilities (34–37). Also damaging to trust is management rhetoric that fails to meet, or indeed disguises, the difficult conditions in which staff operate or inadequately provide the support staff needed for organizational transitions (Herriot et al. 1998: 37–42, 89–92).

One of the features of 'modern' society is its bureaucratization, that is, the degree to which a regulated and codified meritocracy operates on the basis of rationality, administrative law, and natural justice. Even though bureaucratization has been demonized during the last few decades, its historical importance lies in replacing patrimonialism and naked self-interest. The problem with many 'bureaucracies', is not that they operate out of 'bureaucratic principles', but that they have deviated from them by hiring incompetent individuals, allowing micropolitics and toxic cultures to pervade, and may have a surfeit of individuals in the top echelons who have personality disorders or serious neurotic dispositions, situations that are common enough now to drive an industry of scholarship on these problems. In other words, trust has been undermined and damaged by many deviations from the purely bureaucratic. However, embedded in the nature of bureaucracy is a contradiction: once the bureaucracy establishes itself, its rule-based nature replaces relationships of trust (see Bottery 2003). Ciulla argues, with considerable verifying evidence, that a system of 'rules, contracts, and laws' not only at times substitutes for trust, but excessive amounts of such bureaucracy indicate that mistrust dominates (2000: 154). Govier (1992) concurs with this perspective, claiming that surveillance, contracts, and legal institutions cannot replace the need for trust.

There are preconditions to trust that have been explored, necessary for its formation and maintenance. Schindler and Thomas (1993) found, in descending order of importance, that trust among healthcare managers develops in relation to integrity, competence, loyalty, consistency, and openness. Among college undergraduates, Butler and Cantrell (1984) found that the order of importance varied in developing trust in faculty from competence, to integrity, consistency, loyalty, and openness. These can vary also in administration in relation to status: Gabarro's (1978) results demonstrate that trusting subordinates requires integrity, competence, and consistency, but trusting in superiors requires integrity, loyalty, and openness.

However, there are problems in the understanding of trust, its complexity, underlying nature, and relationship to other organizational and personal factors. Hardy, Phillips, and Lawrence have identified a number of these: many sources do not distinguish between relationships of trust and of power; make assumptions about common goals that are unrealistic; underestimate the complex nature of communication required in creating shared meaning; and underestimate domination. In addition, surface dynamics tend to be focused on the way that power can hide 'behind a façade' of trust and rhetoric about collaboration while using manipulation and the 'capitulation of weaker partners' to promote its vested interests. Those authors pursuing trust as a rational practice 'downplay the very real difficulties in creating cooperative relations' (1998: 65). Hardy, Phillips, and Lawrence offer a more robust definition that overcomes these deficiencies, drawing from the work of Sabel (1993) and Gulati (1995) who regard trust as a mutual confidence that neither side will exploit the vulnerabilities of the other: 'trust can be said to exist between partners when relations involve a high degree of predictability, on all sides, that the others will not engage in opportunistic behaviour' and that 'reciprocal communication' exists without sustaining 'asymmetrical power relations or to exploit a position of power' (Hardy, Phillips, and Lawrence 1998: 65). In leadership studies, as Dirks and Skarlicki explain, trust has been recognized for over four decades, however, '*how* trust in leaders contributes to the effective functioning of groups and organizations' has not been adequately researched (2004: 21). They review a number of issues (and provide a literature survey) that would need to be explored for an adequate explanation of leadership trust: 'theoretical perspectives on trust in leadership, positive consequences associated with trust in leaders, key issues related to attaining these consequences, and challenges related to the development of trust' (2004: 21).

When it is a senior administrator or leader who is the source of mistrust, the loss of trust is doubly distressing since it is in the roles of these individuals that the greatest responsibility for creating a trusting environment and the powers of approval lie. Senior officials also have considerable knowledge, access to information, and informal relationships with higher administration where approval and governance rest, as well as greater opportunity to create an informal network, that is, greater potential ability to cause harm to others. If leadership fails to engender trust, and even becomes the source of distrust, it 'degenerates into management and control, power politics and compromise' (Fairholm and Fairholm 2000: 102). Potter takes a close look at the impact of these power relations: 'how trusting one is, and the ease with which one can assume trust, has much to do with one's sociopolitical situatedness as it intersects with one's narrative history' (2002: x). Her analysis ranges from an examination of power differentials affecting the ability of one to trust, the vulnerabilities in trusting, how failures of trust occur, the role that discretionary power plays, the complexities of being in mid-level positions with concurrent trust demands and expectations from subordinates and superiors, to the role organizational ideologies play and the special attributes of trust for vulnerable clients.

Closely associated with senior officials is the governance structure. Buttery and Richter suggest that the division of power in a UK university now more closely resembles feudal baronial power set against a prince. In cases where authorities are found to be untrustworthy, baronial wars could break out, 'at every budget meeting, at every performance appraisal, during enterprise bargaining' (2003: 429). The main losses are lack of trust, which, for Buttery and Richter, in the case of untrustworthy superiors can lead to a withholding of information, substitution of untrusted policies and procedures with 'feudal justice', a failure to contribute resources to authority's projects or innovations (2003: 433).

A climate of mistrust is one of fear. Ryan and Oestreich found that people in organizations most commonly feared retaliation, reprisals, and retribution (1991: 31). Another indication of fear is the existence of 'undiscussables', the most common of which, Ryan and Oestreich found in their extensive study, is the boss's management style; in a university this includes all administrative levels, from the chair up to the president. Presumably even abuses of power can be undiscussable, indicating that colleagues cannot even trust each other to report dissatisfaction. Mistrust is an indication that social relationships have not formed the reliability on each other necessary for collective action, in administrative or organizational settings often originating in punitive, restrictive, or inappropriate policies and rules imposed on a professional work-force (see Sitkin and Stickel 1996).

Indicative also is a culture that either tolerates or promotes a number of what may seem individually to be small and subtle acts, but when pervasive damage trusting relationships and produce a climate of betrayal: 'when we don't do what we say we will do, when we gossip about others behind their backs, when we renege on decisions we agreed to, when we hide our agenda and work it behind the scenes, and when we spin the truth rather than tell it' (Reina and Reina 2006: 7). Those in senior administrative and leadership roles carry a larger proportion of responsibility for allowing such climates to exist, especially when they do not hold people accountable for their damage to others when evidence is apparent (Reina and Reina 2006: 10) or do not manage organizational conflict, blaming the victim or demonizing some of the parties.

Trust can be derived or developed through different aspects of one's organizational persona. Lewicki and Bunker (1996) identify three that can be distinguished in professional relationships, and which can build sequentially: (a) calculus-based trust, primarily a deterrence-based trust, either doing what one says because the consequences of not doing so need to be avoided or to earn the rewards through being trustful; (b) knowledge-based trust, coming from knowing the other person well enough to rely upon their behaviour; and (c) identification-based trust, where mutual understanding exists sufficiently to confidently act for one another. This last form is recognized by Kramer (1993) in groups where identification grows through embracing the organization's goals and culture. Features of character and personality are also important, particularly ethical integrity, which Craig and Gustafson (1998) found strong evidence for in examining job satisfaction. Of course, a persona can be manufactured and projected, that is, not authentic to the individual's character and personality, in order to achieve a position of power, a practice that has been noted in political theory and sociology of politics since Machiavelli and examined in some detail in the many recent studies on narcissism.

Fairholm and Fairholm (2000) identify a broad range of 'forces' that can hinder the development of trust, in other words, forces that contribute to distrust. On an individual level are risks in interpersonal communication, apathy and alienation, the lack of effective accountability, cynicism, self-interest, and lack of leader sensitivity. Organizational forces include an authoritarian authority structure, a history of negative trust events, and a complicated hierarchy that diffuses responsibility. Contributing external forces can include the general societal decay of moral values such as integrity, honesty, dependability, and commitment that serve as preconditions for trust. Accompanying these are institutional and personal barriers that if not surmounted lead to mistrust and potentially betrayal. Contributing factors are also organizations or organizational components that have outlived their usefulness, traditionalism that can impose conformity that stifles innovation, reforms relating to uncontrolled growth (e.g. a programme that is being distributed or 'sold' to too many cohorts), and office politics that engender fear. A broad range of attitudes and behaviours exist on a personal level that contribute to mistrust: unwillingness to share power, sociopathic behaviour, excessive striving after status, open cynical behaviour, subversion (e.g. slander, rumour-mongering), and burn-out.

PROFESSIONAL TRUST

Trust in and by professionals is part of the work and employment literature, examined by a number of authors reflecting a broad range of approaches and aspects. Banks and Gallagher (2009) concentrate on a philosophical grounding to professionalism, based on virtue ethics consisting of respect, trustworthiness, justice, courage, and integrity (see also Barber 1983). Marsden (1998) explores the fragility of co-operation exhibiting a 'low-discretion-low-trust' character, for which organizational transaction rules and employment organizations (e.g. unions) and customs are necessary in preventing the 'slide' into low-trust relations. Teven, McCroskey, and Richmond (2006) found, in their results of a study on perceptions of supervisor Machiavellianism with full-time employees who were part-time graduate students in a corporate and organization communication programme, that high Machiavellian supervisors were found to be significantly less trustworthy. High Machiavellian students are more skilled at manipulation in achieving higher academic grades and in earning greater levels of occupational prestige, are frequently chosen and identified as leaders, and appear to be more socially attractive in the short run; however, in the long run their detached and calculating style leads to negative perceptions by others. In other words, they are willing to use any strategies or tactics that get them what they want, but end up sacrificing long-term credibility.

Vulnerability and risk are high in professional relationships, due to clients' relative lack of expertise, the qualities that grant professionals considerable 'discretionary powers' (Frowe 2005: 44), and a self-governing professional association. It is linked to the notion of caring, as Frowe argues, and involves trusting professionals, such as teachers, faculty, and educational administrators, to take care of one's own or one's children's education, in many cases with little effective choice in the matter or having to be reliant on those distrusted the least (2005: 34–35). Frowe also introduces an important distinction between what he calls 'primary trust' and 'secondary or background trust', the former voluntary or personal relationships and the latter a tacit relationship 'with individuals or institutions that we do not encounter directly' (2005: 36). For example, primary trust would be a relationship parents could have with a school principal (or university faculty members with chairs or deans) and secondary trust would be the majority of the educational system with a government department of education and the minister and cabinet.

Another important distinction for professionalism is that of legal legitimacy and moral legitimacy. The first involves the profession's establishment in law that provides powers for self-regulation, and the second involves the degree to which the public trusts the profession to maintain its standards. While Frowe (2005) concentrates on moral legitimacy as the arena in which public trust resides, I would argue here that a 'secondary' trust exists in which the public assumes that legal authority adequately manages the profession. However, the problem of the overseer offender is multilevel. They can take responsibility through rituals of responsibility, such as public apologies, but these may be undertaken as political tactics that prevent further inquiry into the moral responsibility of all those involved. When only individuals are investigated, individual offenses can seem incidental compared to the collective wrong-doing (Thompson 2005: 250–51).

Institutional insight failures take two main forms, according to Thompson. First is a prospective failure to support and maintain the structures and practices that prevent or record wrong-doing, such as implementing ethics policies on conflict of interest and reducing organizational memory by failing to keep adequate personnel records or communication procedures. The second is a retrospective failure to institute investigations or reforms, including the failure to protect whistle-blowers or investigate the overseers who failed, along with an organizational culture that reinforces suspicion of other agencies (Thompson 2005: 251–52). Effectively holding overseers responsible for their obligations requires that acts of omission rather commission, and gross negligence as well as intentional wrong-doing, be investigated (Thompson 2005: 253).

Where authority derives from legal-rational values, the basis on which meritocracy operates, all organizational members are dependent upon, and therefore must trust, their administrators to adhere to policy, rules, and procedures, as well as relevant legislation on labour and the constitutional rights of students, faculty, and staff. In some highly diverse jurisdictions like Canada where multicultural legislation exists, the community also needs to trust in its rights and interests being accommodated. Administrative authority trades on trust. Subordinates (students, teachers, faculty, etc.) have to trust in the ability and intent of administrators to be fair and equitable, eschewing personal networks, cliques, factions, or other basis for favouritism. In places where administrative law is based on natural justice, one should be able to have the expectation that such politics will be challenged by an administrator acting in the equitable interests of all.

On an individual level, there are many issues arising out of personality and character. Govier argues that self-trust is an important precondition for personal autonomy, self-respect, and self-esteem. I would argue here that it is also necessary for professionalism and collegiality, since, as Govier explains, self-trust is necessary in order to rely upon one's own critical reflection and judgment, basic competence, and worth (1993: 103–4). One form of neurotic disposition common to academia is 'neurotic imposters', who are high achievers but believe they are fakes or frauds, regard their success as meaningless and a burden, and display a number of dysfunctional behaviours, including the inability to trust others since they cannot trust themselves. They are abrasive, unable to delegate, catastrophize mistakes, centralize decision-making, and are impatient, creating 'a gulag-like atmosphere in their organizations' (Kets de Vries 2005: 114). Trust is given in relation to something, such as truth-telling or honesty, reliability, quality of knowledge, and expertise. When the standards of education are undermined, through credential inflation or misassignment of 'old boys' or members of one's personal network to positions of educational authority, mistrust in education will follow by students and the general population and among one's colleagues.

Trust is an important moral and psychological concept by which social action is enabled, but it is also a critical political concept upon which governance (including the shared governance in academic institutions), administration, management, and leadership rest, and an important value during change and reform processes. Most of our professional relationships rely on trust for collaboration and co-operation, for faith in policies and procedures to be adhered to, for fairness in treatment, for scholarly values to be protected from micropolitics and individual bias. And we trust in grievances to be remedied.

TRUST UNDER THE MARKET ECONOMY

One of the casualties of education entering the market economy, fueled not only by declining government funding but also by a number of other changes that came with the New Public Management (such as contracting out and short-term employment) is trust. Instead of a social conception of interacting individuals, the notion of *homo oeconomicus* is assumed in the market, raising self-interest to a fundamental behavioural principle.

Sennett argues that the current short time frames undermine trust, loyalty, and commitment, all of which require social bonds that take time to develop and which cannot simply be captured in formal agreements or contracts, excluded by virtue of the uncertainty and instability that comes with 'vigorous capitalism' (1999: 24, 31). There is little state buffer now to protect educational systems that in many countries are still largely public, but which have been redesigned through legislation and policy to become competitive profit-making enterprises.

Sennett distinguishes between two types of difficulties with trust in this environment: the absence of trust and 'a more active suspicion of others'. For him, the bonds of trust develop not through the formal channels and connections of bureaucracy, but 'informally in the cracks and crevices' as people learn whom they can depend upon. Absence of trust exists where the relational foundation does not exist among those who work independent of each other, relying on their own abilities, or where the exercise of power sends messages that it can do without those who do not take care of themselves (1999: 141–42). Suspicion of others, or mistrust, Sennett argues, occurs when people feel insecure, vulnerable, or unduly dependent (1999: 142). He has an interesting view of team-work in this regard: since it doesn't recognize power or privilege differences by expecting that people share a common motivation, it forms weaker bonds than those through engagement in differences over time (1999: 143), thereby creating weaker bonds of trust.

Kramer (1994) has examined similar ideas, demonstrating that when people are self-conscious or are under evaluative scrutiny they tend to overestimate how much they are scrutinized and treat it as personalistic, which creates a climate of distrust and suspicion of others' motives and intentions which he regards as paranoid (see also Fein and Hilton 1994). This work suggests that distrust probably increases significantly under regimes of evaluation and accountability like those that accompany the imposition of the current market model for education by neo-liberalism. Bottery (2003) has examined the effects of such government policy enacted through legislation in the UK on education, a move by government interpreted by the profession as a lack of trust and erosion of autonomy. Groundwater-Smith and Sachs (2002), drawing primarily on the neo-Marxist tradition of Freire and Giroux, explore the options for professional practice in this 'audit society', finding that the only alternative to entrepreneurialism is to act as an activist professional who requires the reinstatement of trust through the educational community in order to work against managerialism.

THE UNIVERSITY AND TRUST

Trust and betrayal have been common themes over the last 25 years in the study of the university, as both sources of betrayal and as instruments for betraying social, political, and cultural values. One of the early texts is Broad and Wade's *Betrayers of the Truth* (1982), which examines how the search for truth, particularly in biology and medicine, has been compromised by deceit, fraud, and self-deception, as well as the corruption of the system of checks and balances through peer review, in part a result of professionalism in science. It was followed by Judson's *The Great Betrayal: Fraud in Science* (2004). Another common theme is the corporatization and commercialization of the university; a very small sample includes Huer's Tenure for Socrates: A Study in the Betrayal of the American Professor (1991) on corruption of the tenure system by the professoriate who are wooed by politics and economics of the academic marketplace; Readings's *The University in Ruins* (1996) on the undermining of liberal education; Mujeeb-ur-Rahman's *The Betrayal of Intellect in Higher Education* (1997) examining the bureaucratization of the university that subverts intellectualism; Tudiver's *Universities for Sale: Resisting Corporate Control over Canadian Higher Education* (1999); and Conlon's 'Betrayal of the Public Trust: Corporate Governance of Canadian Universities' (2000). Kors and Silverglate examine the betrayal of civil liberties in *The Shadow University: The Betrayal of Liberty on America's Campuses* (1998).

The underlying critique of most of these books is that academia has lost its way valuationally, and, either through the human weaknesses of greed and jealousy or the unceasing external pressures on the university to play a stronger political and economic role, eventually betrays the very values that justified its existence intellectually. The phenomenon is not as new, though, as much of the literature would lead one to believe. The university and its professoriate has been under this pressure since modernized, technologized society took hold—an early critique of which was provided by Benda's 1927 essay *The Treason of the Intellectuals*, on the betrayal of intellectual values by the professoriate itself for other political and commercial ends.

The necessity for trust in universities takes many forms and is required at many levels. Liebeskind and Oliver (1998) examine the roles it plays in intellectual property and academic research, as people derive trust through 'personal experiences, through reputation, and through institutional supports', all of which are vulnerable in the commercialized climate of the US, the UK, and Israel. The main effects have been an erosion or severing of trust-based relationships; the new formalized contract relationships have in many cases undermined trust between researchers, and intellectual property contracts have 'disembedded' traditional research relationships. Even though in some cases commercialization interests can 'foster trust-based relationships' where interests converge, the threat to 'open science' and the values of publicity and impartiality are at grave risk (1998: 118, 139–40). There are many organizational structures that have been introduced because people cannot be trusted: faculty associations, professional unions, harassment offices, ombudsman's offices, etc. The literature on academic bullying and mobbing has demonstrated that the problem of betrayal has grown significantly in universities.

Maintaining trust in a university is a collective responsibility through collegial governance, even if senior university administrators like presidents have gained much more authority through structural transformations over the last couple of decades. Faculty members collectively still have considerable influence over research and teaching. The problem, as these books suggest, is not simply a failure of other social institutions to recognize university faculty jurisdiction, but an abrogation of responsibility originating within (see Samier 1997). On an individual level faculty members have to trust administrators on a day-to-day basis, particularly in North America, where so many activities are subject to approval (e.g. courses, research applications), in many cases by academic administrators who are not necessarily familiar with the discipline. Very little of a faculty member or student's organizational life is not touched by the need to trust in administrators.

There are also a number of trust issues in academic research. Trust has been the subject of research questions and design. Many instruments have been developed to measure trust (e.g. Comrey 1970; Guilford and Zimmerman 1956; MacDonald, Kessel, and Fuller 1972; Rosenberg 1957; Shostrom 1975; Wrightsman 1974) and mistrust (e.g. Heretick 1981; Kanter and Mirvis 1989; Rotter 1967). There are also instruments that, while not measuring trust directly, measure interpersonal relations, such as 'inability to get along' and 'hostile cynicism' (Hathaway and McKinley 1951). In reviewing these and other instruments, mostly of a psychological nature, Omodei and McLennan (2000) claim that a number of problems still exist in finding instruments that adequately measure trust and mistrust at the global level. More specialized instruments also exist to measure particular forms of mistrust, such as the Cultural Mistrust Inventory (Terrell and Terrell 1981), which measures Blacks' mistrust and suspiciousness of Whites in politics and law, interpersonal relations, education and training, and business and work.

Another major issue is the trust that is required between researchers and subjects. Lincoln and Guba argued for the importance of building and maintaining trust in field research since more credible data is likely to be produced, reviewing various theories on how trust is formed: exchange theory, in which one barters for trust; individual-morality theory, in which one needs to build up a 'good guy' image; adoption-of-a-membership theory, in which the research has to commit to the behavioural mores of a group; and psychological-need theory, in which research subjects see the inquiry fulfilling a personal need (1985: 256).

Form (1974) contributes an important part of the discussion through his portrayal of distrust encountered in international research. One must establish a rapport with officials; rely on the influence of sponsors and suspicion of researchers in particularly vulnerable communities or ones experiencing high levels of repression, conflict, or violence; demonstrate loyalty (in this case to a union); be willing to negotiate, mediate, and bargain; accept compromises; resist attempts to manipulate researchers for special interests (for example, corporate executives); tolerate surveillance; and recognize and appreciate sensitivities, among the many complexities and contradictions of some international (and even national) social science research. In some countries, with authoritarian governments for example, it is simply not possible to carry out many forms of research, including gaining access to libraries and archives.

A causal factor more specific to the educational institution is a form of mistrust that many have argued is wise. That is, the distrust of positivistic research particularly in fields of human interaction where critical and interpretive modes may be better suited. An excessive dependence upon science, and the spread of scientism, was regarded by many to lead to a disbelief in an everyday world, resulting in nihilism through the inability of this type of abstraction (mathematical and often materialist) to relate to human experience, particularly intersubjectivity. The list is long and early in the modern era: Max Weber, Georg Simmel, Max Scheler, William James, Oswald Spengler, Edmund Husserl, and George Santayana (Vaitkus 1990: 288). Science is often reduced to what Vaitkus refers to as a 'practical attitude', 'which is the world of my bodily locomotions and physical things that offer resistances and place tasks before me, and which through working acts of effort I gear into to change in order to carry through my plans'. This contrasts with the 'fiduciary attitude' which is 'a spontaneity involving the most basic elements of trust and belief in others in all their personal and non-identical human complexity' (1990: 293). The latter in organizational form consists of 'sedimented social history, "institutions" with their underlife and officially printed texts, and the "symbolic cosmos" ranging from its routine activity to its highly creative production of reflective symbolism' (1990: 293). For the individual, 'social action is reduced to natural behaviour and the inner freedom of the actor vanishes in the mechanisms of systemic and manipulatable orders' (1990: 293).

REFERENCES

Bachmann, R., and Zaheer, A. (2006) *Handbook of Trust Research*. Cheltenham: Edward Elgar.

Banks, S., and Gallagher, A. (2009) *Ethics in Professional Life: Virtues for Health and Social Care*. Basingstoke: Palgrave Macmillan.

Barber, B. (1983) *The Logic and Limits of Trust*. New Brunswick, NJ: Rutgers University Press.

Benda, J. (1927/1969) *The Treason of the Intellectuals*. Trans. R. Aldington. New York: W.W. Norton.

Bottery, M. (2003) 'The management and mismanagement of trust'. *Educational Management Administration & Leadership* 31 (3): 245–61.

Braithwaite, V., and Levi, M. (eds.) (1998) *Trust and Governance*. New York: Russell Sage Foundation.

Broad, W., and Wade, N. (1982) *Betrayers of the Truth: Fraud and Deceit in the Halls of Science*. New York: Simon & Schuster.

Butler, J., and Cantrell, R. (1984) 'A behavioural decision theory approach to modelling dyadic trust in superiors and subordinates'. *Psychological Reports* 55:19–28.

Buttery, E., and Richter, E. (2003) 'On Machiavellian management'. *Leadership & Organization Development Journal* 24 (8): 426–35.

Ciulla, J. (2000) *The Working Life: The Promise and Betrayal of Modern Work.* New York: Three Rivers Press.

Comrey, A. (1970) *Manual for the Comrey Personality Scales.* San Diego: EdITS.

Conlon, M. (2000) 'Betrayal of the public trust: Corporate governance of Canadian universities'. In *The Corporate Campus: Commercialization and the Danger to Canada's Colleges and Universities*, ed. J. Turk. Toronto: Lorimer.

Cook, K. (2001) *Trust in Society.* New York: Russell Sage Foundation.

Cook, K., Hardin, R., and Levi, M. (2005) *Cooperation without Trust?* New York: Russell Sage Foundation.

Craig, S., and Gustafson, S. (1998) 'Perceived leader integrity: An instrument for assessing employee perceptions of leader integrity'. *Leadership Quarterly* 9 (2): 127–45.

Dirks, K., and Skarlicki, D. (2004) 'Trust in leaders: Existing research and emerging issues'. In *Trust and Distrust in Organizations: Dilemmas and Approaches*, ed. R. Kramer and K. Cook. New York: Russell Sage Foundation.

Driscoll, J. (1978) 'Trust and participation in organizational decision making as predictors of satisfaction'. *Academy of Management Journal* 21 (1): 44–56.

Fairholm, M., and Fairholm, G. (2000) 'Leadership amid the constraints of trust'. *Leadership & Organization Development Journal* 21 (2): 102–9.

Fein, S., and Hilton, J. (1994) 'Judging others in the shadow of suspicion'. *Motivation and Emotion* 18 (2): 167–98.

Form, W. (1974) 'The politics of distrust: Field problems in comparative research'. *Studies in Comparative International Development* 9 (1): 20–48.

Frowe, I. (2005) 'Professional trust'. *British Journal of Educational Studies* 53 (1): 34–53.

Gabarro, J. (1978) 'The development of trust, influence, and expectations'. In *Interpersonal Behavior*, ed. A. Athos and J. Gabarro. Englewood Cliffs, NJ: Prentice Hall.

Govier, T. (1992) 'Trust, distrust, and feminist theory'. *Hypatia* 7 (1): 16–33.

———. (1993) 'Self-trust, autonomy, and self-esteem'. *Hypatia* 8 (1): 99–120.

Groundwater-Smith, S., and Sachs, J. (2002) 'The activist professional and the reinstatement of trust'. *Cambridge Journal of Education* 32 (3): 341–58.

Guilford, J., and Zimmerman, W. (1956) *Guilford–Zimmerman Temperament Survey.* Orange, CA: Sheridan Psychological Services.

Gulati, R. (1995) 'Does familiarity breed trust? The implications of repeated ties for contractual choice in alliances'. *Academy of Management Journal* 38 (1): 85–112.

Hardin, R. (1999) 'Do we want trust in government?' In *Democracy and Trust*, ed. M. Warren. Cambridge: Cambridge University Press.

———. (2002) *Trust and Trustworthiness.* New York: Russell Sage Foundation.

———. (ed.) (2004) *Distrust.* New York: Russell Sage Foundation.

Hardy, C., Phillips, N., and Lawrence, T. (1998) 'Distinguishing trust and power in interorganizational relations: Forms and façades of trust'. In *Trust within and between Organizations*, ed. C. Lane and R. Bachmann. Oxford: Oxford University Press.

Hathaway, S., and McKinley, J. (1951) *The MMPI Manual.* New York: Psychological Corporation.

Heretick, M. (1981) 'Gender-specific relationships between trust—suspicion, locus of control, and psychological distress'. *Journal of Psychology* 108 (2): 267–74.

Herriot, P., et al. (1998) *Trust and Transition: Managing Today's Employment Relationship*. Chichester: John Wiley and Sons.

Huer, J. (1991) Tenure for Socrates: A Study in the Betrayal of the American Professor. New York: Bergin & Garvey.

Judson, J. (2004) *The Great Betrayal: Fraud in Science*. Orlando: Harcourt.

Kanter, D., and Mirvis, P. (1989) *The Cynical Americans: Living and Working in an Age of Discontent and Disillusion*. San Francisco: Jossey-Bass.

Kets de Vries, M. (2005) 'The dangers of feeling like a fake'. *Harvard Business Review* 83 (9): 108–16.

Kors, A., and Silverglate, H. (1998) *The Shadow University: The Betrayal of Liberty on America's Campuses*. New York: Free Press.

Kramer, R. (1993) 'Cooperation and organizational identification'. In *Social Psychology in Organizations: Advances in Theory and Research*, ed. K. Murhighan. Englewood Cliffs, NJ: Prentice Hall.

———. (1994) 'The sinister attribution error: Paranoid cognition and collective distrust in organizations'. *Motivation and Emotion* 18 (2): 199–230.

Kramer, R., and Cook, K. (2004) 'Trust and distrust in organizations: Dilemmas and approaches'. In *Trust and Distrust in Organizations: Dilemmas and Approaches*, ed. R. Kramer and K. Cook. New York: Russell Sage Foundation.

Kramer, R., and Tyler, T. (eds.) (1996) *Trust in Organizations: Frontiers of Theory and Research*. London: Sage.

Lane, C., and Bachmann, R. (eds.) (1998) *Trust within and between Organizations*. Oxford: Oxford University Press.

Lewicki, R., and Bunker, B. (1996) 'Developing and maintaining trust in work relationships'. In *Trust in Organizations: Frontiers of Theory and Research*, ed. R. Kramer and T. Tyler. London: Sage.

Liebeskind, J.P., and Oliver, A.L. (1998) 'From handshake to contract: Intellectual property, trust, and the social structure of academic research'. In *Trust within and between Organizations*, ed. C. Lane and R. Bachmann. Oxford: Oxford University Press.

Lincoln, Y., and Guba, E. (1985) *Naturalistic Inquiry*. Newbury Park, CA: Sage.

MacDonald, A., Kessel, V., and Fuller, J. (1972) 'Self-disclosure and two kinds of trust'. *Psychological Reports* 30:143–48.

Marsden, D. (1998) 'Understanding the role of interfirm institutions in sustaining trust within the employment relationship'. In *Trust within and between Organizations*, ed. C. Lane and R. Bachmann. Oxford: Oxford University Press.

Mujeeb-ur-Rahman, M. (1997) *The Betrayal of Intellect in Higher Education*. Toronto: OmniView.

Nooteboom, B., and Six, F. (eds.) (2003) *The Trust Process in Organizations: Empirical Studies of the Determinants and the Process of Trust Development*. Cheltenham: Edward Elgar.

Omodei, M., and McLennan, J. (2000) 'Conceptualizing and measuring global interpersonal mistrust-trust'. *Journal of Social Psychology* 140 (3): 279–94.

Potter, N.N. (2002) *How Can I be Trusted? A Virtue Theory of Trustworthiness*. Lanham, MD: Rowman & Littlefield.

Putnam, R. (1993) *Making Democracy Work*. Princeton, NJ: Princeton University Press.

———. (2000) *Bowling Alone: The Collapse and Revival of American Community*. New York: Touchstone.

Readings, B. (1996) *The University in Ruins*. Cambridge, MA: Harvard University Press.

Reina, D., and Reina, M. (2006) *Trust & Betrayal in the Workplace*. 2nd ed. San Francisco: Berrett-Koehler.

Rosenberg, M. (1957) *Occupations and Values*. Glencoe, IL: Free Press.

Rotter, J. (1967) 'A new scale for the measurement of interpersonal trust'. *Journal of Personality* 35 (4): 651–65.

Ryan, K., and Oestreich, D. (1991) *Driving Fear Out of the Workplace: Creating the High-Trust, High-Performance Organization*. San Francisco: Jossey-Bass.

Sabel, C. (1993) 'Studies trust: Building new forms of cooperation in a volatile economy'. *Human Relations* 46 (9): 1133–70.

Samier, E.A. (1997) 'The capitalist ethic and the spirit of intellectualism: The rationalized administration of education'. In *L'éthique protestante de Max Weber et l'esprit de la modernité*, ed. G. Raulet. Paris: Éditions de la Maison des Sciences de l'Homme.

Schindler, P., and Thomas, C. (1993) 'The structure of interpersonal trust in the workplace'. *Psychological Reports* 73:563–73.

Sennett, R. (1999) *The Corrosion of Character: The Personal Consequences of Work in the New Capitalism*. New York: W.W. Norton.

Shostrom, E. (1975) *Personal Orientation Dimensions*. San Diego: EdITS.

Sitkin, S., and Stickel, D. (1996) 'The road to hell: The dynamics of trust in an era of quality'. In *Trust in Organizations: Frontiers of Theory and Research*, ed. R. Kramer and T. Tyler. Thousand Oaks, CA: Sage

Sztompka, P. (1999) *Trust: A Sociological Theory*. New York: Cambridge University Press.

Terrell, R., and Terrell, S. (1981) 'An inventory to measure cultural mistrust among Blacks'. *Western Journal of Black Studies* 5 (3): 180–84.

Teven, J.J., McCroskey, J.C., and Richmond, V.P. (2006) 'Communication correlates of perceived Machiavellianism of supervisors: Communication orientations and outcomes'. *Communication Quarterly* 54 (2): 127–42.

Thompson, D.F. (2005) *Restoring Responsibility: Ethics in Government, Business, and Healthcare*. Cambridge: Cambridge University Press.

Tudiver, N. (1999) *Universities for Sale: Corporate Control over Canadian Higher Education*. Toronto: Lorimer.

Tyler, T., and Huo, Y. (2002) *Trust in the Law: Encouraging Public Cooperation with the Police and Courts*. New York: Russell Sage Foundation.

Vaitkus, S. (1990) 'The crisis as a bankruptcy of trust: The fiduciary attitude, human nature, and ethical science'. *International Sociology* 5 (3): 287–98.

Warah, A. (2001) 'Trust-building in organizations: A fundamental component of risk management models'. *Optimum* 30 (3–4): 94–98.

Wrightsman, L. (1974) *Assumptions about Human Nature: A Social Psychological Approach*. Monterey, CA: Brooks/Cole.

Zand, D. (1972) 'Trust and managerial problem solving'. *Administrative Science Quarterly* 17 (2): 229–39.

Part II

Research Approaches

4 Reconceptualizing Educational Administration as a Hermeneutics of Trust

Stephanie Mackler and Séamus Mulryan

In this chapter, we consider how current practices in educational administration as both a professional practice and a scholarly field would have to be approached differently if the claims of philosophical hermeneutics—namely, a *hermeneutics of trust*—were taken seriously. Put simply, a hermeneutic, meaning-centred approach would conceive of educational administration more as a task of making meaning than as a technical enterprise, and it would conceive of scholarship as having a stronger interpretive dimension than current practices would admit to. Adopting such an approach would displace positivism's epistemological privilege in the field and, further, it would displace the hermeneutics of suspicion as the predominant alternative to positivist methods. Before we describe a hermeneutics of trust and its implications for educational administration, however, we first briefly outline recent critiques of the current conceptualization of administration.

Since its inception as a field of study, educational administration has been largely dependent on empiricist and behaviourist models of understanding, which has led to mechanistic, functionalist, bureaucratic, formulaic, and technocratic approaches to the field as both an intellectual and a practical endeavour (for an excellent survey of the history of the field, see English 2002; Greenfield 1979/1980; Samier 2005). According to John Smith and Joseph Blase:

> Empiricism assumes that as researchers discover objective knowledge of how social and emotional processes really operate, i.e. discover their underlying structures, we thereby gain both an intellectual and practical mastery of those processes. For intellectual mastery the idea is that the properly directed study of educational organizations and of the teaching–learning process will result in the discovery of law-like generalizations, theory, and so on. (1991: 8)

Within this framework, the educational administrator is assumed to be a 'technical expert both in instructional and organizational matters' (Smith and Blase 1991: 8) who masters and implements predetermined knowledge about organizational and pedagogical matters.

Yet recent criticisms of this understanding have challenged the notion that the social world can be manipulated and controlled in such a technical fashion. According to Smith and Blase, 'no law-like generalizations have been discovered with regard to instructional processes—or to any other schooling processes' (1991: 10). Spencer Maxcy similarly claims: 'Efforts to use traditional rational and technical methods to solve [problems facing educational administrators today] have failed' (1994: 1).

One reason for this failure, Fenwick English argues, is that educational administration relies upon the social sciences, and the very methods upon which the social sciences rely actually deny the possibility of achieving genuine understanding of educational leadership (2002: 117). Eugenie Samier explains:

> An understanding of the human condition is not only submerged in organisational levels of analysis, but is suppressed by the very assumptions and methods employed in constructing large-scale theories about human behaviour, efficient organizational design, and effective management techniques . . . [that] gloss over the complexities in the human character, power and politics dynamics, ethics in organisational life, and opposed contextual forces shaping the world and mentality of the administrator. (2005: 8)

It is important to note that while some critiques focus on the sheer ineffectiveness of social scientific research, some question whether we should attempt to manipulate the social world to begin with. For example, Maxcy worries that the privileging of scientific understanding has led to a mentality that has stressed 'the value of control and bureaucratic manipulations of children, teachers, and parents' and led to the 'powerless status of teachers, parents, and children within its boundaries' (1994: 2). In other words, within the current social scientific approach to educational administration, the administrator is conceived as one who makes decisions based upon efficiency, control, stability, and predictability, and whose various constituents are merely objects to be manipulated rather than active agents to be related to in various processes.

To speak of educational administration in *hermeneutic* terms is to make a break from this positivist emphasis on knowledge, mastery, and control. It is to shift away from the notion that educational institutions are ultimately predictable and manipulable and to reconceptualize the activities of educational administrators as fundamentally interpretive: educational administrators must interpret educational policy in order to make it relevant to the unique contexts of their own institutions; they must interpret the claims made by teachers, students, and community members about what is actually going on in their schools; they must interpret scholarly research and consider how it might be meaningful for their own institutions. And, they must relate each of these spheres to one another, considering how accounts of actual pedagogical situations complicate what is explained by policy and research, and vice versa. In this hermeneutic approach, educational administration:

> is essentially a task of creating meaning, interpreting significance, and choosing one's path for the future against the backdrop of what came before. It also focuses on what kind of people we become in administration—not just how tasks are carried out and organisational goals are fulfilled, but how cognizant we are of the moral dimensions, effects on personality and character, as well as the consequences for one's personal life . . . The intent is not to aim for better managerial principles of efficiency and effectiveness, but to an authentic appreciation of the human truths in organisations and the social good. (Samier 2006: 126–27)

Furthermore, from the perspective of hermeneutics, educational administration must come to terms with the lack of scientific objectivity when approaching these questions. As Smith and Blase assert, 'Leadership is therefore much more than strategic planning which calls upon the supposed law-like generalizations of empirical inquiry; leadership is rather an openness to issues of human significance' (1991: 16). Being open to 'issues of human significance' requires engaging with the ways people make sense of their lives, who they understand themselves and others to be, and how they conceive of their lives, values, and goals. Such openness presupposes that although we cannot seek universal laws for explaining, predicting, or controlling people, we can seek to understand them. As such, the task of a hermeneutics of educational administration is to understand the interpretations that people continually create to make sense of experiences in their lives insofar as these experiences and interpretations of them take place within and in relation to educational institutions. Such understanding positions educational administrators to make the best possible decisions within the always changing landscapes of their own institutions.

In what follows, we offer a descriptive account of educational administration from the perspective of the hermeneutic tradition in order to lay the groundwork for a hermeneutic approach to educational administration. Given that hermeneutic scholarship seeks not to prove or disprove, but rather, to illuminate, we hope to shed light on some aspects not yet touched upon by others who share our concerns. In particular, although Samier (2005) begins with the premise that educational leadership is fundamentally hermeneutic and proposes a humanistic approach to the graduate preparation of administrators, she does not fully outline what it means to ground educational administration in hermeneutics. Maxcy also claims that '[while Hans-Georg] Gadamer's version of poststructuralism [and hermeneutics] is fruitful for the teacher in the classroom, it is not evident that his techniques will help in dealing with the political and moral/ethical dimensions of school leadership' (1994: 8–9). We believe Gadamer can indeed contribute to a discussion of school leadership. In this chapter, we consider with more depth what it means to say that educational administration is hermeneutic work, and we draw largely on the philosophical hermeneutics of Gadamer to do so. Specifically, our aim is to describe the existential experience of relating to the world in a hermeneutic way and to consider how that experience plays itself out in the context of educational administration. In addition, we wish to add caution to those who adopt a 'critical hermeneutic' approach, or what Paul Ricouer calls a 'hermeneutics of suspicion' (for instance, see Lugg and Shoho 2006). While we agree that there is a place for a critical hermeneutics, we argue that ultimately hermeneutics must be trusting, thereby making a normative claim about a preferable type of hermeneutic stance. Finally, we conclude by offering some implications for the field of educational leadership as both a scholarly and a practical endeavour. (It is important to note that although our intent is to address educational administration as both a scholarly field and a professional practice, at times our claims will more clearly address one or the other.)

UNDERSTANDING HERMENEUTICS

To understand what it means to say that educational administration is a hermeneutic endeavour requires that we clarify what hermeneutics is. Hermeneutics is broadly the study of interpretation. Prior to groundbreaking work by Martin Heidegger and Gadamer, hermeneutics took *understanding* to mean what it does in everyday language, for example, 'I understand the solution to that problem', 'I understand what the author is saying', 'I understand how you are feeling'. The task of interpretation in these cases is to help us understand something initially foreign to us. In such cases I understand *through* some interpretive framework, be it my own experiences, propositional logic, mathematics, or a research approach such as 'a Marxist analysis'. With Heidegger came the reversal of the relation between interpretation and understanding—in interpreting we articulate what we *already* understand. This might seem counterintuitive, as one would think the task of interpretation is to reach out and gain something new rather than to simply reflect upon what we already think. In order for this reversal to make sense, one has to consider that understanding for Heidegger is not the cognition of something, but the way in which we already know our way around something. For example, when we walk into a room with a door, we open the door without having to cognize, 'That is a door. First I bring my hand to the knob, then I turn, then I push'. I understand what a door is by the fact that I do *not* have to cognize it prior to opening it and walking through it, and the fact that a door has come to be understood means that it has meaning. Thus any kind of cognition or conceptualization is a derivative of what is already understood. The non-conceptualized dimension of the carrying out of our activities is the interpretation of those things which have meaning, which in their totality comprise that which is already understood.

Understanding, then, is the background of intelligibility that allows us to be in the world without computing every move or every statement. We always already have and are guided by an understanding of our world that helps us make further sense of it, though we are not ordinarily aware of it or of its hold on our lives. Further, interpretation is thus defined not as the acquiring of information about what is to be understood, but the working out of possibilities allowed by one's understanding (Heidegger 1962: 189). That is, what we perceive as possible in our lives depends upon the understanding that serves as the backdrop for our perceptions. Our actions are interpretations of the understanding that lies in the background of everything we do. Likewise, when we seek more explicitly to interpret something, we rely upon our background understanding so that even when we state, 'I understand what you are saying', we already draw upon a specific understanding of the world and its numerous significances without which we could not cognize and articulate the statement to begin with.

One way to think of this in relation to our particular topic is to say that educational administrators have preconceived understandings of the aim of schooling. If we look to the particular aspects of schools, we can see that administrators apply their understandings of those aims in the way they shape their schools. (Although our examples here will be related to K–12 schooling, similar examples could be made in relation to post-secondary institutions as well.) For instance, if an educational administrator understands schooling as job preparation, then the administrator will frown upon the art teacher whose class creates a public mural and praise the economics teacher who teaches business math. The administrator's responses to each particular in the school might vary; however, what is not questioned is the understanding of what schooling is. The administrator will perceive everything that happens according to preconceived assumptions about what should be done. Indeed, it is most likely that the administrator is not at all times thinking about underlying aims, but rather is simply making decisions that are resonant with them. In this way, the background understanding shapes what is perceived as important. Likewise, if assumptions were to change, then what the administrator would perceive as possible would change as well. For instance, if an administrator understands schooling as cultivating civic dispositions, then the administrator might champion the public mural and encourage the economics teacher to teach social entrepreneurship. Obviously, these are simplistic, broad-strokes examples, but they attempt to show the ways in which our possibilities are always inevitably constrained and shaped by a generally inaccessible background understanding of what things are and what they mean for us.

Though we will discuss later the process of questioning and possibly modifying preconceived assumptions, what is essential to point out here is that understanding is thus conceptualized by Heidegger as all-encompassing. It sets the stage upon which one can perceive and thus act. As such, it is important to remember that interpretation is much broader than the specific instances of textual or artistic interpretation that we ordinarily think of when we talk about interpretation in an academic setting; seen in this light, even the seemingly objective scientific endeavour is a derivative of interpretation.

The implications of Heidegger's thought are profound in that they suggest that our conceptualization of the world cannot ever be universal because there is always an implicit understanding that stands in the background of whatever we explicitly attempt to know or make sense of. He asks this question: 'But if interpretation must in any case already operate in that which is understood, and if it must draw its nurture from this, how is it to bring any scientific [scholarly] results to maturity without moving in a circle, especially if, moreover, the understanding which is presupposed still operates within our common information about the man and the world?' (1962: 194). To understand this point, it is helpful to think of the example of the ship of Theseus, which is often used in philosophy courses to complicate the idea of persistent identity. This legendary ship of ancient Greece was a wooden ship that, one by one, had all of its original planks replaced as each one decayed.

This scenario raises the question: was it at all points still the same ship? A slightly modified version of the ship of Theseus can serve to demonstrate the circularity to which Heidegger refers. Let's put the ship out to sea and assume that it has all of its replacement lumber on board. Certainly, as each plank is replaced, the crew would have to stand on the planks that have not yet started to rot and/or those planks that have been replaced. The same holds true for understanding. Understanding is never transformed *en toto* instantaneously. It can only be transformed through the interpretation of understanding itself. The circularity of interpretation and understanding is what has come to be called the hermeneutic circle. In short, there is no point of pure Archimedean objectivity, no transcendental truth to be found, even within the natural sciences. Everything that is conceptualized and cognized rests on presupposed understanding. This circularity should not cause us to resign to futility or relativism but, as Heidegger suggests, 'what is decisive is not to get out of the circle but to come into it the right way' (1962: 195). As we will suggest in the following, a hermeneutics of trust, rather than a hermeneutics of suspicion, is the 'right way' to relate to this circularity.

Before we can consider what it means to intentionally position ourselves in relation to the hermeneutic circle, however, it is helpful to consider what it means to say that the hermeneutic condition is a way of being. What would it thus mean to *be hermeneutic—and, more specifically, what would it mean to be hermeneutic as an educational leader?* In one sense, hermeneutics is a fundamental issue for anyone who seeks any form of conceptualization, or from Heidegger's perspective, we are all already hermeneutic in how we carry out our activities in the world. The hermeneutic condition is inescapable. But simply saying that we are all always hermeneutic does not help us in thinking about a particular wilfulness a researcher or practitioner of educational administration might have in order to come to terms with the hermeneutic question. For this aspect, we must turn to Heidegger's student, Gadamer, who fleshed out more fully a comprehensive philosophical hermeneutics.

Gadamer draws from Heidegger to suggest that whenever we approach something new, we take along our prior understanding of it. We are not ordinarily aware of this 'fore-understanding' (or 'prejudice') because it is so deep in our conception of the world that it takes effort to bring it out into the light to be questioned. Our fore-understanding becomes an issue for us when we encounter something that clashes with our fore-understanding. Such an encounter is what Gadamer, following Hegel, calls an 'experience'. Against the notion of the natural sciences that an experience should be repeatable for the sake of verification, Gadamer asserts that experience is negative, which is to say that it always negates or 'thwarts an expectation' (2004: 350). In this view, an experience cannot be repeated because it is defined by its surprising nature. What we thought would be the case turns out not to be. In the case of our interpretive views, an encounter with another interpretation disrupts our ordinary way of understanding, making us aware of our prior taken for granted assumptions:

> experience is initially always experience of negation: Something is not what we supposed it to be. In view of the experience that we have of another object, both things change—our knowledge and its object. We know better now, and that means that the object itself 'does not pass the test'. The new object contains the truth about the old one. (Gadamer 2004: 348)

As a result of the experience, we not only see the object in a new way (according to the new experience's enrichment of it), but we also have a deeper awareness of our own understanding of it.

Returning to our hypothetical educational administrators, let us say that they take a trip to a nation that has a very strong civic component to its public education. As they watch students in this foreign country create public service projects and study history with an eye toward civic responsibility, they realize that the curriculum in their own schools is, by contrast, lacking in civic awareness. They see that they have privileged job preparation, assuming unthinkingly that this is the best or only goal for public education. Having now seen an alternative, however, they recognize and are able to question their own assumptions.

And this is precisely the task of hermeneutics for Gadamer: to put one's own assumptions at risk so that, ultimately, we can gain a greater awareness of our own understanding. As Gadamer tells us, we 'understand in a *different* way, *if we understand at all*' (2004: 296). We can say, then, that hermeneutics is predominantly concerned with questioning and thinking differently rather than with arriving at definite answers. The question, and not the propositional statement, is the priority of the hermeneutic task (2004: 356–57). Though in the earlier example, the 'experiences' that helped the administrators become aware of their own assumptions was travel to a foreign country, this is not the only way to have such experiences. For Gadamer, we can specifically put our assumptions at risk through dialogue with others and textual interpretation. This will become important later as we consider the graduate and ongoing education of educational administrators.

Note that in the hermeneutic experience we do not necessarily return to our original understanding or adopt the new one. In fact, Gadamer would say both alternatives are impossible. For Gadamer, all interpretation involves application so that to truly understand others' ideas requires applying them within one's own specific context. Generally speaking, one's new understanding is the result of the interplay between one's prior view and that gained in the experience, so that what is understood now includes both awareness of otherwise taken-for-granted views *and* an understanding that is a fusion of former and new ideas. Thus, regardless of whether the administrator continues to aim for job preparation or adopts a new aim of civic responsibility—or chooses a new aim altogether—the point here is that the experience of engaging with another worldview gives the administrator a new perspective. Now when meeting with the economics teacher or the art teacher, the administrator has a new awareness of taken-for-granted aims and can relate to the teachers accordingly.

To have such an experience that allows us to understand differently requires that we put our beliefs at risk and open ourselves up to the claims of others. Gadamer stated, in his 1989 address at the Heidelberg Colloquium, that 'the possibility that the other person may be right is the soul of hermeneutics', and this view of hermeneutics is essentially trusting (Grondin 1994: 124). That is, we approach another's point of view with the assumption that it might have something to tell us rather than with suspicion. The aforementioned administrators did not immediately assume that civic awareness was merely propaganda and dangerous nationalism as they certainly might have done. Rather, they considered that teaching civic awareness might be a good idea. Though ultimately they still might privilege job preparation, their new, explicit stance toward this aim will be informed by engagement with the alternative aim. In this type of hermeneutics, we assume that the other's viewpoint or way of doing things might be right and is worth taking seriously. The point is not to submit wholesale to others' ideas, but rather to engage honestly with them so that our own viewpoints are brought to the fore, challenged, and enriched.

THE DIFFERENCE BETWEEN SUSPICION AND TRUST

It is important to further explore this distinction between being suspiciously hermeneutic and being trusting, particularly to the extent that this chapter speaks to educational research, which often attempts to replace a positivist approach with a critical, suspicious hermeneutic one. Ricoeur's famous distinction between what he called the 'hermeneutics of suspicion' and the 'hermeneutics of retrieval' illuminates the difference. Ricoeur points out that the purpose of an interpretation is to tell us something about something: 'To say something of something is, in the complete and strong sense of the term, to interpret' (1970: 22). However, because the suspicious reader begins with a non-trusting stance toward the interpretation, she has only what she already believes to draw from, thereby positing her prior views as superior to the text's. Ricoeur points out that such an approach to interpretations prevents us from actually engaging with the interpretation's claims:

> For would I be interested in the object [what is described by the interpretation], could I stress concern for the object, through the consideration of cause, genesis, or function, if I did not expect, from within understanding, this something to 'address' itself to me? . . . It is this expectation, this belief, that confers on the study of symbols [and interpretations] its particular seriousness . . . But it is also what today is contested by the whole stream of hermeneutics that we . . . place under the heading of 'suspicion.' [Suspicious hermeneutics] begins by doubting whether there is such an object and whether this object could be the place of transformation of intentionality into kerygma, manifestation, proclamation. This hermeneutics is not an explication of the object, but a tearing off of masks, an interpretation that reduces disguises. (1970: 29–30)

In the last sentence, Ricoeur emphasizes that suspicious hermeneutics is not concerned with learning something *about* something, but rather with proving the interpretation wrong. He is specifically concerned with textual interpretation, but we can understand it more broadly. In educational research, the suspicious approach often consists of uncovering ulterior motives held by people in positions in power, and in this case what gets interpreted (the 'text') are policies, claims, or actions rather than academic texts per se. Following a Cartesian-like method of doubting, this kind of hermeneutics doubts that the interpretation is capable of 'proclamation'— of telling us something. Stronger still, from a Gadamerian standpoint, the hermeneutics of suspicion is hermeneutic in name only because it does not allow one to understand *differently*.

Ricoeur (1970) suggests that there is an alternative to suspiciousness, which he calls 'hermeneutics of retrieval', or 'recovery'. We employ hermeneutics of retrieval when we read an author and take what the author says seriously—as giving us a possibly true explanation of what the world is like. Gadamer's hermeneutics described earlier is essentially a hermeneutics of retrieval. Rather than depending on suspicion, this hermeneutics depends on belief, or what Ricoeur calls faith: 'It is a rational faith, for it interprets; but it is a faith because it seeks, through interpretation, a second naïveté' (1970: 28). By calling it a 'second naïveté', Ricoeur suggests that a hermeneutics of retrieval does not seek to return to an imagined state of absolute naivety in which an interpretation can write on the blank slates of our minds. Rather, to seek a second naivety is to knowingly look for a new way to see the world without trying to arrive at an absolute trust in any one interpretation.

It should be noted at this point that this is true for both interlocutors; neither Ricoeur nor Gadamer is advocating an asymmetrical approach to understanding in which one person (or view) submits and the other dominates. In a hermeneutic situation, we accept the possibility that the other person may be right, just as the other person accepts that we might be right as well. In such an engagement, both participants 'fuse' their horizons of understanding to the subject matter and thus each has a broader horizon of such understanding. Gadamer even says that such a fusion is possible when we engage not with a person but with a text; policy, scholarship, and research findings achieve their meaning when readers interact with them, taking their claims seriously and relating them to their own views.

In relation to research in educational administration, the hermeneutics of trust approach suggests that to do hermeneutic scholarship requires taking seriously what others say. Whether those others are texts (policy, scholarly research, etc.) or dialogical partners (research subjects, teachers, etc.), to truly interpret requires trusting that what the other says might be correct. This means suspending one's preconceived notions (e.g. 'theoretical frameworks' in research) to the extent that it is possible, in order to truly take a claim seriously. The purpose of such interpretation, then, is not ultimately to criticize. Rather, it is to understand differently, which entails engaging with alternative viewpoints that challenge one's own and gaining a greater awareness of the possibilities for making sense of situations.

IMPLICATIONS

As Smith and Blase point out, 'The particular way we choose to think of ourselves as researchers and/or leaders can be understood only against a broader view of ourselves as person' (1991: 12). If we take the claims of hermeneutics seriously, we are forced to reconceptualize educational administration. Further, if we recall the characterization earlier in this piece of administrators as technocratic, mechanistic calculators of action, we see how a hermeneutically trained consciousness (of a practitioner or a researcher) might challenge the very foundation of what it means to *be* an administrator in the first place.

Conceiving of educational administration in hermeneutic terms begins with the assumption that to be an educational administrator is to play a sort of intermediary role in educational institutions. Although administrators have great decision-making power, their effectiveness depends upon the degree to which they can mediate different and often competing interest groups, perceptions, and claims. This relational aspect of administration is, indeed, the basis upon which this volume rests, as the claim that *trust* is essential to administration presupposes the relational nature of the job. Administrators must trust the interpretations of their teachers and/or community in validating, complicating, informing, or disputing the worthiness of any policy, and they must also trust that scholarly research has something to say to the day-to-day pedagogical life of the school. They must, therefore, have the capability to make sense of the conceptual logic of the policy, the nuances and vicissitudes of everyday life in the school(s), and to question the aims and ends of schooling with an appreciation of the former two.

Such educational administrators do not grant *a priori* epistemological privilege to any one faction, but rather maintain the attitude that each party may be right, and in the process of making sense of them, fuse them together into a comprehensive whole that provides a broader horizon of seeing the problem. From the standpoint of hermeneutics, administrators are continually reinterpreting what is and what ought to be done in schools by fusing the perspectives of teachers, policymakers, other administrators, and community members. In other words, we suggest that educational administrators should not seek merely the one best practice or best policy, but rather, that they become adept at engaging with the fundamental assumptions that underlie the claims made by various constituents of educational institutions and use that ability to make judgments about policy based on a broader and more complex understanding.

For instance, consider a new research finding that suggests that students learn a second language best through immersion. The good administrator would want to share this research with the language instructors and help them develop a curriculum that reflects these findings. But what should the administrator do when the teachers report back that immersion does not work in their classrooms? To further complicate matters, the conflict might not only exist *between* research and classroom practice. Conflicts can be found *within* them as well. For instance, one research study might state that language immersion is best, while another states that traditional drilling is most effective. Similarly, staff and faculty within an educational setting might have different perceptions about what is or should be happening within the school.

Although we said earlier that to be human is to some extent to be hermeneutic, that does not mean we are naturally good at probing our own understanding. Developing the ability to listen to multiple views (be they voices of research or staff—or, for that matter, politicians, PTA's, school boards, etc.), to sort through them, and to arrive at a judgment regarding them requires deliberate attempts to do so. Unfortunately, the predominant research and 'current fad of "leadership training"' (Samier 2006: 126) influencing administration over the last century has been uninterested in and, indeed, unable to address the more human aspects of the role, reducing it to a technical enterprise. To move beyond critique of current approaches to educational administration as both a research field and a practical endeavour requires replacing the predominant positivist model with a new intellectual framework. We have tried to provide the outlines of this framework here. The next task would be to bring this hermeneutic approach into the education of academicians and administrators in educational administration. In this vein, Samier (2005) has suggested a return to studies in the humanities as part of a larger effort to reconceptualize the educational administrator as a more human character, someone in touch with the complex and ambiguous aspects of human life.

If we take this idea seriously, then we would have to refashion our professional education (and with it the research that informs it) to specifically develop the ability to think hermeneutically so that educational administrators would be adept at making sense of the many varied interpretations that come into play in educational institutions. We agree with Samier's proposal that we teach philosophy, history, anthropology, and the arts and conceive these disciplines in explicitly hermeneutic terms. Such an education, we propose here, and have argued elsewhere (Mackler 2009; Mulryan 2010), would have to teach aspiring or current administrators how to think hermeneutically and develop character traits that lend themselves to hermeneutic thinking. This would include creating experiences that challenge students' worldviews and help them become aware of their own preconceived understanding. A hermeneutic education would specifically include two components. First, students would have to become 'apprentices' to exemplary interpretations. This would serve to help students become aware of their own understanding so that they realize the extent to which being human means being hermeneutic. That is, it is only through such experiences that we begin to approach the degree to which our own preconceived understanding shapes our lives. Further, engaging with exemplary interpretations gives students more ways to understand the world and, in particular, the many social, political, and pedagogical issues affecting educational institutions. As such, it provides them with more lenses through which to interpret when they encounter complex, ambiguous situations in their institutions. Second, students would need practice offering their own interpretations in order to develop the ability to make sense of complex, nuanced situations. We suggest that this type of hermeneutic education, though it does not offer any explicit models or theories of human behaviour, would go a long way toward preparing administrators.

Up until this point, we have considered recentring the administrator as the nexus of understandings and have considered briefly the education that would help cultivate such understanding. However, although recentring the administrator as the nexus of understandings is necessary, it is not sufficient in making the position one of leadership, particularly not if we think about the administrator in public K–12 education, who is often still defined by the constraints of hierarchy of executive authority and thus is not yet free from her technocratic tasks. That is, although they might stand at a unique position allowing them the broadest understanding of education from the standpoint of their school, they are still asked to carry out the demands of those who do not stand at that position. More specifically, the shift to a hermeneutic administrator would require us to recentre the top-down authority structure into one in which the administrator stands at the centre of multiple perspectives on the truth of what does or ought to go on in educational institutions. Thus, to complete the transition from mere *educational administrator* to *educational leader*, the authority structure (particularly in public schooling) must be modified such that the administrator is allowed to be considered authoritative on the matter of the ends of schooling, not just its means. Allowing the possibility for administrators to be authoritative on such matters requires that they not merely come to a conclusion on a matter and grasp it dogmatically, but that, in taking up the hermeneutic task, they understand the multiplicity of understanding and use it to continually ask questions about their own understandings and that of others. Their questions compel them to question further—something Gadamer considers 'the art of thinking' (2004: 360).

In this chapter, we have attempted to lay the groundwork for conceiving of educational administration and leadership in hermeneutic terms by both sketching a picture of what it means to be hermeneutic and offering preliminary practical implications for researchers and practitioners. This view of educational administration stands in stark contrast to argumentation or the calculation of quantitative study as an end in itself, as educational administration is typically conceived. Reconceptualizing educational administrators as question-askers and meaning-makers rather than technical experts would open up a whole new set of possibilities for educational administration, a set of possibilities based upon a richer understanding of the human condition than that which predominates today.

REFERENCES

English, F.W. (2002) 'The point of scientificity, the fall of the epistemological dominos, and the end of the field of educational administration'. *Studies in Philosophy and Education* 21 (2): 109–36.

Gadamer, H.-G. (2004) *Truth and Method*. 2nd ed. Trans. J. Weinsheimer and D.G. Marshall. New York: Continuum.

Greenfield, T.B. (1979/1980) 'Research in educational administration on the United States and Canada: An overview and critique'. *Educational Administration* 8 (1): 207–45.

Grondin, J. (1994) *Introduction to Philosophical Hermeneutics*. Trans. J. Weinsheimer. New Haven, CT: Yale University Press.

Heidegger, M. (1962) *Being and Time*. Trans. J. Macquarrie and E. Robinson. New York: Harper and Row.

Lugg, C.A., and Shoho, A.R. (2006) 'Dare public school administrators build a new social order: Social justice and the possibly perilous politics of educational leadership'. *Journal of Educational Administration* 44 (3): 196–206.

Mackler, S. (2009) *Learning for Meaning's Sake: Toward the Hermeneutic University*. Rotterdam: Sense Publishers.

Maxcy, S.J. (1994) 'Introduction'. In *Postmodern School Leadership: Meeting the Crisis in Educational Administration*, ed. S.J. Maxcy. Westport, CT: Praeger.

Mulryan, S. (2010) 'The courage of dialogue'. In *Philosophy of Education 2009*, ed. D. Kerdeman. Urbana, IL: Philosophy of Education Society.

Ricoeur, P. (1970) *Freud and Philosophy: An Essay on Interpretation*. Trans. Denis Savage. New Haven, CT: Yale University Press.

Samier, E. (2005) 'Toward public administration as a humanities discipline: A humanistic manifesto'. *Halduskultuur* 6:6–59.

———. (2006) 'Educational administration as a historical discipline: An *apologia pro vita historia*'. *Journal of Educational Administration and History* 38 (2): 125–39.

Smith, J.K., and Blase, J. (1991) 'From empiricism to hermeneutics: Educational leadership as a practical and moral activity'. *Journal of Educational Administration* 29 (1): 6–21.

5 Studying the Psychological and Cultural Wages of Mistrust

An Essay on Organizational Torment under a Suspicious Regime

Eugenie A. Samier

For the wages of sin is death . . .

(Romans 6:23, King James Bible)

Man's chief enemy and danger is his own unruly nature and the dark forces pent up within him.

(Jones 1957)

Education internationally has become increasingly fraught with stress, conflict, and professional disappointment, producing an increasingly difficult work environment. The external causes are multiple: downsizing and restructuring brought about through the New Public Management in the early 1980s, forcing schools and universities into the competitive marketplace; decreasing levels of public confidence; demographic changes; globalization and internationalization; and technologization. All of these place new demands and pressures on the university that have diminished trusting relationships. Speeding up the educational process, using distance education and streamlining students into cohorts, does not provide the time necessary for relationships to form, particularly cross-cultural or multicultural classrooms, a condition Case and Selvester refer to as the McUniversity (2002: 240; Parker and Jary 1995; Ritzer 1993).

But there are also internal causes, evident in the political polarization of teachers and faculty against their administrators and governing bodies, the politics of equity, internal restructuring along business lines, restaffing from the private sector (who have little experience of the values and culture of academia), and entrepreneurial-style budgeting. Those in senior positions carry a greater measure of responsibility, in part because they have bureaucratized behaviour and introduced high levels of monitoring and surveillance that produce an environment that is 'explicitly legalistic' with 'defensive rhetoric' (Case and Selvester 2002: 242). Combined with administrators' access to informal and disproportionate influence and decision making power, the effect is a culture of mistrust, if not betrayal.

There are many approaches available from sociology, psychology, political science, cultural studies, et cetera, through which to study the problem of mistrust and betrayal in education. The subject of this chapter here, though, is psychoanalysis, which Anderson and White claim brings to an otherwise heavily objectivized and rational-technical field a more humanistic approach by examining the unconscious lives of people in organizations—hidden and covert dynamics and the 'psychic disruption [that is] often the cause of resistance to organizational change'. It offers a 'powerful approach that can enhance personal and organizational performance' and 'help to alleviate the psychic stress' accompanying radical organizational change (2003: 190). The main focus is on people's anxiety in response to change or a lack of clarity in goals, tasks, and hierarchical relationships, and the problem of defenses becoming ritualized or institutionalized (2003: 191). Psychoanalytic studies of management are closely related to or overlap into other traditions that play a marginal but persistent role in the field: Heideggerian phenomenological, existentialism, and hermeneutics (see Jahoda 1977: 118–19), Marxism, and the hermeneutics of Critical Theory (Kvale 1996: 78).

Currently, the most prolific and influential author is Kets de Vries (with over 30 books and countless international articles), who brings an extensive clinical experience with executives, that is, '*real* leaders at the strategic apex of their organizations' (2007: 30; 2006a: xv) and a strong theoretical background. His main objective is '*to bring the person back into the organization*', to counteract a field that uses objectification and an overly rational emphasis on structures and systems at the expense of the individual by examining the 'extrarational forces' that 'influence leadership, group functioning, and organizational strategy, structure, and culture' (1991a: 2; 2006a: xv). His clinical approach provides a 'lens through which to look at people and concepts—a lens that makes unusual behavior (in self and others) more understandable' (2006a: xvii). Kets de Vries relies primarily on storytelling, aimed at the complexity of personality and the internal world of individuals in relation to their social and organizational context (2006b: xix–xx), as well as an interpretive method that looks for thematic unity, pattern matching, psychological urgencies, and multiple levels of meaning (1991a: 16–18). This brings 'an extra level of magnification through which to look at organizational phenomena' that allows for an understanding of 'what drives people', their 'personality problems', 'what certain symptoms signify', making 'sense of interpersonal difficulties, and [to] see through group phenomena and social defenses' as part of a holistic approach (2009: xxi).

Kets de Vries investigates the inner world of those in positions of power who display psychological irrationality and how this translates into widespread organizational problems, manifesting as overall neurotic culture and managerial dysfunctions (see Kets de Vries and Miller 1984: 2–4). In those organizations where power and decision-making are concentrated at the senior level, the neurotic dispositions of executive administrators create a dominant neurotic organizational style that Kets de Vries terms 'the rot at the top', producing the five most common dominant 'constellations': dramatic, suspicious, detached, depressive, and compulsive' (2006b: 108–9, 110–12; Kets de Vries and Miller 1984: 6). In other words, parallels can be drawn between individual pathology and organizational pathology (Kets de Vries and Miller 1984: 17)—defensive processes and personality disorders that permeate organizational life and become integrated into social structures (Kets de Vries 1991a: 4).

While most organizations have combinations of these types, such as suspicious-compulsive, Kets de Vries concentrates on delineating the 'pure' types for clarification and analytic purpose, however, at some points in an organization's history one of these may predominate. Each compromises trust by engendering mistrust and, at times, betrayal. It is also important to note that organizational pathology may be attributed to factors other than leadership style, such as other strong personalities at senior administrative levels, a dwindling clientele or strong competition, domination by another organization, or too few resources (2006a: 110). In other words, these types are 'ideal types', in the Weberian sense, that is, analytic types used collectively to study empirical cases.

This chapter focuses on the 'suspicious' type in which mistrust and betrayal, or at least the fear of them, have become pervasive, leading to the micropolitics of secretiveness, envy, and hostility. Trust is antecedent to healthy administrative and leadership practices, contributing to individual well-being, achievement, and the overall positive conditions within which to teach and research. Its loss in a suspicious organization can be exacerbated by the entrepreneurial characteristics of the market model, placing new stresses on professional roles and relationships, compromising academic integrity, standards, freedom, and collegial governance.

THE FREUDIAN LANDSCAPE

Organizational psychoanalysis is not well understood or used in management and leadership studies although it has been around for at least 50 years (Anderson and White 2003: 191), going through periods of relative development and decline. Equally, psychoanalysts have largely ignored the world of work (Kets de Vries 2009: xx). From the 1950s to the 1970s works included those by Adorno et al (1950), Fromm (1973), Horney (1950), Jaques (1976), Lasswell (1960), Levinson (1972), Maccoby (1976), and Zaleznik (1966), but were eclipsed at the time that organizational culture and leadership became popular. Since the early 1990s there has been a resurgence, in part through the problem of narcissists, most often approached through psychoanalytic theory (e.g. Baum 1993; Diamond 1993a, 1993b, 1998; Hirschhorn and Barnett 1993; Levinson 1994; Obholzer 1996; Obholzer and Roberts 1994; Zaleznik 1995). Central to this literature is the quality of interpersonal relations, including the role that trust, distrust, mistrust, and betrayal play.

Kets de Vries's clinical perspective is complemented by ethnology, developmental psychology, family systems theory, object-relations theory, and neurology (see 1991a: 4), exemplifying the increasing sophistication of psychoanalytic theory since Freud (Kets de Vries 2006a: 6). His work goes beyond the directly observable, from 'the presenting internal and social dynamics; to the intricate playing field between leaders and followers; and to the unconscious and invisible psychodynamic processes and structures that influence the behavior of individuals, dyads, and groups in organizations'. To this end, the 'stuff' of which organizations are made are 'unconscious fears, hopes, and motivations' as well as 'needs, impulses, desires, wishes, fantasies, and dreams' (2006b: 3). Even though consciously people may deny unconscious processes, argues Kets de Vries, 'at the level of behavior and action we live out such processes every day' (2006a: 4).

The beginnings of a psychoanalytic examination of authority and leadership lie with Freud himself. While Freud was fascinated with the dynamics of unconscious erotic and aggressive desire early in his career, his later attention turned to issues of authority that were centred in the superego. The superego is partially the internalization of mores, or 'social strictures' of society 'the collective will works to impose' (Edmundson 2008: 143). Freud was most concerned with authority gone bad in the form of tyranny, which he viewed as the complementary desires for power and to be dominated. Through *Group Psychology and the Analysis of the Ego* (1922/1975), *Totem and Taboo* (1913/1985), and *The Future of an Illusion* (1927/1964) he studied how people respond to tyrants through obedience, love, and honour, essentially surrendering their will [and judgment] (see Freud 1913/1985: 56–69; 1927/1964: 19, 35). This desire for domination by others he regarded as part of the sadistic side of humanity constituting forces that divide us from 'ego, reason, civilization', but which can be minimized by bringing such repressed desires to consciousness (Edmundson 2008: 52, 53). The desire to be dominated, that is, to have a stabilizing contact with power and authority can override all other desires. The need to create solid identities instead of exploring one's own human possibilities can even lead to domination contrary to collective interests (Edmundson 2008: 153, 157). In part, this explains why staff often waits for a 'saviour' appointment, like a new chair or dean, instead of tackling problems themselves.

Group Psychology and the Analysis of the Ego examines crowd behaviour, emphasizing roles leaders play in providing the illusion of being loved, a clear or 'true' vision for change, and certainty 'about all things', even though they may be emotionally independent or even narcissistic ('self-enclosed self-love') (Edmundson 2008: 54). Leaders can provide a new set of values in which the differences among people that lead to anxiety are removed, satisfying 'the human hunger to rise above time and chance and join with something more powerful and more enduring than merely transient, mortal enterprises' (Edmundson 2008: 100). Unconsciously adopting an ego ideal from a leader satisfies the need for 'a strong man with a simple doctrine that accounts for our sufferings, identifies our enemies, focuses our energies, and lets us indulge our forbidden desires with the best of conscience' and promises 'to deliver people from their confusion and to dispense unity and purpose' (Edmundson 2008: 103; Freud 1922/1975). The leader, as a super-ego figure, can provide permission to act violently, discharging the anxiety of wanting to do something forbidden (Edmundson 2008: 100–101), going some way to explaining how normally moral individuals will engage in academic bullying or mobbing.

One related topic that Freud did not live to develop was on the role sublimation can play in creating new achievements in governance, commerce, and scholarship as alternatives to the old 'patterns of domination' (Edmundson 2008: 148), but one can see in this idea how psychological processes of sublimation can lie at the heart of organizational change. Adorno et al. pursued one aspect of this susceptibility in *The Authoritarian Personality* (1950), examining what personality, group membership, and socio-economic factors make people receptive and resistant to anti-democratic propaganda.

These texts, along with *Civilization and Its Discontents* (1929/2005) and *Moses and Monotheism* (1939/1985), constitute his primary writings on society in which he investigated the nature of social institutions and political authority, and the price oppressors and the oppressed pay (Wollheim 1971: 219, 222). Edmundson's discussion of leadership in *Moses and Monotheism* highlights many issues relevant to this chapter. Freud presents Moses as the image of a positive leader whose authority resides in his honesty and ability to dramatize his own internal conflicts, intelligently sublimate his impulses, and provide a pattern for others to follow (Edmundson 2008: 164–65, 236). In contrast, the third chapter contains Freud's critique of 'perverse authority and its uncanny appeal'. Initially, fascism begins with the 'allure of the leader, the man of a masterly and charismatic nature who appears to be absolutely certain of himself and all that he does', essentially an erotic relationship in which the followers are 'hypnotized' and, as a substitute for the super-ego, provides 'psychological dispensation' (Edmundson 2008: 85, 97, 100). Its attractiveness lies partly in its eye-intense presentation through 'pageantry, color, light, and noise', trafficking in 'miracle, mystery, and authority' (Edmundson 2008: 235, 240).

It is from this foundation that neo-Freudians have constructed an explanation for how leadership forms psychologically, evident in Erikson's (1958, 1969) studies of Martin Luther and Mahatma Gandhi, demonstrating how they were able to externalize internal and private concerns into public ones, creating the platform from which trust forms.

THE 'INNER THEATRE' OF ORGANIZATIONAL MEMBERS

Kets de Vries uses a psychoanalytic approach to personality as a more 'complete and far more integrated view of intrapsychic functioning and behavior' than most other psychological studies of management that tend to focus on narrow traits or behaviours (Kets de Vries and Miller 1984: 18). In this way, clusters of behaviours, the quality of interpersonal interactions, and development that affects the way an individual perceives, interprets, and reacts, produce fantasies and dysfunctional neurotic traits exhibited in even the most 'normal' of people (1984: 19). Important to this approach is an understanding of the 'inner theatre': the 'mental schemas that are the outcome' of an interface between 'our motivational needs with environmental factors (especially human factors, in the form of caretakers, siblings, teachers, and other important figures)'. These produce the 'mental representations of our self, others, and relationships' that 'govern our motivations and actions' (Kets de Vries 2006a: 12–13), including our construction of and ability to trust others.

Kets de Vries draws heavily upon the British psychoanalyst Wilfred Bion's theory of group dynamics, characterized by three general types of shared fantasy, each of which shapes the capacity for and effect on trust. These were summarized by Kets de Vries and Miller in terms of their negative qualities. First, 'flight/fight' groups are occasioned by an imagined common enemy leading to 'inappropriate and disruptive acts of aggression' by splitting the world into 'good' and 'bad' parts, projecting hostile impulses onto others, and denying responsibility for misfortunes through a lack of insight and self-reflection. The organizational effects include vague strategic goals, rigid perceptions, short time horizons, a lack of inspiration and vision, and insular management style. In terms of trust, in this culture not only can 'no one be trusted' but 'enemies' are tracked down and 'disloyal' employees are fired. In other words, there is rampant and undiscriminating distrust (1984: 7–8).

'Dependency' groups express a need to idealize their leaders as all-powerful and all-good, while denying evidence to the contrary, as providers of unity and security to the point of being unable to take independent action. Leaders surround themselves with 'compliant, subservient second-tier executives', subordinates who are unquestioning, have an autocratic style, lack deliberation and critical judgment, and, through a lack of moderation, pursue 'poorly conceptualized and risky strategic moves', losing strong personalities in the process. The implication for trust is that the non-subservient will not be able to become a part of the overly trusting attitude required for the leader.

'Utopian' groups believe in deliverance from their current problems through a 'Messianic' hope, creating the illusion that a new leader or idea can resolve conflict and provide gratification. In this type of culture, pressing current problems and lessons from the past are ignored, there is a focus on goals to the exclusion of means (e.g. plans, procedures, programmes) and an unrealistic expectation that innovations will improve matters, a striving for grandiosity, drifting from one managerial panacea to another to create the ideal climate (e.g. TQM, quality circles, participative management), and too much risk-taking (Kets de Vries and Miller 1984: 51–70).

Kets de Vries also draws on Bale's theory of group mentality that explains how a 'chain-reaction process' allows for unified fantasies to occur in groups leading to 'an accelerated growth curve of interest, excitement, and involvement' (Kets de Vries and Miller 1984: 48). These combined influences produce an effect that is sometimes called organizational ideology, culture, imagery, or identity.

Central to Kets de Vries's organizational theories is Freud's concept of transference—the re-enactment of past important relationships through current ones, usually involving 'intense and inappropriate behaviour', particularly with 'those in which power plays a key role' (Kets de Vries and Miller 1984: 8; Kets de Vries 1991b: 124). Since all meaningful relationships have transferential characteristics, it is not hard for authority figures to 'revive previously unresolved conflicts', causing regressive behaviour in subordinates who 'endow their leaders with the same omniscience and omnipotence that in childhood they attributed to parents or other significant figures' (Kets de Vries 2009: 137).

Kets de Vries and Miller identify three patterns of transference that can occur in superior/subordinate relationships. The first is an 'idealizing transference', common in charismatic leadership (Kets de Vries 2009: 45). In extreme form it is a dependence upon someone who is perceived as 'omnipotent and perfect' due to an inability to feel worthy without such a person to admire. Subordinates can therefore be easily controlled and manipulated, causing them to lose the 'capacity for independent judgment'. This transference allows for people to regard a leader as a saviour, who will 'deliver the group from hatred, destructiveness, and despair' (2009: 140), or it causes a desire to 'merge' in order to acquire their power (1991b: 125–27). The second, 'mirror transference', or narcissism, is the perception of oneself as perfect and all-powerful, leading to grandiosity and a need for others to affirm and confirm one's perfection; it requiring constant attention and admiration. This leads to a lack of empathy for others, the need to take credit for everything, disregarding others' rights and being exploitative. The final form, 'persecutory transference', is the management of anxiety by splitting the world into good and bad, thereby preserving 'the sense that one is good' and projecting unwanted feelings such as rage and guilt onto others, leading to expressing attitudes of hostility, envy, and moral masochism as a defensive reaction (Kets de Vries and Miller 1984: 79–92).

In idealization, trust is inevitably undermined as the transferee is never able to live up to expectations; in mirroring, those subordinates who do not play a worshiping role will be demonized; and in persecution there is no opportunity to establish trust.

Most problematic for management are personality disorders, or what Kets de Vries calls 'character disorders', many of which are derived from psychoanalytic theory. Among the 15 he discusses, 10 of which appear in the *Diagnostic and Statistical Manual of Mental Disorders* (American Psychiatric Association 2000), all have direct implications for trust or indirectly inhibit or incapacitate the individual in either forming trust or being trustworthy, and all are 'represented in workplaces' and 'capable of wreaking havoc' (Kets de Vries 2006b: 14):

1. The paranoid is distrustful and is the dominant personality type for the next section of this chapter, the suspicious organizational form.
2. Borderline personalities do not have the ability to trust because of impulsivity, instability of affect, inappropriate anger, and the avoidance of close relationships.
3. The avoidant, with similar but less extreme behaviours of the borderline, are socially inhibited, 'suffer from feelings of inadequacy, are timid, and hypersensitive to negative evaluation'; they mistrust others, exhibiting a general distrustful manner.
4. The narcissist is generally distrustful of others and is not able to provide trustworthiness due to an unreasonable grandiosity, 'a need for admiration and a tendency toward interpersonal exploitation'.
5. The obsessive-compulsive's behaviour compromises their ability to live up to trust through a preoccupation with 'orderliness, perfectionism, control, and conformity' that leads them to be rigid and dogmatic.
6. Histrionics tend to be manipulative and crave attention, display excessive emotion, are self-centred, and have a 'fleeting attention span'.
7. The depressive are pessimistic and 'suffer from feelings of worthlessness and self-denigration'.
8. The antisocial, while often able to exhibit good social skills, is devoid of conscience and therefore is not trustworthy, reliable, or responsible.
9. The dependent is 'submissive, self-effacing, docile, ingratiating, and constantly in search of approval from others', often found in organizations dominated by a patriarchal leader.
10. The schizotypical personality finds interpersonal relations difficult because of their suspicion, inappropriate emotions, and a number of 'eccentricities' of thinking and language.
11. Schizoid personalities are 'aloof, introverted, and of a reclusive nature', and have difficulty in establishing friendships.
12. The sadistic personality is 'power oriented, opinionated, combative, and abusive'.
13. Masochists are self-denigrating, exhibiting deference and self-sacrificial behaviour.
14. The passive-aggressive has difficulty saying no, and then fails to act.
15. The cyclomythic personality has a 'fluctuating mood state'. (2006b: 12–14)

In many cases, problems do not often emerge until the individual is in a position of power, making them unrecognizable to those who knew them, in some cases the power acts like a drug to which they will hang onto 'at all costs' (Kets de Vries 1991b: 121).

Kets de Vries also draws heavily on psychoanalytic theories of defense mechanisms, the hypothesized processes of which resistances are the observed behaviours (Kets de Vries and Miller 1984: 134). These include repression, regression, projection, identification, denial, and reaction formation, all of which play a large role in organizational change where 'authority, status, prestige, and security' are taken from those in power leading to a threat to self-image (1984: 9). Additional defenses discussed in *The Leadership Mystique* are: splitting, undoing, displacement, isolation, conversion, suppression, rationalization, altruism, and humour (Kets de Vries 2006b: 15–16). Such resistances, when exaggerated or overused, create hindrances to healthy interpersonal relations, especially in organization change when 'destructive political behavior as factions compete for power' or one's past performance comes into question. The problems of 'wounded pride, lowered morale, and increased distrust, hostility and suspicion' can result from change-fueled resistance (Kets de Vries and Miller 1984: 134–35). These defenses are also used to deflect or diminish the inclination to change dysfunctional character patterns and feedback received about their dysfunctions.

There are a number of techniques Kets de Vries discusses that people can use in response to overly aggressive administrators and leaders. One is a concept developed by Anna Freud, 'identification with the aggressor' (Freud 1936/1966: 139), which causes people to create an ambivalent relationship and is characterized by both fear and attraction to protection. In a more developed form, as Kets de Vries discusses, people imitate the aggressor, taking on a threatening role themselves, acting as informers and aggressors while suspending independent thought (2009: 188–89). An alternative is to dissociate, a common defense mechanism when under attack and extraordinary stress; however, if it is persistently used, people become dissociated, which affects organizational culture: disconnected from others, a sense of unreality, an inner deadness, and the assumption of 'a bland mask in public to cover the turmoil within' (2009: 189). In this climate, relationships of trust cannot be formed and maintained. Another option is to 'flee into despair', exhibiting hopelessness and helplessness (2009: 189–90). The most constructive way, in the long run, to cope with aggressors is to challenge or assume a 'fight' posture (2009: 190). In an organizational context, though, isolated individuals will not fare well, particularly when the majority have assumed the prior options.

All of the defense mechanisms referred to here can damage trust. In repression, for example, anxiety is avoided and problems are forgotten. Regression involves reverting to adaptations and behaviour appropriate to early stages of development. In projection, others are blamed. Identification with an aggressor can either turn one into one who threatens or produce yielding conformity to a senior official that can undermine change. Reaction formation is the holding of contradictory attitudes, one of which is kept unconscious through 'emphasizing its dramatic opposite', such as stubbornness by compliance or messiness by compulsive neatness. And denial, regarded by Kets de Vries and Miller as one of the most common in organizational change, is where one denies the existence of an unpleasant reality leading to the temporary delusion that nothing is wrong or has changed (1984: 136–42). In all of these cases, trust is either undermined, damaged, or cannot be formed.

Two other forms of resistance that have organizational effect are secondary gain resistances and super-ego resistances. The former occurs as a form of coping with weakness and insecurities by seeking attention out of dependency needs during change by asking for help or appearing to co-operate yet resisting the actual change (1984: 142–44). In the case Kets de Vries and Miller use to illustrate this resistance, the individual was unable to cope with the loneliness of losing long-term peers (left with subordinates and peers much younger)—a situation that is common in academia, particularly with more senior faculty who have lost their long-term peers, exacerbated by the frequent isolation experienced in teaching and scholarly pursuits. Super-ego resistance, characterized by 'feelings of guilt and the wish to be punished for real or imagined sins', is seen often in those recently promoted who 'become extraordinarily error-prone' (1984: 144).

It is all of these factors that come into play in shaping organizational climate, the way in which responsibilities for selection, reward and punishment, and promotion are carried out. These practices can create a compatible staff and help create and reinforce cultural elements, such as myths, legends, stories, and symbols that produce a neurotic culture (1984: 21). Of all the values present in successful organizations, Kets de Vries argues that trust is the most fundamental upon which others rest—candour, empowerment, accountability, integrity, and openness to change (2006b: 160–61). One important value that when absent can kill trust is respect for the individual (2006b: 162). This means that in universities and schools (or school districts) where senior administrators have strong personalities, an autocratic managerial style, and a neurotic disposition, the relationships, personnel, culture, structures, and strategies will reflect the 'shared fantasies' influenced by the top.

THE SUSPICIOUS ORGANIZATIONAL TYPE

The defining characteristics of the suspicious personality in power are 'mistrust of others, hypersensitivity, extreme alertness, secretiveness, envy, and hostility' that reflect an 'inner theater fantasy that nobody can be trusted' (Kets de Vries 2006a: 114, 115; 2006b: 111–14). In interpersonal relations this leadership style: takes offense easily, responds in anger, easily misreads and distorts others' actions, magnifies minor slights, expects trickery and deception, has an intense and narrowly focused time-span, and come across as 'cold, rational, and unemotional' (2006a: 115). Their most common defense mechanisms are: splitting, dividing the work into two camps; projection, involving blaming others for their own feelings, faults, and errors; and denial, including 'negating the reality of a particular situation (2006a: 112).

Originally called the 'paranoid' type, the suspicious organization is one in which 'managerial suspicions translate into a primary *emphasis on organizational intelligence* and controls' in order to meet their suspicious demand for 'perpetual vigilance' (Kets de Vries and Miller 1984: 23). Relations are 'characterized by a persecutory theme', that consists in mistrust for subordinates, producing a defensive reaction of hostility (Kets de Vries 2006a: 115). Paranoid leaders 'question the trustworthiness of everyone around them and suffer from delusions of conspiracy and victimization', finding in even the most innocent remarks 'hidden meanings', and an endless search for confirmation to the point of creating proof (Kets de Vries 2009: 175). Senior administrators who selectively and distortionally read the actions of others as deception intensify their control and harsh punishment and aggressively react to honesty, producing a flight–fight culture and academic bullying and mobbing.

Its effect is threefold. First, information systems are used to identify threats and challenges by external actors and high levels of control are used through 'budgets, cost centers, profit centers, cost-accounting procedures, and other methods of monitoring the performance of internal operations' (Kets de Vries and Miller 1984: 23; Kets de Vries 2006a: 115–16). In other words, they intensify bureaucratization. Secondly, managerial paranoia affects their decision-making, causing senior executives to excessively share information against external threats, conduct considerable analysis of organizational problems, and repeatedly practice consultation—referred to as 'institutionalization of suspicion' that ultimately lowers morale and trust and wastes time and energy. Features could be constantly putting staff through reorganizations and reviews and having an excessive number of meetings. Accompanying these behaviours is a centralization of power high up in the organizational hierarchy while using subordinates to supply information. This can be done through 'consultative' committees; however, actual decisions are made at the top. Finally, its strategies are characterized by reaction rather than proaction, and a conservatism that stifles innovation and risk-taking leading to muddling through. Decision-making yields to stereotyping, rigidity, and an unnecessary search for organizational problems, which institutionalizes suspicion, causing rather than solving actual problems (Kets de Vries 2006b: 117).

These practices can explain, at least in part, why many universities under the current market model engage in one characteristic identified by Kets de Vries and Miller: over-diversification undertaken to reduce risk (1984: 25–27). This could take the form of commercializing and marketing programmes, in effect, a greater tendency to 'sell' degrees, and appoint people to co-ordinate, teach, and supervise who 'buy into' this model.

Kets de Vries describes suspicious leader styles as 'clusters of behaviour patterns' (2006b: 111) which 'generate organisational cultures that reflect their own distrust and suspicion' producing an atmosphere 'clouded with fear of attack', the blaming of problems on an identified external or internal 'enemy', and a fight/flight set of responses. Its guiding theme, despite rhetoric to the contrary, is: 'Some menacing force is out to get me. I'd better be on my guard. I can't really trust anybody' (2006b: 111). Toxifying the culture takes place through the personnel system by hiring, rewarding, and promoting those who share the leader's views and ignoring or refusing promotion to those who dissent. Information as a power resource is hoarded and bartered as a commodity, internal co-ordination is reduced due to adversarial relationships, 'secrets abound and proliferate, and a '"protect yourself" ethic prevails' (2006a: 116; see also 2009: 176–79). Senior administrators or leaders are in a position to use resources to 'buy' allegiance, or at least alliance for the short term. Differential treatment is provided those motivated by 'power, honor, fame, glory, and wealth' (2009: 184), translated into university terms as leaves from teaching, funds diverted for special projects, teaching or research projects, positions that can be made through appointment favouring compliance, et cetera. This can be combined with a 'reflex-like' obedience to authority, demonstrated in the famous Milgram experiments to 'absolve them for their actions', delegating guilt to others, and trying to please authority, while preferring to rationalize their behaviour than challenge authority (2009: 186). The temporary illusion of power and absolution from moral responsibility (2009: 187) is difficult for many to spurn.

One of the most disturbing of leadership patterns is that of the malevolent antisocial individual, whose behaviour is characterized by 'sadism, extreme aggressiveness, narcissism, and paranoia' expressed commonly through satisfaction achieved through 'intimidating and humiliating others'. As Kets de Vries notes, we can commonly meet those with signs of antisocial behaviour, but the malignant form is less common (2009: 171–72). However, they do occasionally show up in the work world, and the less malignant form can still evidence these traits in muted form, demonstrating towards colleagues callousness, vengefulness, belligerence, and brutality (2009: 171). It is not a stretch for most people who have been in the work world for some time to run across someone who, as Kets de Vries describes, uses 'cruelty as a control device': they are 'irritable, argumentative, abrasive, malicious, and easily provoked to anger', nurturing 'strong hatreds', they demonstrate a persistent need to dehumanize (particularly those who frustrate them), they are 'dogmatic, closed-minded, and opinionated', and they take pleasure in establishing dominance and exerting their will while demeaning others in public (2009: 173).

CONCLUSION: ESCAPES AND INTERVENTIONS

For Kets de Vries, trust is an important value that underpins much of organizational life, and can serve as a strong indicator of health where needs for attachment and affiliation, as well as exploration and assertion, are met. When trust exists, candour characterizes people's communication and their willingness to speak their minds, exhibiting a 'healthy disrespect for their superiors'. With distrust 'realism disappears, and the quality of decision-making deteriorates' (2000: 10). Of great importance for organizational members is a feeling that they have a sense of control and ownership (2009: 219), possible only when they find others trustworthy. Based on cases of nurturing and productive executives, Kets de Vries notes that creating and maintaining trust is a central goal involving 'competence, credibility, consistency, support, respect, and honesty' while living the traits they expected in others (2009: 222). Trust means that there can be risk-taking, and, necessarily, making mistakes, along with a high level of access to information, collaboration, and co-operation, all contributing to creativity, one of the first casualties of a mistrustful environment (2009: 239).

Trust is an important value for organizational success, requiring a number of administrative skills in building a culture that supports the requisite honesty, respect, fairness, and integrity for trusting relationships to form. As Kets de Vries notes in one of his early publications, one responsibility of senior administrators is to create a climate of trust, for: 'without trust, communication breaks down and learning stops. As a result, people become turf defenders, lack a helpful attitude toward other people in the organization, and fail to engage in good corporate citizenship behavior by pitching in when needed' (1995: 97). To do this, they need to show respect and support, and cultivate 'honesty, consistency, and competency' in their own practice (1995: 97). Not only do collaboration and co-operation fall by the wayside, but also features that are important in education, such as creativity and the atmosphere in which risk-taking is possible necessary to true creative ventures (1995: 150).

Kets de Vries also notes that distrust is more apt to be expressed by entrepreneurs since they typically have an ambivalent attitude towards control, sometimes leading them to become secretive and overly security-conscious, in extreme form creating an organizational culture in which 'people may stop acting independently, allowing sycophancy and political gamesmanship to become rampant' (1995: 198–200). This pattern does not auger well for educational systems that have been redesigned along the market model where entrepreneurialism is either fostered or required. The implication is clear here—the market model is inappropriate for universities where trust and trustworthiness is required for the many activities of collegial governance that each member must rely upon.

The portrait of suspicious organizations described earlier seems to be insurmountable. Certainly, as Anderson and White argue, there is a role for organizational psychoanalysis in exposing or 'surfacing, assessing, and interpreting defensive processes' (2003: 192). They recommend the use of an organizational psychoanalyst in public organizations to assist: people in recognizing tasks in an environment where conflict exists; leaders in adapting to structural and strategic realities in public administration; in establishing boundary management; in accepting a realistic understanding of authority; and limiting abuses (2003: 196–200).

The solution to paranoid or suspicious administrators, and the organizational cultures they produce, does not lie in the latest turn in educational administration—the adoption of business-style practices and entrepreneurialism. Kets de Vries has studied the entrepreneur type for many years, concluding that while instrumental in 'the conception and implementation of an enterprise' they are not suitable once an organization is established with a complex structure and division of labour (2009: 8, 36). Entrepreneurs are risk-takers, more comfortable with uncertainty and ambiguity. An entrepreneur has high achievement motivation (although 'often inconsistent and confused about his motives, desires and wishes'), a 'need for autonomy, power, and independence', 'often upsets others by his seemingly irrational and impulsive activities', is unable to submit to authority and organizational rules, has little tolerance for those who challenge his authority, and has little patience for operational planning, serious deliberation, judgment, and the requirements for analytic thinking (2009: 8, 10–12, 34–35). Their career profile consists of a sequence of failed positions produced by their inability to work for others and 'non-conformist rebelliousness', their driving ambition an attempt to 'contradict strong feelings of inferiority and helplessness' (2009: 34).

Most importantly for this chapter, the entrepreneur's need for control is related to a suspicion of others that is 'accentuated and dramatized' in an organizational setting: they have a strong 'distrust in the world around them' and continue to scan the environment for confirmation of suspicions, leading to blowing up trivial issues into false problems while ignoring actual problems. Other consequences for the organization are: sycophants setting the tone (informal relationships overtaking formal duties and responsibilities), cessation of independent actions by others, and rampant gamesmanship, all of which result in low morale, low employee satisfaction, and a decline in productivity (2009: 13–14).

Among actions that can be taken, Kets de Vries recommends 'safeguards' that can be built into organizational structures: 'setting boundaries that will lead to the dispersion of power', distributing 'key power positions' over a number of individuals, and adopting flatter organic structures that allow for lateral communication that can 'help diffuse excessive transferential manifestations' (2009: 143). The restoration of balance to a suspicious organization requires that decision-making and reporting be simplified, that information be shared, secrecy minimized, trust-building activities established, and proactive attitudes to strategy be adopted (2006b: 118).

On an individual level, those in power positions who are suspicious have a number of options to exercise: making a major career change to a new challenge in order to avoid falling into the rut of routine administration; mentoring others to avoid excessive narcissism; moving to a public service role that often requires a reassessment of personal priorities; and 'breaking the routine' with seminars, conferences, and workshops that allow for discussion with peers outside one's organization (Kets de Vries 1991b: 132–37). In some cases, leaders may have outlived their usefulness to the organization and need to let go (1991b: 137–38).

More research on this problem, particularly in tackling suspicious universities and schools, is required. In psychoanalytic research, the primary method is the psychoanalytic interview, consisting of a number of qualitative features that are consistent with many recommendations in recent years in approaching organizational problems in a non-positivistic way. This kind of interview is an intensive individual case study, using an open mode of interviewing and a contextualized interpretation of meaning in statements and actions that are often ambiguous and contradictory. It also has a long-term temporal dimension composed of both repressions of and resistance to the past, and is conducted through a reciprocal emotional human interaction (involving transference and counter-transference). Its focus on abnormal and irrational behaviour reveals less visible conflicts and change in the analysand/subject that requires overcoming resistance when making the unconscious conscious (Kvale 1996: 75–79). Kvale explains how the 'hermeneutics of suspicion' operates in interpretation; when the listener is suspicious of the explicit text or speech, it can mean something different indirectly. It is common to psychoanalysis where the researcher looks for hidden or implicit meaning, a consequence of unconscious forces (1996: 203).

Based on clinical work and studies, Kets de Vries has developed a Leadership Archetype Questionnaire that takes into account many different character styles and organizational environments, based on eight predominant 'leadership archetypes' that are also designed to help senior executives better understand their own style and the situations under which they can be most effective. It is also a valuable instrument in identifying one's limitations and learning how 'to align individual strengths' with others one works with, the combinations that are likely to be most successful and those to avoid (2007: 30). Given the stress that the educational sector has been under, this type of leadership instrument would be a valuable addition to the current repertoire of methods in improving educational leadership practice.

REFERENCES

Adorno, T., et al. (1950) *The Authoritarian Personality*. New York: Harper.

American Psychiatric Association. (2000) *Diagnostic and Statistical Manual of Mental Disorders: DSM-IV.TR*. Washington, DC: American Psychiatric Association.

Anderson, D., and White, J. (2003) 'Organizational psychoanalysis in public administration'. *American Review of Public Administration* 33 (2): 189–208.

Baum, H. (1993) 'Organizational politics against organizational culture: A psychoanalytic perspective'. In *The Psychodynamics of Organizations*, ed. L. Hirschhorn and C. Barnett. Philadelphia: Temple University Press.

Case, P., and Selvester, K. (2002) 'Watch your back: Reflections on trust and mistrust in management education'. *Management Learning* 33 (2): 231–47.

Diamond, M. (1993a) 'Bureaucracy as externalized self-system: A view from the psychological interior'. In *The Psychodynamics of Organizations*, ed. L. Hirschhorn and C. Barnett. Philadelphia: Temple University Press.

———. (1993b) *The Unconscious Life of Organizations: Interpreting Organizational Identity*. Westport, CT: Quorum.

———. (1998) 'The symbiotic lure: Organizations as defective containers'. *Administrative Theory & Praxis* 20 (3): 315–25.

Edmundson, M. (2008) *The Death of Sigmund Freud: Fascism, Psychoanalysis and the Rise of Fundamentalism*. London: Bloomsbury.

Erickson, E. (1958) *Young Man Luther*. New York: W.W. Norton.

———. (1969) *Gandhi's Truth*. New York: W.W. Norton.

Freud, A. (1936/1966) *The Ego and the Mechanisms of Defense*. Madison, WI: International Universities Press.

Freud, S. (1913/1985) *Totem and Taboo*. In *The Origins of Religion*, trans. J. Strachey. London: Penguin.

———. (1922/1975) *Group Psychology and the Analysis of the Ego*. Trans. J. Strachey. New York: Norton.

———. (1927/1964) *The Future of an Illusion*. Trans. W.D. Robson-Scott. Garden City, NY: Doubleday.

———. (1929/2005) *Civilization and Its Discontents*. Trans. J. Strachey. New York: Norton.

———. (1939/1985) *Moses and Monotheism*. In *The Origins of Religion*, trans. J. Strachey. London: Penguin.

Fromm, E. (1973) *The Anatomy of Human Destructiveness*. New York: Henry Holt.

Hirschhorn, L., and Barnett, C. (eds.) (1993) *The Psychodynamics of Organizations*. Philadelphia: Temple University Press.

Horney, K. (1950) *Neurosis and Human Growth: The Struggle toward Self-Realization*. New York: W.W. Norton.

Jahoda, M. (1977) *Freud and the Dilemmas of Psychology*. Lincoln: University of Nebraska Press.

Jaques, E. (1976) *A General Theory of Bureaucracy*. London: Gower.

Jones, E. (1957) *The Life and Work of Sigmund Freud*, vol. 3. New York: Basic Books.

Kets de Vries, M. (1991a) 'Introduction: Exploding the myth that organizations and executives are rational'. In *Organizations on the Couch: Clinical Perspectives on Organizational Behavior and Change*, ed. M. Kets de Vries et al. San Francisco: Jossey-Bass.

———. (1991b) 'On becoming a CEO: Transference and the addictiveness of power'. In *Organizations on the Couch: Clinical Perspectives on Organizational Behavior and Change*, ed. M. Kets de Vries et al. San Francisco: Jossey-Bass.

———. (1995) Life and Death in the Executive Fast Lane, San Francisco: Jossey-Bass.

———. (2000) 'Beyond Sloan: Trust is at the core of corporate values'. *Financial Times*, 2 October, 10.

———. (2006a) *The Leader on the Couch: A Clinical Approach to Changing People and Organizations*. Chichester: Wiley.

———. (2006b) *The Leadership Mystique: Leading Behavior in the Human Enterprise*. Harlow: Prentice Hall.

————. (2007) 'Decoding the team conundrum: The eight roles executives play'. *Organizational Dynamics* 36 (1): 28–44.

————. (2009) *Reflections on Character and Leadership*. San Francisco: Jossey-Bass.

Kets de Vries, M, and Miller, D. (1984) *The Neurotic Organization*. San Francisco: Jossey-Bass.

Kramer, R. (1999) 'Trust and distrust in organization: Emerging perspectives, enduring questions'. *Annual Review of Psychology* 50:569–98.

Kvale, S. (1996) *Interviews: An Introduction to Qualitative Research Interviewing*. Thousand Oaks, CA: Sage.

Lasswell, H. (1960) *Psychopathology and Politics*. New York: Viking.

Levinson, H. (1972) *Organizational Diagnosis*. Cambridge, MA: Harvard University Press.

————. (1994) 'Diagnosing organizations systemically'. In *Organizations on the Couch: Clinical Perspectives on Organizational Behavior and Change*, ed. M. Kets de Vries et al. San Francisco: Jossey-Bass.

Maccoby, M. (1976) *The Gamesman: The New Corporate Leaders*. New York: Simon & Schuster.

Obholzer, A. (1996) 'Psychoanalytic contributions to authority and leadership issues'. *Leadership & Organization Development Journal* 17 (6): 53–56.

Obholzer, A., and Roberts, V. (eds.) (1994) *The Unconscious at Work: Individual and Organizational Stress in the Human Services*. London: Routledge.

Parker, M., and Jary, D. (1995) 'The McUniversity: Organization, management and academic subjectivity'. *Organization* 2 (2): 319–38.

Ritzer, G. (1993) *The McDonaldization of Society*. London: Pine Forge.

Wollheim, R. (1971) *Freud*. London: Fontana.

Zaleznik, A. (1966) *Human Dilemmas of Leadership*. New York: Harper and Row.

————. (1995) 'The case for not interpreting unconscious material mental life in consulting to organizations'. *Psychiatry* 58 (4): 357–70.

6 Developing Trust through Collaborative Research

Mentoring Graduate Students of Colour

Cynthia Gerstl-Pepin
and Marybeth Gasman

In *Teaching to Transgress: Education as the Practice of Freedom*, hooks recalls her own experience in graduate school to explain how faculty teaching styles can harm students of colour: 'The vast majority of our professors often used the classroom to enact rituals of control that were about domination and the unjust exercise of power' (1994: 5). She provides a way of conceptualizing the academy as a site of political and personal struggle over knowledge. How we mentor can lead students to feel silenced, excluded, and as though their personal narratives of racial and ethnic identity are of little consequence (Anderson-Thompkins et al. 2004; Gasman et al. 2004). hooks challenges those working within the academy to create supportive learning environments by transgressing boundaries. The purpose of this chapter is to explore the possibilities of creating trust in collaborative narrative research relationships, particularly when faculty mentor graduate students of colour. Specifically, we examine how power differentials in terms of faculty–student status can be intertwined with inequities in race, ethnicity, socio-economics, and gender. We posit that it is possible to overcome these differences by developing meaningful trusting relationships through the creation of collaborative research projects in which students are mentored and valued as co-researchers.

We have constructed this chapter in a narrative conversational style to elicit our personal experiences and struggles as a way of providing insight into our relationship and the way we build trust with both each other and students. Central to our narrative exploration is the acknowledgment that trust is an interdisciplinary concept that crosses many fields. Trust is central to all human relationships whether conceptualized in society, politics, organizations, or education (Bachmann and Zaheer 2006; Howes, Ritchie, and Bowman 2002; Roderick and Cook 2007; Uslaner 2002). Narrative inquiry provides one way to explore the complex way in which trust may be developed through interpersonal relations. As Hendry suggests: 'By acknowledging the social construction of knowledge, narrative has provided a methodology that has taken into account the situated, partial, contextual, and contradictory nature of telling stories' (2007: 489). Thus, narrative provides us with a way to explore how we as mentors work to build trust with each other and with graduate students of colour.

WHY DEVELOPING TRUST IS
IMPORTANT IN A RACED ACADEMY

Before we begin, we feel that it is important for us to define what we mean by 'trust'. For us, trust is, 'the belief that others will not deliberately or knowingly do us harm, if they can avoid it, and will look after our interests, if this is possible' (Newton 2007: 242). We conceptualize trust within a socio-political context in which power relationships are unequal and complicated by societal inequities such as racism (Moody 2004). Within this inequitable context trust is not a static entity, but operates on a continuum from distrusting a person and maintaining a distance from them because we are concerned that they may hurt us to having a deeply trusting relationship in which we share our most intimate details with another (Case and Selvester 2002; Newton 2007). This distinction highlights a conceptualization of trust that is not static but evolving or devolving in which various levels of trust are possible. One can move from a relationship that reflects minimal trust to a relationship in which there is deep trust and understanding (Newton 2007: 344). Conversely, one can lose trust in an individual or institution when the relationship is seen as putting one at risk for harm such as the potential pain of experiencing institutional or interpersonal racism (Fries-Britt and Kelly 2005; Gasman et al. 2004).

Racism in the academy continues to be a problem that is marked by the under-representation of faculty and graduate students of colour. Establishing trust within this context presents a particular challenge. The legacy of the 40-year Tuskegee 'Study of Untreated Syphilis in the Negro Male' left a lasting impact concerning distrust of research among African American communities that is still felt today (Brandon, Isaac, and LaVeist 2005). Study participants were mostly African American, poor, and illiterate. After researchers discovered that penicillin was an effective treatment for syphilis, they kept the information from study participants thereby allowing some participants to die of the disease and infect their wives and children (via birth). Understanding this historical legacy points to the importance of building trust when engaging in a research endeavour involving inequitable power relations and persons of colour. Building trust, given these inequities, requires believing 'that persons and institutions will act in a manner consistent with our own interests' (Corbie-Smith, Thomas, and St. George 2002: 2462). Most institutional review boards inform student and faculty researchers of the ethics, including the racial dynamics, of conducting research. Thus, acknowledging how these racial and power inequities permeate academia sets an important context for building trust (Dowdy et al. 2000). Building trust across power differentials by sharing power provides a way to strategically counter an unequal system by fostering an equitable trusting relationship (Tynan and Garbett 2007).

MEANINGFUL TRUST BUILDING THROUGH CO-REFLECTION

We elected to explore issues of trust with graduate students through narrative reflection as it offers a venue for uncovering the often paradoxical and complex ways that race may play out in a mentoring relationship. Specifically, we discuss our mentoring roles in terms of our individual reflections and co-reflection. We use the notion of co-reflection as 'a collaborative critical thinking process mediated by language, broadly construed to include all meaningful signs' (Yukawa 2006: 1556). Developing a trusting mentoring relationship across race requires acknowledging power differentials, sharing power, and being vulnerable by sharing our own stories related to racism and power inequity (Fries-Britt and Kelly 2005; Gasman et al. 2004). First we explore our reasons for feeling compelled to mentor graduate students of colour. Then we reflect on the ways in which we evolved as mentors of students of colour and as collaborators together. We do this by sharing our personal narratives related to the role we have played as faculty mentors of graduate students of colour.

While we are both White, we have had separate first-hand experiences that taught us that there was an urgent need for faculty to serve as mentors and supports for graduate students of colour given the dearth of faculty of colour in academia (Moody 2004).

Marybeth

All too often, I find myself in the situation of having a student of colour come to my office—usually in tears—to tell me about a negative experience that she is having in graduate school. Sometimes the student is being mistreated by other students—perhaps they think that she does not belong in graduate school. On other occasions, the student is there to discuss the troubled relationship that he has with his advisor. Based on these experiences and my underlying belief in equity, I care deeply about nurturing and supporting students of colour as they progress through their graduate education. Sometimes people ask me why I am so interested in working with students of colour, given that I am White. I think that my race is all the more reason to be supportive of students of colour. For decades, even centuries, Whites have benefited from their privilege and, in my opinion, we have an obligation to make positive change for students of colour and to share our privilege in the academy with them. We all benefit from this approach in the end.

Cindy

Growing up in poverty in a single-parent household I often hid who I was from my classmates. I was afraid if people knew the kind of home-life I had that I would be ostracized. I felt this way because I had friends at school who when they saw our dingy apartment would cease to be my friend. I had been hurt many times by this. It made it difficult for me to trust others in terms of showing people who I was. In graduate school, I learned a great lesson from my fellow graduate students of colour. I learned about the daily experiences of racism they experienced. My eyes were opened to the ways in which the curriculum and culture of graduate school was racist. I had a faculty mentor who modelled the importance of building trust with graduate students of colour through open conversations about race and an open acknowledgment of the role racism plays in the academy. I knew this type of role was crucial in the academy. It was important that the classroom space provided an open forum for discussing racism. I knew that while I could hide my childhood poverty in the academy, a person of colour could not hide their race. It made me feel responsible for ensuring that when I saw evidence of racism in the academy, I acknowledged it openly. I see it as my responsibility to be supportive of students and colleagues. The primary way I do this is by building trust across racial and cultural lines.

We both learned from personal experience and a growing body of research (see, for example, Dowdy et al. 2000) that graduate students of colour faced many challenges around racism in the academy. Given this, we saw it as our ethical responsibility to acknowledge this racism and develop ways for us to be supportive of students of colour, always being sensitive to their needs.

REALIZING THE IMPORTANCE OF BUILDING TRUST TOGETHER: EVOLVING AS MENTORS

When we first met, we were both assistant professors working towards tenure. We openly acknowledged our struggles around fitting in to the academic norms of our department and the pressure to publish. In our tenuous untenured positions we sought each other out for support given that our department was not always a supportive place for junior faculty, or women for that matter.

Marybeth

From the moment I met Cindy during our new faculty orientation, I could sense a rare kindness in her eyes and, more importantly, in her interactions with others. She wasn't judgmental, taking considerable time to parse through issues and make decisions. Cindy has a different approach to scholarship than I do—she's a qualitative researcher whereas I'm an historian—yet we both advance our research with an eye toward equity and fairness. We strive to tell the underdog's story. We attempt to give voice to those who have long been silenced. I do this in my work on African Americans and higher education—looking for examples of agency and action on the part of everyday Blacks and those in leadership positions. Because we have the common goals of access, equity, and equality, we have developed a trusting relationship in which we both challenge and support one another.

Cindy

Marybeth has an honesty, openness, and smile that invites people in and makes them feel welcome. There is genuineness in everything she does. I knew when I met her that this was someone I could trust. For me, it was not our academic conversations that built trust initially, it was our conversations about our life outside of the academy. As mothers of small children we commiserated with the challenges of finding good child-care and shared our hopes and dreams for our children. While these were conversations that were important to us, they were not common conversations we had in academia. These conversations built up trust for me slowly over time as we little by little revealed more of ourselves to each other. This is not the type of conversation that was easy for me. In the work environment I am always on guard, particularly as a woman academic with children. At the time, we had a colleague who was berated for taking time off to be with his children. We also had another colleague who suggested that women academics having children was tantamount to career suicide. I did not trust many of my colleagues. Because Marybeth shared her personal life with me, I knew I could also share my personal side with her.

Marybeth

Due to the high level of trust in our relationship and our similar worldviews, Cindy and I began to talk about discrepancies that we saw in our department (both of us are at different institutions now) in terms of treatment of students. We noticed considerably poorer treatment of students of colour in particular. Rather than continue an insular conversation between the two of us, we chose to engage our students in the conversation—a conversation that led to the publication of an article based on our interactions. We asked that the students have free conversations and trust us. We recorded the conversations so it was essential that we maintain their trust completely. Despite the power inequalities that are innate between faculty and students, we were able to have an open dialogue that brought to life the good, bad, and ugly of graduate school and the experiences of students of colour.

Cindy

This process also evolved slowly as students who had us in class saw that we lived our philosophy in our teaching. The courses we taught acknowledged racism in content, readings, and class discussions. Our classes were structured to invite inquiry and conversation around race and other equity issues. Through our teaching, we sought to create a safe space to have uncomfortable discussions about issues related to inequities in culture and education. These discussions were then carried on in one-on-one meetings where we allowed space for students to share concerns privately about racism that they may have felt or personally experienced in graduate school. These interactions provided an opportunity for us to build trust with students beyond the classroom. We shared the concerns we were hearing from students with each other and that is what led to our creation of a collaborative project in which we wanted to invite students in so that we created a project around race in the academy that would be created collectively.

From our project, and others conducted since, we learned many things about mentoring and working with students of colour. These lessons will be elaborated on throughout the chapter.

STRATEGIES TO BUILD TRUST IN COLLABORATIVE RESEARCH

As we noted earlier, we believe that central to establishing trust is acknowledging that racism occurs both inside and outside the academy in multiple ways (Gasman et al. 2004). This, for us, is the first step in building trust in working with students of colour. Acknowledging racism and power in the academy is central to any attempt to work collaboratively with students of colour, particularly when the topic relates to race or their own experiences in the academy.

Utilizing a collaborative research model is one way to acknowledge the power inequities and to work against them by sharing power during the research process (Gerstl-Pepin and Gunzenhauser 2002). As the work of Kemmis and McTaggart suggests, collaborative research in particular has emerged as a form of resistance to more conventional research practices that have historically been viewed by the oppressed 'as acts of colonization, that is, as means of normalizing or domesticating people to research and policy agendas' (2000: 572). Unlike more traditional research practices, collaborative research can 'bring together broad social analyses: . . . the self-study of practice, the way language is used, organization and power in a local situation, and [social or political] action' (2000: 568). Thus, social transformation is accomplished through critical self-reflection of the participants and/or researchers with respect to the acknowledging inequities embedded in language, values, culture, and structures.

Collaborative narrative inquiry provides a way to develop trust and interrogate power inequities such as issues of race, power, and status (Gasman et al. 2004). Ellis and Bochner describe narrative inquiry as a 'confessional tale' which allows the 'researcher's experience of doing the study [to] become the focus of the investigation' (2000: 740). This kind of research has the potential to be empowering because it breaches 'the conventional separation of researcher and subject' (Bochner, Ellis, and Tillmann-Healy 1998: 43) and provides an opportunity to share private and personal details of one's life. This approach provides a way of acknowledging emotional experience and valuing subjectivity in the research process (Ellis and Bochner 2000).

In addition, this approach is important because creating trust in the academy through mentoring involves taking risks (Chan 2008). We assert that in order for students to develop trust, faculty mentors have to be willing to make themselves vulnerable and share their own personal narratives of race and share power through the creation of collaborative research opportunities.

SHARING POWER AND BEING VULNERABLE

Sharing power can be challenging for a faculty member who may feel his or her career is linked to research. But in order for students to feel a measure of trust, they must feel as though the risk is shared. So, just as they share concerns and experiences concerning racism, it is important for faculty mentors to acknowledge their own vulnerabilities. Faculty can do this either by sharing personal stories about their own concerns with power inequities or by acknowledging specific ways that they might see instances of racism at work in the academy. At the same time, it is important to share ideas for how these forms of racism can be addressed. We felt compelled as mentors to address these issues in our interactions with students of colour. But once trust was established, we also challenged students' assumptions if they had misperceptions about issues related to equity. We felt this was possible only once trust had been established.

Marybeth

Building trust with students of colour is absolutely essential given the negative experiences that many of these students have with faculty, in particular, majority faculty members. When I first began mentoring students of colour, I was hesitant to challenge or push given the negative experiences that these students were having. However, over time, I realized that high expectations and a method of challenge and support was essential to the relationship. I had to teach the students to have high expectations of themselves and to meet the expectations of others. This combination of pushing while simultaneously supporting helped us to build a healthy amount of trust between us. However, the technique that worked best was when I expressed my vulnerability to the students, when I opened myself up to their challenges and questions. By doing this, I was able to reduce the power differential in the relationship. Of course, it can never go away entirely—even after the student graduates—but in a healthy mentoring relationship there is give and take, back and forth, and honesty.

Cindy

Yes, give and take is essential to the relationship. Acknowledging that there is a racial lens through which many experience the world is critical. While I can never know what it means to experience the world as a person of colour, I can be supportive and acknowledge that I know inequities exist. I agree with Marybeth that being vulnerable as a mentor is critical. It requires sharing your own concerns and limitations. To create trust with students it is important to share some of the pieces of yourself that you normally keep hidden from both colleagues and other students. You learn when working collaboratively that you have to trust that the other person will keep up their responsibilities and be there for you just as they expect you to be there for them. This sets the groundwork for creating a collaborative research project.

NEGOTIATING A SHARED RESEARCH PROJECT

We believe that our roles as mentors require that we prepare our students for their future roles as researchers in an academy that has not had great success in retaining and promoting faculty of colour (Moody 2004). Given the lack of support many junior faculty receive in navigating the publishing process and their general distrust of the racial motivations of academia (Souto-Manning and Ray 2007), we felt building trust was crucial. We believe the best way for students to do this is to engage in research with the goal of publication. Any collaborative project should evolve out of a shared interest. It can originate from a research project the faculty member may be engaged in or a new one initiated by a student. Whichever path from which the project begins, it is critical that there is a shared interest in the topic. The project should move the faculty member's research along as well as the student's own interests and desires. This helps to foster trust as it subverts the top-down focus of academia by placing a high value on the student's ideas and interests. The resulting collaborative project then requires negotiating a topic that will be of interest to both faculty and students.

Collaborative research can be time-consuming and requires a high level of trust. Once a project has been identified then the negotiation of roles, responsibilities, and challenges begins (Hanawalt 2006). We consider trust as a concept that operates on a continuum from a relationship in which there is little trust to a relationship in which there is greater trust. Once initial trust has been established through a mentor/mentee relationship, then the ground is set to explore the possibility of a collaborative research project. For example, a student may believe that a faculty member is sensitive to racial issues and is someone they can talk to about these issues. Collaborating on a research project requires a deeper level of trust that requires not just the sharing of information but moves into the sharing of work and responsibility and, most importantly, power. Collaborative narrative research itself works against the academy's focus on individual achievement and competition and instead seeks to share power and foster co-operation (Bowl 2008; Tynan and Garbett 2007).

The initial project we worked on emerged out of student concern that our department was not a supportive place for students of colour. We saw this as an opportunity to learn from each other. But what was most important to all of us was the idea that the project would be focused on thinking about ways in which to make the academy more supportive to graduate students of colour. First, we talked to each other about the idea and saw it as an opportunity to collaborate around a shared interest as well as provide a training ground for students to engage in research aimed at improving the experiences of students of colour while affording them an opportunity to work towards a publication.

NEGOTIATING ROLES, RESPONSIBILITY, AND CHALLENGES

Conducting collaborative research with graduate students requires a careful balance between mentoring and supporting students in the development of research skills and fostering independence in terms of ownership, accountability, and responsibility. Traditional mentoring relationships function to 'socialize individuals into a preexisting environment . . . intentionally or unintentionally reproducing systems of inequality' (Humble et al. 2006: 2). While students require mentorship, they also require space for the acquisition of strong research skills—space to provide input and the opportunity to develop their own research interests (Gunzenhauser and Gerstl-Pepin 2006). When working with students of colour it is critical to acknowledge the ways in which academia can oppress, while simultaneously giving students the necessary skills they need to survive in an inequitable system (Collins 2000; Davenport, Davies, and Grimes 1999; Humble et al. 2006).

Cindy

One of the first ways we in developed trust in this relationship was through shared decision-making and a sharing of responsibilities. Marybeth and I sought to make ourselves more accessible to students. We shared our concerns with the racial climate in the department and even shared our own challenges with balancing home and family and how devalued we felt our roles as mothers were by our colleagues. The research process then evolved out of our sharing of ourselves. And acknowledging the instances and patterns of racism we witnessed. At the same time, we wanted to hold the students to high expectations and treat them like colleagues. We expected them to shoulder their share of the work while we also supported them by providing the knowledge and skills needed to be full collaborators in a professional research project.

Marybeth

One of the most delicate aspects of our collaborative research with students was the negotiation of responsibilities and ensuring that everyone 'pull their weight'. Each partner had different skills and different strengths in terms of organizing, writing, researching, and analysing. We were all responsible for keeping each other on track and we worked hard to accomplish equity in terms of contributions, especially among the students. Based on my experience, graduate school tends to pit students against each other in a competition—giving them the idea that there is only room for so many of them and that only the strong survive. There may be some truth to this as you need to work incredibly hard in order to make it as an academic; however, it is possible to work collaboratively and watch everyone succeed. Despite all of our efforts, we did experience some competition and a bit of discomfort—at which point the faculty had to intervene. One student was not doing enough in the eyes of his peers; another student was doing too much in the eyes of her peers, and there was also frustration with the quality of some of the contributions as the students were all at different levels intellectually. Regardless, with trust and honest conversation, we were able to overcome these obstacles and challenges.

While it is challenging to negotiate the roles and responsibilities of joint research, it also provides a unique opportunity to prepare students to compete successfully in the academy. Students gain important skills in designing, implementing, managing, and ultimately publishing their research.

This is an opportunity not available to all students in graduate school. Entering the job market as a published author provides one with a solid base from which to work towards tenure.

WORKING THROUGH THE PUBLISHING PROCESS AND AUTHORSHIP

Deciding on authorship is one of the most challenging aspects of collaborative writing even without the added issues of the mentoring relationship or racism (Stith, Jester, and Linn 1992). Fields such as medicine and family studies have developed detailed ethical guidelines for authorship that centre on how much work an author has put into the writing (APA Science Student Council 2006; Newman and Jones 2005; Stith, Jester, and Linn 1992). Deciding authorship becomes even more complicated when the authors hold differing positions of power (Mullen and Kochan 2001). Layering in the historical racial inequities embedded in academia (Souto-Manning and Ray 2007), negotiating authorship then becomes a very delicate process.

Cindy

Our first goal in the project was to do a national presentation on our work. We worked together as a group on the conference proposal and on the presentation itself. We started with a poster session in which we shared photographs and our individual and joint narratives. A journal editor took an interest in our work and encouraged us to submit our work for publication in their journal. We realized that this goal of publishing in the journal was a tremendous opportunity for us all. We split up the work between us by clarifying how much time we each had to devote to the work. We were equally committed to the work but realized that each of us did not have the same amount of time to devote to the writing. So we 'divvied up' the work based on interest and time. We were proud of the way in which we worked together on the paper with each of us contributing to the final piece. One of the greatest challenges in this process was negotiating authorship. This can be one of the most challenging aspects of collaboration. We have found that anyone accorded first authorship needs to bear the primary responsibility for shepherding any manuscript through the publication process. For us, we wrote a manuscript and submitted it only to find that the publisher wanted a drastic and time-consuming revision. The revision came at a challenging time as it was towards the end of the semester when students were engaged in final exams, papers, and projects. Marybeth and I found ourselves with the primary responsibility of ensuring that the article would make it through the final stages of the revision process. This is often the most crucial aspect of the publication process. A revision that does not satisfy the reviewers will not get published.

Marybeth

As Cindy noted, the revise and resubmit process at the journal (a top-tier journal with a 5 per cent acceptance rate) was arduous. The students had never engaged in the publishing process before and were not prepared for the substantive concentrated time needed to ensure the paper met the editors' standards and the short timeline required for the revision. As a result, Cindy and I took the lead in revising the paper substantially. In fact, the original paper was published as a book chapter because the journal article no longer resembled it at all. The journal editor was not interested in the topic of mentoring but was captivated by the process by which we wrote the paper. After revising the paper, we rearranged the authorship. It was originally in alphabetical order and remained that way on the book chapter. However, we felt that the authorship of the peer-reviewed journal article needed to reflect the effort of each person. This caused some strain among the students as one student contributed significantly more than the other two; with one of these two contributing very little to the writing process. As this was the first time that most of these students had written an article for publication, we had to be delicate in the way we handled the situation, explaining how we were rewarding work-load. This aspect of the collaboration was the most dicey and difficult in my opinion.

Moving the collaborative research through the publishing process is where developing a deep level of trust between the collaborative research team becomes critical. Authorship may have to be negotiated more than once during the process as differing collaborators take on differing roles. What is centrally important in this process is to discuss authorship openly and address any concerns. If the writing in the manuscript is distributed evenly, then an alphabetical listing of names can be used as we did with the book chapter we published (Anderson-Thompkins et al. 2004). When, however, substantive work is distributed unevenly, careful attention needs to be paid to the amount of writing and responsibility when determining who first author is as this status receives the most credit for the work. We negotiated this in our journal article by determining the extent to which each of us contributed to the publication (Gasman et al. 2004).

CONCLUSION

Creating trust in the academy through mentoring requires careful attention to the ways in which power differentials can complicate the mentoring process. Developing collaborative research is one specific way in which to build trust and mentor graduate students of colour throughout the publishing process. We assert that in order for students to develop trust, faculty mentors have to be willing to make themselves vulnerable and share their own personal narratives of race and share power through the creation of collaborative research opportunities. These opportunities can be difficult and they take a considerable amount of work, but the benefits are enormous in terms of what all partners learn. We learned how to listen more attentively to students—both what they are saying and not saying. We learned how to negotiate sensitive topics, terrain, and relationships. And, we learned how to trust in the academy—a place that tends to teach new faculty the polar opposite. Our experiences conducting collaborative research provided us with an opportunity to do important research while simultaneously creating a much-needed supportive space for graduate students of colour. The students we worked with repeatedly shared with us how little trust they felt in academia due to their own encounters with racism in their programme. Our project was not overly time-consuming and did not require significant financial resources. What it required was careful attention to trust building in the mentoring relationship, acknowledging the power differentials between us, and the creation of collaborative research expectations that were both supportive and challenging at the same time. We encourage faculty to consider collaborative research as a way to mentor graduate students of colour in a supportive environment to meet the rigours and expectations of the academy.

REFERENCES

Anderson-Thompkins, S., Gasman, M., Gerstl-Pepin, C., Hathaway, K., and Rasheed, L. (2004) '"Casualties of War": African American graduate students in the predominantly White academy'. In *Broken Silence: Conversations About Race by African American Faculty and Graduate Students*, ed. D. Cleveland. New York: Peter Lang.

APA Science Student Council. (2006) *A Graduate Student's Guide to Determining Authorship Credit and Authorship Order*. Online. Available HTTP: http://www.apa.org/science/AuthorshipPaper.pdf (accessed 30 June 2009).

Bachmann, R., and Zaheer, A. (2006) *Handbook of Trust*. Northampton: Edward Elgar Publishing.

Bochner, A.P., Ellis, C., and Tillmann-Healy, L. (1998) 'Mucking around looking for truth'. In *Dialectical Approaches to Studying Personal Relationships*, ed. B.M. Montgomery and L.A. Baxter. Philadelphia: Lawrence Erlbaum Associates.

Bowl, M. (2008) 'Working for change in higher education: The possibilities for collaborative research'. *Critical Studies in Education* 49 (2): 185–98.

Brandon, D.T., Isaac, L.A., and LaVeist, T.A. (2005) 'The legacy of the Tuskegee and trust in medical care: Is Tuskegee responsible for race differences in mistrust of medical care?' *Journal of the National Medical Association* 97 (7): 951–56.

Case, P. and Selvester, K. (2002) 'Watch your back: Reflections on trust and mistrust in management education', *Management Learning*, 33, 2: 231-47.

Chan, A.W. (2008) 'Mentoring ethnic minority, pre-doctoral students: An analysis of key mentor practices'. *Mentoring and Tutoring: Partnership in Learning* 16 (3): 263–77.

Collins, P.H. (2000) *Black Feminist Thought: Knowledge, Consciousness, and the Politics of Empowerment*. 2nd ed. New York: Routledge.

Corbie-Smith, G., Thomas, S.B., and St. George, D.M.M. (2002) 'Distrust, race, and research'. *Archives of Internal Medicine* 162 (21): 2458–63.

Davenport, S., Davies, J., and Grimes, C. (1999) 'Collaborative research programmes: Building trust from diffcrence'. *Technovation* 19 (1): 31–40.

Dowdy, J., Givens, G., Murillo, E., Shenoy, D., and Villenas, S. (2000) 'Noises in the attic: The legacy of expectations in the academy'. *International Journal of Qualitative Studies* 13 (5): 429–46.

Ellis, E.M., and Bochner, A. (2000) 'Autoethnograhy, personal narrative, reflexivity: Researcher as subject'. In *Handbook of Qualitative Research*, 2nd ed., ed. N.K. Denzin and Y.S. Lincoln. Thousand Oaks, CA: Sage.

Fries-Britt, S., and Kelly, B. T. (2005) 'Retaining each other: Narratives of two African American women in the academy'. *Urban Review* 37 (3): 221–42.

Gasman, M., Gerstl-Pepin, C.I., Anderson-Thompkins, S., Hathaway, K., and Rasheed, L. (2004) 'Negotiating power, developing trust: Transgressing race and status in the academy'. *Teachers College Record* 106 (4): 689–715.

Gerstl-Pepin, C.I., and Gunzenhauser, M.G. (2002) 'Collaborative team ethnography and the paradoxes of interpretation'. *International Journal of Qualitative Studies in Education* 15 (2): 137–54.

Gunzenhauser, M.G., and Gerstl-Pepin, C.I. (2006) 'Engaging graduate education: A pedagogy for epistemological and theoretical diversity'. *Review of Higher Education* 29 (3): 319–46.

Hanawalt, P.C. (2006) 'Research collaborations: Trial, trust, and truth'. *Cell* 126 (5): 823–25.

Hendrey, P.M. (2007) 'The future of narrative'. *Qualitative Inquiry* 13 (4): 487–98.

hooks, b. (1994) *Teaching to Transgress: Education as the Practice of Freedom.* New York: Routledge.

Howes, C., Ritchie, S., and Bowman, B.T. (2002) *A Matter of Trust: Connecting Teachers and Learners in the Early Childhood Classroom.* New York: Teachers College Press.

Humble, A.M., Solomon, C.R., Allen, K.R., Blaisure, K.R., and Johnson, M.P. (2006) 'Feminism and mentoring of graduate students'. *Family Relations* 55 (1): 2–15.

Kemmis, S., and McTaggart, R. (2000) 'Participatory action research'. In *Handbook of Qualitative Research*, 2nd ed., ed. N.K. Denzin and Y.S. Lincoln. Thousand Oaks, CA: Sage.

Moody, J. (2004) *Faculty Diversity: Problems and Solutions.* New York: Routledge.

Mullen, C.A., and Kochan, F.K. (2001) 'Issues of collaborative authorship in higher education'. *Educational Forum* 65 (2): 128–35.

Newman, A., and Jones, R. (2005) 'Authorship of research papers: Ethical and professional issues for short-term researchers'. *Journal of Medical Ethics* 32 (7): 420–23.

Newton, K. (2007) 'Social and political trust'. In *The Oxford Handbook of Political Behavior*, ed. R.J. Dalton and H. Klingemann. Oxford: Oxford University Press.

Roderick, K.M., and Cook, K.S. (2007) *Trust and Distrust in Organizations: Dilemmas and Approaches.* New York: Russell Sage Foundation Publications.

Souto-Manning, M., and Ray, N. (2007) 'Beyond survival in the ivory tower: Black and Brown women's living narratives'. *Equity and Excellence in Education* 40 (4): 280–90.

Stith, S.M., Jester, S.B., and Linn, J.L. (1992) 'Student–faculty collaborative research'. *Family Relations* 41 (4): 470–74.

Tynan, B.R., and Garbett, D.L. (2007) 'Negotiating the university research culture: Collaborative voices of new academics'. *Higher Education Research and Development* 26 (4): 411–24.

Uslaner, E. M. (2002) *The Moral Foundations of Trust.* Cambridge: Cambridge University Press.

Yukawa, J. (2006) 'Co-reflection in online learning: Collaborative critical thinking as narrative'. *International Journal of Computer-Supported Collaborative Learning* 1 (2): 1556–1607.

Part III

Critical and Current Issues

7 Toxic Leadership and the Erosion of Trust in Higher Education

Sheri R. Klein

There is an assumption that individuals who assume leadership positions and become educational administrators have good will and intent for peers, subordinates, and their organizations. Typically, leadership is associated with positive behaviours and outcomes that illustrate the principles of effective leadership and the ability of a leader to establish trust (Bennis 1995; Blackmore 2006; Fairholm 1994; Farnsworth 2006; Goleman 2006; Greenleaf 2002; Klein and Diket 2006; Sergiovanni 2005; Starratt 2005; Thomas 2003; Tschannen-Moran 2004). However, there is a growing body of scholarship within the fields of education, leadership, management, and psychology that acknowledges the darker side of leadership (Griffin and O'Leary-Kelley 2004; Kellerman 2004; Klein 2009; Klein and Stokes 2008; Padilla, Hogan, and Kaiser 2007; Samier and Atkins 2009; Westhues 2004, 2006b), that there are leaders who cause harm to others, violating the trust of organizational members. This darker side of leadership is widely known as 'destructive leadership' (Einarsen, Aasland, and Skogstad 2007; Padilla, Hogan, and Kaiser 2007). Other terms associated with destructive leadership include 'toxic leadership' (Lipman-Blumen 2005), 'abusive supervision' (Harvey et al. 2007; Tepper 2000), 'petty tyrants' (Ashforth 1994), 'bad leadership' (Kellerman 2004), 'derailed leaders' (Einarsen, Aasland, and Skogstad 2007), 'strategic bullying' (Ferris et al. 2007), and 'bullying and mobbing' (Harvey et al. 2007; Namie and Namie 2000;Westhues 2003, 2006a).

Researchers have also addressed the socio-psychological dimensions of leaders, suggesting that destructive leaders are destructive narcissists (Samier and Atkins 2009, forthcoming). I will use the terms 'destructive' and 'toxic' interchangeably because the research suggests that toxic leadership is destructive to individuals and organizations, and the outcomes of destructive leadership result in toxic work-places. The research also suggests that destructive or toxic leadership occurs in varying degrees, and that the outcomes may vary for individuals and institutions. It is also clear that destructive or toxic leadership is both an act(ion) and an outcome of leaders 'who abuse their position' (Harvey et al. 2007).

While there is no consensus as to a definition of toxic or destructive leadership, there is a general consensus among many researchers that the individual destructive/toxic leader does not work alone: 'leadership does not take place in a vacuum . . . leaders cannot lead unless followers follow' (Kellerman 2004: xiv). Harvey et al. argue that that these pathologies in leadership involve more than an analysis of the 'deviant behavior of an individual (innate characteristics that manifest into antisocial behavior) . . . one must take a careful multilevel analysis that examines the individual, the group, as well as organisational conditions' (2007), a view with which Zimbardo (2008) concurs.

Einarsen, Aasland, and Skogstad believe that a 'more nuanced concept of destructive leadership' may be necessary to understand the facets of toxic leadership. One facet is that they may be 'derailed leaders' (2007: 208, 213), or those who act destructively towards subordinates and an organization. Another suggests that leaders may display characteristics of both destruction and construction, as in 'a leader who bullies or harasses subordinates [but who] may still act in accordance with the goals of the organization' (2007: 211). Yet another suggests that leaders may act in opposition to organizational goals and be supportive of subordinates—known as 'supportive-disloyal leaders' (2007: 213). Finally, 'laissez-faire leadership' as described by Kellerman (2004), suggests that leaders may be toxic not out of intent to harm but due to sheer incompetence. Generally, the research suggests that the intent and targets of toxic leadership varies by leader, situation, and context, and that the dynamics of an organization greatly influence the emergence and longevity of toxic leadership. As such, it may be concluded that toxic leadership that is tolerated and sustained is embedded in a dysfunctional web of institutional relations that can be described as a toxic triangle (Padilla, Hogan, and Kaiser 2007). Viewing toxic leadership from this multifaceted lens may help to explain its complexities, variations, and outcomes.

A general consensus among researchers is that the behaviours and actions of a toxic leader are not a one-time singular act of aggression (Harvey et al. 2007; Westhues 2006b), but rather 'systemic and repeated behaviour by a leader, supervisor or manager that violates the legitimate interest of the organisation by undermining or sabotaging the organisation's goals, tasks, resources, and effectiveness and/or the motivation and well-being and job satisfaction of his/her subordinates' (Einarsen, Aasland, and Skogstad 2007: 207). While this definition takes into account a leader's behaviour, it does not fully address how a leader engages other administrators and/or subordinates in anti-subordinate acts, namely mobbing.

A closer analysis of toxic leadership is timely and warranted so we may better understand under what conditions people abuse power and why. Zimbardo (2008; Padilla, Hogan, and Kaiser 2007) and others remind us, we must consider the leader, the followers, and the environmental factors to fully understand how and why toxic leadership occurs and the irrevocable damage it causes. In addition, the current climate within higher education that embraces a consumerist model will be discussed for how it may foster a breeding-ground for toxic leadership and the erosion of trust of leaders, colleagues, and institutions of higher learning.

The focus here will be on the individual leader or administrator who aims to 'undermine the motivation well-being and job satisfaction of [his/her] subordinates' (Einarsen, Aasland, and Skogstad 2007: 212) without necessarily being destructive of the overall organization. Based on my experiences in higher education, and an analysis of the literature, this kind of tyrannical leader is often referenced, describing those who are firmly established in mid-level to senior administrative positions such as chair, dean, provost/vice president, president, and chancellor. As area/unit heads/supervisors of faculty and staff, they may display 'anti-subordinate behaviours like bullying, humiliation, manipulation, deception and harassment' (Einarsen, Aasland, and Skogstad. 2007: 212) toward subordinates while maintaining a positive image to their own supervisors and upper management. Their intent is to: (a) increase their power and rise within the organizational hierarchy; (b) eliminate any rivals or resistance in their way; and (c) control the larger work group.

CHARACTERISTICS, TARGETS, AND TACTICS

The toxic leader engages in anti-subordinate behaviours and in 'psychological violence and emotional abuse [toward some targets that is] . . . intended to harm or control the victim [target and thereby] . . . affecting an employee's dignity or psychological integrity, and that results in a harmful work environment' (Westhues 2007: 8). Many researchers have identified the toxic leader as a narcissist (Padilla, Hogan, and Kaiser 2007; Samier and Atkins 2009, forthcoming) who displays an 'illegitimate sense of entitlement, need for admiration, lack of empathy, and projection of negative traits onto others' (Samier and Atkins, forthcoming: 1). What is consistent about narcissistic leaders in universities is that they are 'likely to violate policies, principles of administrative law, and natural justice' (Samier and Atkins 2009: 219), they refuse to be accountable for their words and actions, they 'ignore others' viewpoints or welfare . . . [and] demand unquestioning obedience' (Padilla, Hogan, and Kaiser 2007: 181). Toxic leaders also use rewards with organizational participants such as summer contracts, new office furniture, grants, and hiring spouses to align subordinates and create a loyal work group. In dysfunctional and punitive work cultures, participants are motivated by survival, rewards, and the avoidance of punishment (pain).

Padilla, Hogan, and Kaiser believe that 'destructive leadership and charisma are empirically linked' (2007: 180). One of the reasons that toxic leaders may be so effective and undetected within their own organizations is due to their ability to project a positive public persona to others outside the sphere of their intended targets; their behaviour is 'essentially manipulative ranging from superficially charming . . . to arrogant and haughty . . . and finally divisive, contemptuous, and destructive if the individual is in their road, or perceived as a threat' (Samier and Atkins 2009: 215–16). The necessity of toxic leaders to project their shadows and dark side onto targets may be due to wounded egos and psychological damage arising from 'parental discord, low socioeconomic status, paternal criminality, material psychiatric disorder, and child abuse', but 'while the traumas of childhood may contribute to the development of a toxic leader, it does not excuse their viciousness, cruelty and possessing an ideology of hate' (Padilla, Hogan, and Kaiser 2007: 180, 182).

Westhues (2006b) and others report that the targets of toxic leaders are typically faculty who are highly capable, those who have a strong sense of ethics, who may 'file grievances and make noise' (Gravois 2006: 4), and who question a toxic leader's unfair practices. Targets within university settings typically excel well above departmental or college norms and expectations, tend to be highly productive scholars, popular/effective teachers, grant recipients, and are known to be 'personally invested in a secure job' (Westhues 2003: 29). Some researchers believe that targets may be aligned with 'vulnerable groups that lack influence . . . or lack political skill' (Harvey et al. 2007), or are 'conscientious, literal minded, and introverted' (Ferris et al. 2007: 196). It is not uncommon to see 'tenured faculty [as] members [who] are pursued relentlessly' (Jefferson 2007: 6–8) by toxic leaders.

One characteristic worth noting with respect to targets is social class. Padilla, Hogan, and Kaiser report that 'poor people living in daily fear are easier to control' (2007: 183). Faculty or staff who may be financial vulnerable, from working-class backgrounds, or who may deviate from a White middle-class university culture may be vulnerable to abuse by toxic leaders.

Once toxic leaders have identified their targets, they work to control and intimidate them with 'implicit threats' with the desired outcome of 'influencing the target/individual(s) to act in some preconceived direction . . . [and] subordinate the focal individual to a position weakness' (Ferris et al. 2007: 198) to make them fearful and compliant. They aim to instill fear about job security, position or assignments, and future advancement, while eroding their self-esteem and sense of safety. The toxic leader uses a variety of aggressive tactics over time, and this may be understood as 'strategic bullying' (Ferris et al. 2007). The toxic leader engages in the 'enlargement of some real or imagined misdeed or fault in order to smear the target's whole identity, so that he or she is seen as personally abhorrent . . . a dangerous, repugnant entity . . . [and acts on] a shared conviction that the target needs a lesson' (Westhues 2006a: 2–3). This may be repeated at various intervals of a target's employment if the toxic leader remains in power and if the target remains a perceived threat.

Attacks are aimed at the self-image and reputation of a target in an organization with the full knowledge that one's personal/professional reputation is linked to personal power, self-esteem, confidence, professional identity, and status within organizational work groups. Character assassination is attempted through repeated hostile and demeaning verbal and nonverbal communication whereby the toxic leader makes false claims to upper management about the target or a target's peers or about a target's performance, appearance, and/or personality. Behind the scenes, toxic leaders may also engage in petty but consistent harassment, for example, constantly losing a target's travel paperwork or requests, not answering emails from a target, 'not giving target needed information, mean pranks against a target, and continued accusations of error' (Parker-Pope 2008a: 4).

Seeking to widen the audience for these attacks, the toxic leader may begin to attack a target in public at meetings with verbal accusations. In higher education contexts, the toxic leader, without just cause, may observe a target's classes to intimidate the faculty/target, cause suspicion among students, and erode the trust and confidence of students for that faculty member. They may also solicit student complaints about a target, and even go so far as to help students write complaints against a target. They may solicit negative feedback about a target without his/her knowledge from peers and use it in a personnel review and by-pass established personnel rules and procedures. They may engage in a pattern of writing unsupportable insubordination charges against a target replete with manipulations and lies with the aims of ruining a target's reputation and creating a trail of negative personnel documents.

What is consistent about all these tactics is that the claims made about a target are never supportable and verifiable. These emotionally laden claims work to infuriate the target so he/she may overreact. They also are created to play on the emotions of a target's peers and upper management, who by now may have been indoctrinated and believe the rhetoric of hate about a target. Furthermore, the toxic leader: (a) often blames the target (scapegoat) for matters beyond his/her control; (b) punishes a target for not satisfying unreasonable work assignment(s); and (c) uses rhetoric that may be considered by most reasonable persons as slander and character defamation. The toxic leader becomes part of a web of social aggression (Simmons 2002) and rumour spreading with aims to stigmatize and separate a target from the larger group through shunning. Labels, such as 'uncollegial', 'troublemaker', 'vindictive', 'liar', 'difficult', and 'corrosive' are used to describe targets, and signal 'that the target should not be listened to and [be] ignored [and] that positions the target outside of a circle of respectability and dialogue' (Westhues 2001: par. 1–3). As gossip can never be attributable to one individual, groups of colleagues (mobbers) work with anonymity and lack of accountability, and in doing so, are never held directly responsible for the aggression. Using their administrative authority, toxic leaders may also physically isolate a target to separate them from department colleagues to remind their faculty and subordinates that they are capable of 'creating scapegoats who they punish harshly to serve as a warning to others' (Einarsen, Aasland, and Skogstad 2007: 212).

Targets may receive awards, positive teaching evaluations, grants, and successfully publish; however, the toxic leader never acknowledges these accomplishments to the target or the larger group. To further punish a target, toxic leaders may alter a target's duties and responsibilities without discussion with the faculty/target. They may increase their work-load beyond a level of expectations for others within their department or unit, and without any additional compensation. In addition, they may also decrease their work-load and remove a target's courses and projects for no justifiable reason, and without discussion. Again, all of this may occur to both untenured and tenured faculty and is aimed to erode a target's self-esteem, confidence, professional identity, and opportunities as well as cause worry, stress, confusion, and disruption.

Always working under the legal threshold, toxic leaders use psychological violence to destroy and eliminate targets, rivals, and dissenters. In addition, they use their administrative authority, political capital, and upper-management alliances to circumvent any and all university policy and rules, influence grievance committees and upper-management decision-making about a target, particularly when confronted with wrongdoing or grievances. What may be considered a final attempt in a toxic leader's aggression toward a target is to initiate and/or support a target's non-renewal, denial of tenure, if untenured, and dismissal, if tenured. True to the toxic leader's behaviour, charges are fabricated and exaggerated about a target's work, conduct and/or personality, and events, timelines are manipulated, and when facts support a target, they are disregarded.

ROLE OF PARTICIPANTS AND ORGANIZATIONAL CULTURE

The experiences of targets and those who witness toxic leadership have verified that toxic leaders do not act alone, that they enlist others in what is known as 'mobbing'. When Swedish psychologist Hans Leymann coined the term 'mobbing' in the 1980s as he studied occupational health and safety (cited in Westhues 2003: 1), it was not well documented in higher education. In Westhues's work documenting cases of mobbing of professors in higher education, he has identified it as an 'impassioned, collective campaign by co-workers to exclude, punish, and humiliate a targeted worker initiated most often by a person in a position of power or influence' (2003: 9). Consequently, mobbing requires compliance and/or involvement of a toxic leader, and 'will only take place if a bully feels he or she has the blessing, support or implicit permission of superiors' (Harvey et al. 2007). In academic environments, there may be varying levels of aggression and participation from mobbers (faculty, staff, and/or students) depending on a target's gender, status, and rank; untenured faculty and adjuncts may also participate in mobbing of tenured faculty. Toxic leaders may also enlist vulnerable staff (secretaries, graduate students, and new employees) in mobbing that includes antisocial behaviours of shunning, gossiping, or spying on a target for the toxic leader. What is clear is that these processes result in the dehumanization of a target that is sanctioned and led by the toxic leader.

Zimbardo writes that influential situational forces, such as 'roles, rules, norms', need to be examined to better understand how groups engage in dehumanization of a target (2008: 291). The roles that organizational participants play include being a conformist (mobber) and a bystander. Conformists are those who 'become what the aggressor wants' (2008: 205). In order to survive in a hostile work environment, their needs for approval and to be a team player are 'perverted into compliance and [having an] in/out mentality' (2008: 233). In order to carry out the orders of the toxic leader, they must first label their target as the enemy to dehumanize them and then morally disengage to 'minimize the link between actions and outcomes . . . reconstructing a perception of the victim [target] as deserving' (2008: 311).

In the web of toxic leadership, there are bystanders who choose to turn a blind eye because they believe they 'have neither the power to control the authority or to sanction the bully . . . involvement may also draw attention [to them] as a potential target of bullying' (Harvey et al. 2007). The aggression of toxic leadership is enabled because of bystanders and their fear of the leader and other bully peers who through intimidation, subtle and covert, make examples of others (through marginalizing, ostracizing, etc.). The result is a 'spiral of silence' (Moy, Domke, and Stamm 2001: 7) and a climate of fear that leaves its organizational participants debilitated and silenced.

NORMS

The norms of institutions and departments play a key role in how faculty and staff conform or deviate, become bystanders or conformist/mobbers, and shape the consequences. Zimbardo reminds us that 'situational power often triumphs over individual power' (2008: x), which becomes a powerful force in shaping individual and group behaviour. Norms are also communicated through formal and informal policy, gossip, social interactions, patterns of speech, and in the written and spoken culture of the organization and their leaders.

Targets who may bring toxic leadership to the attention of key administrators or senior management may be at a loss. In a recent survey it was reported that in '62% of the cases, when made aware of bullying, employers worsen the problem, or simply do nothing' (Workplace Bullying Institute 2007). Upper management may choose to be a bystander, but in many cases, upper management engages in mobbing. If there are toxic leaders at several levels (chair, dean, provost, and president), and there are identified targets whom they all agree on, the toxic leaders will act in unison to support and enable one another.

CONSUMERIST MODELS IN HIGHER EDUCATION

A current climate within higher education that has transformed the landscape by enabling toxic leadership is the business/consumer model. In recent years, universities and colleges across the globe have moved sharply in practice and mission from being 'democratic public spheres' (Giroux 2002: 17), shaped by faculty governance and democratic ideals, to academic institutions based on a consumerist model of education and labour management. The culture of universities has shifted to a corporate culture of higher education where there is an aim to create 'compliant workers' (Giroux 2002: 2), and where a 'culture of business' has replaced an academic culture (Bowen 2005: 72). The corporatization of higher education is a widespread and global problem in higher education affecting institutions worldwide (Agostinone-Wilson 2006; Clark 2008; Giroux 2002; Jeon 2004; Nelson and Watt 2004).

Agostinone-Wilson regards the accountability movement in K–16 American education as a parallel to 'the growth of corporate power and a retreat from workers' rights . . . this includes [employee/faculty] goal setting, [and] use of standards' to shape student and faculty behaviors' (2006: 40). The business model has also elevated the opinions of student/consumers about faculty performance, giving undue empowerment and entitlement to students. Colleagues who 'dare to disagree, civilly and reasonably' (O'Connor 2003: 1) with peers or administration about any issue related to personnel, curricular, or governance matters are targeted and vulnerable to attacks. Furthermore, reasonable requests to administration for transparency in decision-making in the business model are perceived as a challenge and threat to authority, resulting in these actions being regarded as transgressions that warrant discipline.

Within the corporate paradigm, many university administrators see their roles as managing, controlling, neutralizing or diminishing faculty power, and punishing faculty who do not conform and/or resist corporate-centred norms and policies. As a result, the 'dialogic process located in civic democratic values' (Blackmore 2006: 192) is greatly diminished where 'unions and senates are eviscerated, neutralized, or eliminated altogether . . . [with a] a chilling effect on free speech' (Clark 2008: 1) in academe. Environments susceptible to toxic leadership have been described as those 'where there is extensive change (restructuring or downsizing)' (Ferris et al. 2007: 196). This phenomenon is currently occurring in universities worldwide with the downsizing of tenure track faculty positions, the increase of part-time and adjunct positions, and customized tuition and online programmes that increase profits while eroding faculty authority and professionalism.

These conditions have resulted in higher education work-places becoming vulnerable environments for many faculty and staff, even for those working without the protections of collective bargaining and contracts.

OUTCOMES FOR TOXIC LEADERSHIP

There are direct and negative outcomes of toxic leadership for targets, organizational participants, and institutions. The outcomes of toxic leadership for targets include emotional and psychological distress due to 'loss of social status, credibility, reprisal, and [continuous] professional ostracism' (Zimbardo 2008: 471). In addition, targets also suffer social isolation, and often financial loss and ongoing psychological attacks that are akin to those who experience physical combat. Physical symptoms of targets of toxic leadership can include chronic stress (Parker-Pope 2008b), 'sleep disruption (ranked number two for health consequences for bullied individuals at 84 percent), anxiety (94 percent), and depression which affect the victim and the people who care about him or her' (Workplace Bully Institute 2008). Other health consequences include 'loss of concentration, panic attacks, feelings of paranoia, recurrent nightmares, suicidal thoughts and thoughts about being violent to others' (Workplace Bullying Institute 2008). Targets typically experience symptoms of post-traumatic stress disorder (PTSD) due to repeated violations and stress.

Outcomes for organizational participants are numerous. First, the conformer/mobbers learn that engaging in violence and the dehumanization of colleagues is acceptable behaviour. Bystanders learn to silence their voices and stay invisible for survival. Ultimately, in organizations where toxic leadership is tolerated, participants learn that faculty solidarity, respect for governance, and acting ethically and morally are not as important as self-preservation and remaining under the radar of a toxic leader.

IMPACTS ON INSTITUTIONS

One impact of toxic leadership on institutions is the 'devaluation of valuable colleagues who are not admirers' of targets and who are bullied and mobbed to the point of resignation or termination 'leaving others to adopt a state of 'passive acquiescence' (Samier and Atkins 2009: 217). Furthermore, another impact of toxic leadership are the 'continued tests of obedience demanded' (Bates 2009: 170) of organizational participants that erode dignity and self-respect.

Without sanctions for toxic leaders, bullies, and mobbers, there is chronic scapegoating; one employee after the other is singled out as the bad guy and subjected to collective exclusion and punishment (Wyatt and Hare 1997). Finally, a devastating impact of toxic leadership on institutions is the destruction of the university as a space for 'engaged intellectuals' (Giroux 2002: 19) and a trusting teaching and learning community. Faculty who are perpetual targets may have difficulty focusing on teaching and research that may result in teaching ineffectiveness and/or lack of scholarly productivity.

As toxic leaders act in ways that betray trust among and between organizational participants, the spaces for justice within the academy decrease significantly. In a review of Fricker's *Epistemic Injustice: Power and the Ethics of Knowing* (2007) Code writes:

> Testimonial injustice and hermeneutical injustice, each of which consists most fundamentally, in a wrong done to someone specifically in their capacity as a knower. Hermeneutical and testimonial injustice are interconnected in the harms they perform . . . Yet, they operate differently in that testimonial injustice is an individual-to-individual harm . . . whereas hermeneutical injustice, with its roots in the collective hermeneutical resource, invokes different culpability issues, some of which refer to institutional, social policies and practices held in place. (2008: 13)

Where toxic leadership prevails, there is both testimonial and hermeneutic injustice for targets and institutions. As toxic leaders never admit to any errors, any kind of restoration that results in a regained sense of trust is difficult, if not impossible, in the absence of acknowledgment of wrong-doing. As such, the damage caused by toxic leadership penetrates into the fabric of university life and society, alters it, and thereby defines the university not as a site of democracy and freedom, but rather as a work-place marked by constraint, torture, and injustice.

PROBLEMATIZING TOXIC LEADERSHIP

Toxic leadership is systemic 'violent managerial practices occurring all over the globe in which women [and men] are the targets of ruthless violence' (Cotter 2001: 87). From a labour perspective, it is ultimately a 'strategy to reproduce a labor force that will be more easily exploitable' (Cotter 2001: 170). To fully understand toxic leadership, one needs to look to the individuals (targets, leaders, bystanders), the work-place setting, institutional culture and norms, and other external factors that may permit toxic leadership to thrive. Toxic leadership is damaging on many levels that include individuals and institutions and can only be stopped internally if it is 'vigorously challenged by authorities they could not manipulate or undermine' (Samier and Atkins 2009: 219). Ultimately, toxic leadership destroys a basic human sense of trust that is critical for working relationships, effective leadership, the university as site of democracy, and a healthy society.

Targets remain relatively unsupported by colleagues within their institutions out of fear by association by peers. Targets remain relatively unprotected due to a lack of or unclear institutional policies, lack of work-place violence laws, and the existence of toxic leadership at many levels within an institution. Targets can be damaged while employed and may be further pursued by toxic leaders who slander targets to future employers and thereby destroy a target's future employment prospects. Online social networking systems and blogs also pose problems for targets who may be vulnerable to social aggression by revengeful toxic leaders and their mobs.

Finally, there is relatively little extant scholarship and activism on the part of academics on the subject of toxic leadership within higher education. While blogs about academic mobbing and bullying allow for anony·mous postings, there are difficulties in getting targets to come forward in a public forum due to the realities of fear and reprisal. Furthermore, targets may be debilitated by the endless cycle of attacks, which may leave them incapable of participating. Such factors may impede the growth of scholarship surrounding toxic leadership and impede our understanding of current climates within higher education.

In a review of Nelson and Watt's *Office Hours: Activism and Change in the Academy* (2004), Fine writes that academics have 'committed their professional lives to social criticism but have failed to analyse the conditions of their own workplaces' (2005). Giroux similarly writes:

> Refusing to take positions on controversial issues [such as toxic leadership] or to examine the role of intellectuals in lessening human suffering, such academics become models of moral indifference. (2002: 18)

Westhues reminds us that there needs to be opposition to those who are 'ignoring, twisting, or misappl[ying] reasonable rules', adding that 'the prevention of mobbing [and toxic leadership] in universities depends on us academics doing what we are supposed to be especially skilled at: keeping ourselves conscious' (2006c: 22, 38). Yet, the price for being conscious may result in becoming a target. What is apparent is the necessity of a critical mass of organizational participants who decide they will not be morally indifferent.

One must also critically analyse the perspectives of those who write about toxicity in the work-place. For example, a number of researchers (Furnham and Taylor 2004; Kusy and Holloway 2009; Twale and DeLuca 2008) support a management perspective about toxicity, suggesting that the toxic work-place is due to the toxic and abrasive personalities of employees, not management. They describe the toxic employee as a 'difficult person, a control freak, narcissist, manipulator, bully, and poisonous individual' (Kusy and Holloway 2009: 3). Furthermore, Kusy and Holloway list strategies for managers to deal with such employees, such as, 'ignoring emails, not involving the employee in team work, working around him/her, excluding them from important decisions and removing them from responsibilities' (2009: 45).

However, these are identical to the strategies that Westhues and other researchers have identified as tactics of toxic leaders and bullies. Toxic leaders justify their violence: the 'unwarranted attacks on others . . . even to the extent of manufacturing dismissal could be seen instead by narcissists as warranted staff discipline' (Samier and Atkins 2009: 219). There are clearly distinct differences about who is toxic in the work-place depending on whether one is a manager, administrator, a subordinate, or a target, and whether one is writing from the field of leadership studies or business management. While all perspectives may be important to illuminate the phenomenon of toxicity in the work-place, the reality is that toxic leaders do exist, their damage is far-reaching, and targets of toxic leaders never deserve such abuse.

CONCLUSION

It is important that faculty and graduate students in educational administration, higher education, and those preparing for careers in teaching in higher education contexts reflect on the darker side of leadership, and the factors that allow this pathology to occur. The following questions are intended to guide such reflection, future research, debate, and social action within the academy, professional associations, and unions.

What professional, moral, and ethical responsibilities should academics have in response to witnessing and/or experiencing toxic leadership? How do toxic leaders silence the collective judgment, speech, and voices of other academics in the academe, and with what consequences? How does toxic leadership inhibit and oppress teaching and learning spaces and alter the roles of faculty as public intellectuals? How does toxic leadership alter the path of vital academics and scholars? What is the role as academics, 'to act to help others, prevent harm to others, or not act at all?' (Zimbardo 2008: 486). How do toxic leaders destroy trust—and is it repairable? What kinds of changes are necessary within organizations, unions, and labour law to protect targets and stop toxic leadership?

There needs to be greater awareness of and advocacy about toxic leadership in higher education to increase understanding about the tactics, motives, aims, and outcomes of toxic leaders and their followers. This is a beginning for change and transformation of organizational cultures and work-spaces.

Transformation and reform is not an easy road: Banfield reminds us that 'human emancipation is an active struggle and requires our engagement' (2003: 7). The work that lies ahead to disable toxic leadership requires a raising of one's consciousness and a commitment to engagement and activism if higher education is to become a space where all 'people feel significant' (Bennis 1989/2009: 22–23), where basic human rights of dignity, safety, and democracy are fostered and ensured for all, and where faculty may 'gain a public voice and come to grip with their own power as individuals and social agents' (Giroux 2002: 10).

Trust in leadership is an issue not just for the higher education community. It is a global issue affecting political, economic, corporate, and educational organizations and work sectors. Recent events worldwide have revealed that those in positions of authority and leadership can and do betray the trust of their constituents in highly destructive ways and with moral indifference. The educational community is no different; the reporting of cases of bullying, mobbing, and toxic leadership within higher education appears to be increasing.

The hope and the challenge for higher education communities and its members is to restore the academy, which has been decimated through the toleration of psychological violence in a current climate of academic corporatism as well as a climate of anti-intellectualism and unreason that extends well beyond the ivory tower (Jacoby 2008), to a site of trust and democracy. The restoration of trust is by far more difficult than the establishment of trust, and in some cases the restoration of trust may not be feasible. The glimmer of trust and democracy in the academe, however, can be achieved when faculty and administrators operate on the principle of free speech without fear of retaliation, where toxic leaders and their followers are justly sanctioned, when organizations realize that 'leaders need people around them who have contrary views' (Bennis 1989/2009: 190), and where trust simply guides leadership practices and human relations.

REFERENCES

Agostinone-Wilson, F. (2006) 'Downsized discourse: Classroom management, neo-liberalism, and the shaping of correct workplace attitudes'. *Journal of Critical Educational Policy Studies* 4 (2). Online. Available HTTP: http://www.jceps.com/index.php?pageID=article&articleID=69 (accessed 20 February 2007).

Ashforth, B. (1994) 'Petty tyranny in organisations'. *Human Relations* 47 (7): 755–78.

Banfield, G. (2003) 'Getting real about class: Towards an emergent Marxist education'. *Journal for Critical Education Policy Studies* 1 (2). Online. Available HTTP: http://www.jceps.com (accessed 1 June 2008).

Bates, R. (2009) 'The political economy of the emotions: Individualism, culture and markets, and the administration of self, in education'. In *Emotional Dimensions of Educational Administration and Leadership*, ed. E.A. Samier and M. Schmidt. Milton Keynes: Routledge.

Bennis, W. (1989/2009) *On Being a Leader*. Cambridge: Perseus Books.

———. (1995) 'The art form of leadership'. In *The Leader's Companion: Insights on Leadership through the Ages*, ed. T. Wren. New York: Free Press.

Blackmore. J. (2006) 'Social justice and the study and practice of leadership in education'. *Journal of Educational Administration and History* 38 (2): 185–200.

Bowen, R.W. (2005) 'Academic freedom undermined: Self-censorship'. *Academe* 91 (4): 72.

Clark, G.A. (2008) 'How academic corporatism can lead to dictatorship'. Online. Available HTTP: http:universitypolitics.blogspot.com (accessed 28 May 2008).

Code, L. (2008). 'Review of Miranda Fricker's *Epistemic Injustice: Power and the Ethics of Knowing'*. *Notre Dame Philosophical Reviews*, 12 March. Online. Available HTTP: http://ndpr.nd.edu/review.cfm?id=12604 (accessed 25 July 2008).

Cotter, J. (2001) 'Sexual harassment as/and (self) invention: Class, sexuality, pedagogy, and (creative) writing'. In *Marxism, Queer Theory, Gender*, ed. M. Zavarzadeh, T.L. Ebert, and D. Morton. Syracuse, NY: Red Factory.

Davenport, N., Schwartz, R., and Elliot, G. (1999) *Mobbing: Emotional Abuse in the Workplace*. Ames, IA: Civil Publishing.

Dellasega, C. (2005) *Mean Girls Grow Up: Adult Women Who Are Still Queen Bees, Middle Bees and Afraid to Bees*. Hoboken, NJ: Wiley.

Einarsen, S., Aasland, M.S., and Skogstad, A. (2007) 'Destructive leadership behavior: A definition and conceptual model'. *Leadership Quarterly* 18 (3): 207–16.

Fairholm, G.W. (1994) *Trust and Leadership*. Santa Barbara, CA: Greenwood.

Farnsworth, K.A. (2006) *Leadership as Service*. Santa Barbara, CA: Praeger.

Ferris, G.R., et al. (2007) 'Strategic bullying as a supplementary balanced perspective on destructive leadership'. *Leadership Quarterly* 18 (3): 195–206.

Fine, M. (2005) 'Office hours: Activism and change in the academy'. *Academe* 91 (4): 61–63.

Furnham, A., and Taylor, J. (2004) *The Dark Side of Behavior at Work*. New York: Palgrave MacMillan.

Giroux, H. (2002) 'The corporate war against higher education'. *Workplace* 5 (1). Online. Available HTTP: http://www.louisville.edu/journal/workplace/issue5p1.giroux.html (accessed 5 August 2008).

Goleman, R. (2006) *Primal Leadership*. Cambridge, MA: Harvard Business School.

Gravois, J. (2006) 'Mob rule: In departmental disputes, professors can act just like animals'. *Chronicle of Higher Education* 52 (32): A10.

Greenleaf, R. (2002) *Servant Leadership*. Mahwah, NJ: Paulist Press.

Griffin, R.W., and O'Leary-Kelley, A.M. (eds.) (2004) *The Dark Side of Organizational Behavior*. San Francisco: Jossey-Bass.

Harvey, M., et al. (2007) 'A bully as an archetypal destructive leader', *Journal of Leadership & Organizational Studies*. Online. Available HTTP: <http://www.entrepreneur.com/tradejournals/article/171136508.html> (accessed 28 July 2008).

Jacoby, S. (2008) *The Age of American Unreason*. New York: Random House.

Jefferson, A. (2007) 'The bullying boss'. *Academic Leadership* 4 (4). Online. Available HTTP: http://www.academicleadership.org (accessed 31 July 2008).

Jeon, J.A. (2004) 'Corporatization of higher education policies of Australia and Korea in the era of global markets'. Stanford University School of Education. Online. Available HTTP: www.stanford.edu/dept/SUSE/ICE/monographs/jeon-04.pdf (accessed 10 February 2009).

Kellerman, B. (2004) *Bad Leadership: What It Is, How It Happens, Why It Matters*. Boston: Harvard Business School.

Klein, S. (2009) 'Workplace violence in higher education'. *Journal of Cultural Research in Art Education* 27:145–52.

Klein, S., and Diket, R. (2006) 'Aesthetic leadership: Leaders as architects'. In *Aesthetic Dimensions of Educational Administration and Leadership*, ed. E.A. Samier. New York: Routledge.

Klein, S., and Stokes, S. (2008) 'Academic mobbing: Is gender a factor?' *Women in Higher Education* 17 (5): 24–25.

Kusy, M., and Holloway, E. (2009) *Toxic Workplace: Managing Toxic Personalities*. San Francisco: Jossey-Bass.

Lipman-Blumen, J. (2005) *The Allure of Toxic Leaders*. New York: Oxford University Press.

Moy, P., Domke, D.S., and Stamm, K. (2001) 'The spiral of silence and the public opinion on affirmative action', *Journalism & Mass Communication Quarterly* 78 (1): 7–25.

Namie, G., and Namie, R. (2000) *The Bully at Work*. Naperville, IL: Sourcebooks.

Nelson, G., and Watt, S. (2004) *Office Hours: Activism and Change in the Academy*. New York: Routledge.

O'Connor, E. (2003) 'Brooklyn College's death wish'. *Critical Mass*, 7 December. Online. Available HTTP: http://www.erinoconnor.org/archives (accessed 22 July 2008).

Padilla, A., Hogan, R., and Kaiser, R.B. (2007) 'The toxic triangle: Destructive leaders, susceptible followers and conducive environments'. *Leadership Quarterly* 18 (3): 176–94.

Parker-Pope, T. (2008a) 'Have you been bullied at work?' *New York Times*, 24 March. Online. Available HTTP: http://well.blogs.nytimes.com/2008/03/24/have-you-been-bullied-at-work/ (accessed 31 January 2009).

———. (2008b) 'Meet the work bully'. *New York Times*, 11 March. Online. Available HTTP: http://well.blogs.nytimes.com/2008/03/11/meet-the-work-bully/#more-284 (accessed 31 January 2009).

Samier, E.A., and Atkins, T. (2009) 'The problem of narcissists in positions of power: The grandiose, the callous, and the irresponsible in educational administration and leadership'. In *Emotional Dimensions of Educational Administration and Leadership*, ed. E.A. Samier and M. Schmidt. Milton Keynes: Routledge.

———. (Forthcoming) 'Preventing and combating administrative narcissism: Implications for professional graduate programs'. *Journal of Educational Administration*.

Sergiovanni, T.J. (2005) 'The virtue of leadership'. *Educational Forum* 69 (2): 112–23.

Simmons, R. (2002) *Odd Girl Out: The Hidden Aggression in Girls*. New York: Harcourt.

Starratt, R. (2005) 'Responsible leadership'. *Educational Forum* 69 (2): 124–33.

Tepper, B. (2000) 'Consequences of abusive supervision'. *Academy of Management Journal* 43 (2): 178–90.

Thomas, G.L. (2003) 'Are you a constructive or destructive leader?' *weLEAD*. Online. Available HTTP: http://www.leadingtoday.org/Onmag/2003%20Archives/august03/gt-august03.html (accessed 5 March 2008).

Tschannen-Moran, M. (2004) *Trust Matters: Leadership for Successful Schools*. San Francisco: Jossey-Bass.

Twale, D., and DeLuca, B. (2008) *Faculty Incivility: The Rise of the Academic Bully Culture and What to Do about It*. San Francisco: Jossey-Bass.

Westhues, K. (2001) 'Basic critique'. Online. Available HTTP: http://mueller.educ.ucalgary.ca/Difficult/default.html (accessed 31 January 2008).

———. (2003) 'At the mercy of the mob'. Online. Available HTTP: http://arts.uwaterloo.ca/~kwesthue/ohs-canada.htm (accessed 31 January 2008).

———. (2004) *Workplace Mobbing in Academe: Reports from 20 Universities*. Lewiston, NY: Mellen.

———. (2006a) 'Checklist of mobbing behaviors'. Online. Available HTTP: http://arts.uwaterloo.ca/~kwesthue/checklist.htm (accessed 5 August 2008).

———. (2006b) *The Envy of Excellence: Administrative Mobbing of High-Achieving Professors*. Lewiston, NY: Mellen.

———. (2006c) 'Waterloo strategy for prevention of mobbing'. Online. Available HTTP: http://arts.uwaterloo.ca/~kwesthue/waterloostrategy.htm#one (accessed 5 August 2008).

————. (2007) 'Before drafting your policy on workplace decency, compare these two alternatives'. Online. Available HTTP: http://arts.uwaterloo.ca/~kwesthue/dignitypolicies01.htm (accessed 5 August 2008).

Workplace Bullying Institute. (2007) 'Results of the WBI-Zogby U.S. Workplace Bullying Survey'. Online. Available HTTP: http://www.workplacebullying.org/research.html (accessed 20 June 2009).

————. (2008) Online. Available HTTP: http://www.workplacebullying.org/research.html (accessed 20 June 2009).

Wyatt, J., and Hare, C. (1997) *Work Abuse: How to Recognize It and Survive It.* Rochester, NY: Schenkman.

Zimbardo, P. (2008) *The Lucifer Effect: Understanding How Good People Turn Evil.* New York: Random House.

8   In Schools We Trust?

Leadership *in loco parentis* and the Failure to Protect Students from Bullying and Harassment

Dominique E. Johnson

When high school student Eric Mohat was repeatedly targeted with name-calling, teasing, constant pushing, shoving, and hitting in front of school officials, they did nothing. Insults and harassment by his peers, mostly in math class, who taunted him by calling him 'fag, queer, homo, and gay' were done all too often in front of teachers with no consequences for the students responsible for the bullying (Lenderman 2009). He was a quiet student, involved in theatre and music, he did not self-identify as gay. One day in class, a bully told him 'why don't you go home and shoot yourself, no one will miss you'—and he did.

Eric's parents have filed a lawsuit against the school that should have protected him from such harassment hoping for an outcome that mandates anti-bullying programmes at the school and an official acknowledgment that their son's death was a bullycide (Lenderman 2009). This past spring, Carl Walker-Hoover of Springfield, Massachusetts, took his own life (Valencia 2009) and Jaheem Herrera of DeKalb County, Georgia, took his own life 10 days later (Simon 2009). Like Eric, both boys were targeted by their peers with extreme bullying, including anti-gay taunts despite neither boy identifying as gay. Schools are active players in the formation of masculinities and femininities, and traditional, dichotomous gender roles are mostly reinforced in schooling. Though boys are also agents in the construction of their own masculinities, schools are distinct contexts for student gender role development, regulation to an ideological norm, and student resistance to these regulatory practices. Indeed, gender and bullying are inextricably coupled with distinct deployments of femininity and masculinity, and bullying is utilized as a means of regulating these rigid gender roles and norms.

These boys were subjected to taunts that are specifically employed to police their boundaries of perceived gender roles and lack of masculinity. But this taunting goes beyond equating weakness with femininity and homosexuality. Boys who repeatedly harass their peers by calling them 'fag, queer, homo, and gay' are policing boundaries of sex, gender, and sexual orientation and invoking the powerful conflation between the three to make these attacks particularly painful (Valdes 1995).

The violent policing of gender role boundaries is particular harmful as boys must make the masculine grade in schools or face isolating consequences and social stigma. But its conflation with biological sex is potentially even more dangerous when used as a taunt—boys are accusing other boys of not just being perceived as too effeminate but no longer boys. For a boy to call another boy a girl is to ostracize him from his male peers and instantly remove him from the social structure of the school. It is only when we better understand how deeply embedded these relational hierarchies are, driven by male privilege and static, conflated notions of gender, biological sex, and sexual orientation, that we can then move forward in implementing prevention and intervention efforts that take these issues as seriously as they actually are.

Some educational scholars maintain that research findings in the field remain contradictory and without consensus for best practices (McClintock 2007). What will improve schools, McClintock argues, 'is adequate resources for the job, human and financial, and lots of hard work, day by day, in an ethos of support and high expectation, in school and out' (2007: 1). But even enhanced resources might not lead to improvements in some areas of school-life. For example, Lugg (2006) posits that public school administrators have historically functioned as sexuality and gender police, often acting as agents of state-sponsored stigma for those who do not conform to traditional notions and roles. Wilkinson and Pearson (2009) found that while heteronormativity may marginalize a wide range of youth in schools, students whose schools had a greater presence of football and religion would have a more difficult time. This policing of borders results in a panopticon in public schooling that lends to not only distrust but also betrayal for those stigmatized or forced to cover (Yoshino 2006).

This leads to the question of whether American students and families can trust schools to ensure safety from bullying and harassment, particularly in light of this recent group of bullying-related suicides. The experiences of Carl Joseph Walker-Hoover, Eric Mohat, and Jaheem Herrida should be situated in context of *in loco parentis* and the responsibilities of school leadership to ensure student safety from bullying and harassment. Bullying is a way for youth to police traditional gender roles among peers, yet the tolerance of such peer abuse by school administration, either through a lack of prevention or intervention, is a form of systemic violence in schools.

Boys like Carl, Jaheem, and Eric experience the all too frequent negative social and physical experiences of bullying and other forms of victimization because they transgress traditional gender boundaries or are perceived to be less masculine than their school norm. Even though evidence suggests a strong relationship between gender role nonconformity and the increased likelihood of experiencing bullying (Johnson 2009), research and practice in educational administration have yet to address how schools might better support gender nonconforming students. Acting in the place of the parent, schools and their leadership betray the trust of those students and their families who experience bullying and harassment, particularly when it is based in peer gender role regulation.

IN SCHOOLS WE TRUST? THE FAILURE TO PROTECT STUDENTS *IN LOCO PARENTIS*

We are just beginning to understand how school staff and faculty consider their role in bullying and harassment prevention and intervention. One such study (Anagnostopoulos et al. 2009) examined how school staff members made sense of and respond to bullying and harassment violence. Findings indicate that school staff members felt compelled to intervene when male students sexually harassed quiet girls but they were ambivalent about their responsibility toward intervening in bullying that targeted perceived lesbian and gay students. This administrative ambivalence and inaction threatens the relationships of trust between parents, the community, and its school. This trust is most evident in the *in loco parentis* doctrine.

The doctrine of *in loco parentis* is primarily applied in the United States to its educational institutions. The legal responsibility of a person or organization that acts 'in the place of a parent', or *in loco parentis*, allows schools to determine and act in the best interests of the students as they see fit unless it violates students' civil liberties. *New Jersey v. T.L.O.* (1985) upheld that students are not afforded the same rights as adults and reiterated that school officials are still representatives of the state *in loco parentis*. The Supreme Court ruling in *Hazelwood School District v. Kuhlmeier* (1987) echoed this case, indicating that students do not have the same rights as adults in the school setting and they may be censored (for example, in school-sponsored publications such as the school newspaper or yearbook). Publicly funded schools cannot claim the same level of freedom to create and impose arbitrary rules on their students as private educational institutions. One area where this doctrine will likely be tested in the coming years is with regard to school dress codes.

Whether student freedom of expression is limited by application of the *in loco parentis* doctrine remains a significant issue. *Lander v. Seaver* (1986) did allow schools to punish student expression that was believed to be contrary to the interests and educational goals of the school. However, this was only for acts of legal malice or acts that caused permanent injury, neither of which was involved in the *Tinker v. Des Moines Independent Community School District* (1969) case where students were suspended from school for wearing black armbands in protest of the Vietnam War.

Since it is assumed that young people have no right to free speech against their parents under law, as well as being subject to discipline to enforce rules and maintain order, this thought is extended to public schools under the *in loco parentis* doctrine. As public education in the United States was historically intended to create assimilated citizens, free speech among students might have been in contrast to these aims. Depending on the interpretation of the *in loco parentis* doctrine, there seem to be very few limitations on the kinds of rules that schools can set for their students as well as the consequences for those who break them. One interpretation of the underlying logic of *in loco parentis* suggests that parents who disagree with the decisions made by their children's school have the option of private or home-schooling, or they can take up the issues they might have at their local school boards or through the political process via their elected representatives. Alternatively, they would have to move and leave the district. But do educational choice and local community empowerment in district operations in theory exist in practice?

This debate about interpretations of *in loco parentis* in the context of US public education and student freedom of speech and expression was most notably defined in *Morse v. Frederick*. This case (known widely as the 'Bong Hits 4 Jesus' school speech case) determined that the First Amendment does not inhibit educators' abilities to restrict student speech, particularly when it is promoting drug use (i.e. against school policy) and doing so at a school-sponsored venue. While this decision might seem to have a narrow reach in that it deals specifically with protecting students from an endorsement of drug use while at school, it might hold precedent for further decisions limiting student freedom of expression about other issues.

IN THE ABSENCE OF LEADERSHIP: THE CONSEQUENCES OF DISREGARDING GENDER

Most bullying is often used as a way to police gender among peers, or uses gender role transgression as an often effective vehicle for students to bully one another. Systemic violence in schools can encompass the tolerance of student abuse such as bullying and discriminatory policies and practices. Ross Epp defines it as the 'consequences of procedures implemented by well-meaning authorities in the belief that the practices are in the best interests of students' (1996: 1). When a student is seen as non-compliant the blame is attributed to the individual student and/or that student's parent(s) rather than the school. Watts and Erevelles (2004) expand this line of research by investigating the structural violence of such oppressive educational conditions and how they contribute to the social construction of the deviant student. They argue that violence is normalized in schools and individualized such that individual students are assigned blame and responsibility.

Crothers and Levinson (2004) discuss how childhood bullying has become recognized as a significant, pervasive form of school violence because of its deleterious effect on both victims' and bullies' current and future roles. Sandra Bem (1977, 1993, cited in Arnett 2004) argues that those concepts of masculinity, femininity, and androgyny place emphasis upon personal characteristics rather than the socio-cultural force of gender socialization. Watts and Erevelles (2004) contend that violence in the school is a product of the systemic violence of schools and their oppressive environment, shaping both identity and social practices.

The social psychology literature tells us that gender stereotypes are automatic (Zemore, Fiske, and Kim 2000). Some argue that schools reinforce these stereotypes and encourage violence among students, including learning to hate the 'other' (Harber 2004). For example, Nayak and Kehily (1997) discuss the gendered aspects of these performances of prejudice used to regulate particularly boys' traditional gender role conformity. Many scholars suggest that schooling and its activities make masculinities among boys and young men (Frank 1996). All students are affected by rigid gender roles, often limiting their choices in academic classes and extra-curricular sports and activities (Grayson 1987). The majority of the millions of students bullied every year are targeted for their perceived nonconforming gender (National Mental Health Association [NMHA] 2002).

Goffman's (1977) work on gender inequality and the socio-cultural factors that create such structures of interaction hold implications for the creation of gender boundaries and their maintenance. Goffman's (1979) concept of 'genderism' is present in student interactions, where stereotypes of masculinity and femininity create and maintain borders between these two gender identities. Interactions that reify these boundaries constitute a pattern of borderwork (Thorne 1993) that, if violated, might hold serious consequences for the transgressor (Sroufe et al. 1993). One instance of borderwork would be the carrying out of bullying and/or violence in order to enact masculinity. Bullying is a public performance intended to reiterate the in-group status of the bully, perhaps driven out of a fear of lost or low masculinity, by relegating the bullied to an out-group of femininity and weakness.

The work of Connell (1996) has been particularly instrumental in articulating how schools are active players in the formation of masculinity. And while traditional, dichotomous gender roles are mostly reinforced in schooling, students are also agents in the construction of their own masculinities. For example, Maccoby (1987) maintains that while feminine boys participate in sex role atypical activities, masculine boys enjoy rough-and-tumble play at recess with other boys. Connell (1996) argues that curricular divisions, discipline practices, and sports are the areas of concentration around masculine development in schools. Arnot (2002) asserts that students, like all people, actively reproduce such categories of gender.

Frank et al. (2003) discuss hegemonic compulsory masculinity and its relation to compulsory heterosexuality. Boys must 'make the masculine grade' and can do so by knowing about hegemonic masculinity and then performing it in a public space, in this case the school. This normalized masculinity is often defined by hypermasculine identification, athletics, fighting, distance from homosexuality, dominant relationships with women, and disdain for academics (Klein 2006). Indeed, heterosexuality informs masculinity and its social practice (Frank et al. 2003: 125; Connell 1996). And gender hierarchies are constructed by and maintained by student cultures in school. Certainly, gender is constructed within various cultural and institutional contexts where multiple though not altogether mutually exclusive masculinities are formed (Connell 1996).

Adults often insist that young people maintain what Goffman (1963) might describe as an *unspoiled* identity, particularly as it relates to gender identity and its expression. Youth agency, however, can be better understood through the work of Davis (2001a, 2001b), Messner (2000), and Thorne (1993), all of whom offer engaging critiques of and insights into: the ways in which children are agents in the creation of their own social worlds (Thorne 1993) and experience gendered moments in everyday life (Messner 2000) and how boys have agency in gender construction and the construction of their own masculinities (Davis 2001a, 2001b). Pascoe (2003) argues that we should see masculinities, and the individual agency involved in their creation, as more fluid, resisting static and rigid typologies. Despite this emerging research about the lived experiences of the dynamics of gender, especially among boys, Pascoe's work (2007) reminds us of the all too frequent negative social and physical experiences of bullying and other forms of victimization for boys who transgress gender boundaries in school.

GENDER AS SPEECH? THE *TINKER* DOCTRINE REVISITED

The *Tinker* doctrine focuses on the question of disruption in the school environment, especially whether freedom of speech and expression among students is a disruption to the education of their peers. And, while limits on free speech exist and the First Amendment is not absolute in practice, cases such as *Tinker* and those that followed on its precedents illustrate how age (i.e. youth) can be a salient factor in the decision to limit such freedoms. Classrooms free from disruption, notions of community standards, and the achievement of educational objectives drive the field in navigating the boundaries of student expression in schools.

The armbands the students wore in Des Moines, Iowa, in protest of the Vietnam War were considered 'symbolic' school speech and the dissent argued that they were not constitutionally protected. If this thought is extended to gender, particularly if it concerns students' dress (especially sex atypical dress), gender might also be equated with symbolic school speech.

This relationship might also apply to perceived gender nonconformity in various forms. Tepidly negative anti-gay speech is allowed in school; when school officials enforce district policies against derogatory comments they have been found to be reaching too far. Therefore, taking cues from such cases as *Nuxoll v. Indian Prarie School District* and *Bethel School District v. Fraser*, tepidly negative speech is within the moral values and the boundaries of socially acceptable behaviour in school by students. This interpretation allows us to consider that the lack of clear policies and/or their enforcement against students who bully and harass fellow students about perceived gender nonconformity equals a sanctioning of these peer-enforced norms.

Is the *in loco parentis* doctrine appropriate for framing student experiences in public schools? There is an implicit contract between parents and school leadership invoked by *in loco parentis*. Public schools are essential to the United States and they are by design agents of the states. Even if public schools are acting as agents of the state and not directly as parents, school leadership and parents hold an implicit contract to keep young people free from harm. Authority over the experiences of students in schools is a large responsibility of school leadership. If school administration is not responsible for and in authority of the members of the school community, namely its students, then disorder and disruption would follow. This authority, aided in practice via the *in loco parentis* doctrine, is not mutually exclusive with their identities as and roles of agents of state. It is a matter of trust, embodied as the *in loco parentis* doctrine, and not a fallacy that bind parents and school leadership in an implicit contract that students will be free from harm while attending school. Views of *in loco parentis* should therefore be expanded to include public agents of government entities such as public school principals if communities of trust are to prevail.

It is essential to remember that issues of gender prejudice are substantial components of the very basis of homophobia and sexual prejudice. This is tragically apparent when we consider the experiences of Lawrence King, a junior high school student who was murdered by a fellow classmate while attending school in the Los Angeles metropolitan area in Southern California. Classmates reported to the press that he sometimes wore feminine clothing, make-up, jewelry, boots with high heels, and painted nails. A 13-year-old classmate in the eighth grade was quoted as saying that this (his queer gender expression) 'was freaking the guys out' [at school] (Saillant and Griggs 2008). Apparently, Lawrence and a group of boys fought during lunch period the day before he was shot, and presumably one of these boys was his assailant, a boy with whom he had a falling out because Lawrence had come out as gay (his queer sexuality).

If student expression and speech are limited only when they threaten another's physical safety, schools and their leadership are missing much of the disparaging speech used in bullying by students every day in schools everywhere. The most horrific and tragic reminder of this are the motives behind Lawrence King's murder by a fellow student. Student speech and expression should not be pre-emptively limited, however, out of fear that it could bring harm onto the student from bullying by his/her peers as with, for example, the rigid deployment or enforcement of dress codes. After Lawrence was murdered his school responded by, among other things, introducing a more rigid enforcement of school dress codes, intimating that Lawrence would somehow be alive if it weren't for his dress. Yet even the restricted form of free speech in schools unfortunately does not deter all students who would bully and harass students using harmful speech.

With *R.A.V. v. City of St. Paul,* the Supreme Court established that hate speech or expressions of hate could be within First Amendment rights. R.A.V., the initials of the teenager responsible for the hate crime, burned a cross on the lawn of an African American family in the neighbourhood where s/he was staying. The representation for R.A.V. argued that the bias-motivated crime ordinance was too broad and overreaching, and that, coupled with its delineation of what constitutes bias crime, resulted in a violation of First Amendment rights.

The Court, in reviewing the case and its precedents, engaged in debate about the principles of free speech. In the case of unpopular speech, the First Amendment prevents the government from prohibiting speech and 'expressive conduct'. This invocation of free speech necessitates a further discussion of the nature of harm and offense. While it can be argued that most hate speech falls under a definition of offense, it is difficult to prove the psychological and emotional harm brought about by hate speech and expressions of hate. Social science has yet to equivocally determine whether psychological harm is physical harm, a distinction that is important for the Court. The harm principle in free speech has been a guiding doctrine throughout the history of the First Amendment.

With *R A.V. v. City of St. Paul* as a touchstone for free speech, it is necessary to consider how this doctrine is applied to the public school in particular. For example, is bullying protected in schools under freedom of speech and expression, even though it could be and usually is hateful speech in nature? Public schools might be the major social and institutional player in this continued debate where order and freedom, expression and offense, are mostly seen as mutually exclusive. Of great interest in this complex relationship is the potential for schools to be sites of intersection and agreement between freedom from harm and order.

What constitutes harm and what offends is largely subjective and has remained so throughout American history. Social change has, however, been reflected in the legal narrative of the Supreme Court. Where public schools are concerned, it is important to remember that students have limited rights (as in *Hazelwood School District v. Kuhlmeier*). Schools, therefore, might be better suited by the offense principle as opposed to the harm principle with regards to student speech and expression. This might especially be the case since students must attend school and the school leadership, as argued here, is acting *in loco parentis*. While there is no documented case of a student claiming freedom of expression as justification for bullying another student, important questions remain.

These questions are crucial to the ongoing debates about freedom of speech and First Amendment rights in American society at large, and public schools might be the fitting location to consider how we might begin to reconcile individual and collective rights with the offense principle. It is also important to consider once again how most bullying is a function of peer norm regulation and as such might not be classified so clearly into a category of hate speech. Yet the *in loco parentis* doctrine suggests that hate speech would be intolerable for the establishment and maintenance of order in the public school and the protection and safety of the individual student. The harm principle, in the context of *in loco parentis* within the public school, is ultimately too broad.

MOVING TOWARD TRUST IN EDUCATIONAL LEADERSHIP

While some schools are known to be potentially dangerous places, particularly in both the extreme case of the violence at Columbine and also on a more frequent basis in unsafe schools in high poverty neighbourhoods in urban America, bullying is anecdotally considered as a somewhat acceptable part of daily life for youth as they make their way socially into young adulthood. Viewing schools as places of either incarceration or education, as is so often the case, lends itself to the estrangement of public education from the jurisdiction of the US Constitution and toward a false binary of what the purpose of education is and should be in the public school.

Trust in schools and their leaders might be compromised because of the illusive opportunities of school choice in the modern American public educational system and the importance placed upon them by current policy imperatives accompanying 'No Child Left Behind'. But this dwindling trust in the American public education system by some parents should not be construed for betrayal—at least not yet. It is important that schools (re)gain trust in the communities they serve before they lose legitimacy as partners in the educational process. Possibilities for school leadership to move from (potential) failure to protecting students from bullying and harassment must begin with the promise of regaining the trust of students and families.

Current federal law provides important federal support to promote school safety but does not comprehensively and expressly focus on issues of bullying or harassment. In a step toward this end, Califorina Representative Linda Sánchez recently introduced a federal anti-bullying bill, the Safe Schools Improvement Act, in the House of Representatives this past year to amend the Safe and Drug-Free Schools and Communities Act (Sánchez et al. 2009). The bill, now referred to committee, requires schools that receive Safe and Drug-Free Schools and Communities Act funding to

150   *Dominique E. Johnson*

implement a comprehensive anti-bullying policy that enumerates categories often targeted by bullies, including race, religion, sexual orientation, gender identity/expression, and others. Bullying and harassment would be delineated as prohibited in school discipline policies that would be mandated to include bullying and harassment. Mechanisms allowing parents and students to file official complaints with schools when infractions occur will also be required. Perhaps, most importantly, bullying and harassment would be included in the definition of violence used in the federal law.

Some additional possibilities for school leadership to move toward trust and away from betrayal include the conscious examination of school dress codes that require different attire for boys and girls. These might further institutionalize binary markers of expression among students that could exacerbate in-group/out-group dynamics. Restorative justice, when institutionalized from the administration on down through the school community, might also provide an opportunity for reconciliation and intervention when bullying and harassment occur. The conflation of sex, gender, and sexuality and the relationships of all three to both gender roles and gender nonconformity call for entire communities of practice to consider gender as queer. Considering gender and its relationships with gender role nonconformity will ultimately pose necessary challenges to school administration.

REFERENCES

Anagnostopoulos, D., et al. (2009) 'School staff responses to gender-based bullying as moral interpretation: An exploratory study'. *Educational Policy* 23 (4): 519–53.
Arnett, J.J. (2004) *Adolescence and Emerging Adulthood: A Cultural Approach.* 2nd ed. Upper Saddle River, NJ: Pearson Education.
Arnot, M. (2002) *Reproducing Gender? Essays on Educational Theory and Feminist Politics.* London: RoutledgeFalmer.
Bem, S.L. (1977) 'On the utility of alternative procedures for assessing psychological androgyny'. *Journal of Consulting and Clinical Psychology* 54:196–205.
———. (1993) *The Lenses of Gender: Transforming the Debate on Sexual Inequality.* New Haven, CT: Yale University Press.
Connell, R.W. (1996) 'Teaching the boys: New research on masculinity, and gender strategies for schools'. *Teachers College Record* 98 (2): 206–35.
Crothers, L.M., and Levinson, E.M. (2004) 'Assessment of bullying: A review of methods and instruments'. *Journal of Counseling & Development* 82 (4): 496–503.
Davis, J. (2001a) 'Black boys at school: Negotiating masculinities and race'. In *Educating our Black Children: New Directions and Radical Approaches*, ed. R. Majors. London: Taylor & Francis.
———. (2001b) 'Transgressing the masculine: African American boys and the failure of schools'. In *What about the Boys? Issues of Masculinity in School*, ed. B. Mayeen and W. Martino. Buckingham: Open University Press.
Frank, B. (1996) 'Masculinities and schooling: The making of men'. In *Systemic Violence: How Schools Hurt Children*, ed. J. Ross Epp and A.M. Watkinson. London: The Falmer Press.

Frank, B., et al. (2003) 'A tangle of trouble: Boys, masculinity and schooling—future directions'. *Educational Review* 55 (2): 119–33.

Goffman, E. (1963) *Stigma: Notes on the Management of Spoiled Identity.* New York: Simon & Schuster.

———. (1977) 'The arrangement between the sexes'. *Theory and Society* 4 (3): 301–31.

———. (1979) *Gender Advertisements.* Cambridge, MA: Harvard University Press.

Grayson, D.A. (1987) 'Emerging equity issues related to homosexuality in education'. *Peabody Journal of Education* 64 (4): 132–45.

Harber, C. (2004) *Schooling as Violence: How Schools Harm Pupils and Societies.* London: RoutledgeFalmer.

Johnson, D. (2009) 'The dynamics of gender in single sex schooling: Implications for educational policy'. Unpublished doctoral dissertation, Temple University.

Klein, J. (2006) 'Cultural capital and high school bullies: How social inequality impacts school violence'. *Men and Masculinities* 9 (1): 53–75.

Lenderman, M. (2009) 'Teen commits suicide due to bullying: Parents sue school for son's death'. ABC News. Online. Available HTTP: http://abcnews.go.com/Health/MindMoodNews/Story?id=7228335&page=3 (accessed 29 September 2009).

Lugg, C.A. (2006) 'Thinking about sodomy: Public schools, legal panopticons, and queers'. *Educational Policy* 20 (1): 35–58.

Maccoby, E.E. (1987) 'The varied meanings of "masculine" and "feminine"'. In *Masculinity/Femininity: Basic Perspectives*, ed. J.M. Reinisch, L.A. Rosenblum, and S.A. Sanders. New York: Oxford University Press.

McClintock, M. (2007) 'Educational research'. *Teachers College Record.* Online. Available HTTP: <http://www.tcrecord.org/content.asp?contentid=13956> (accessed 22 December 2009).Messner, M.A. (2000) 'Barbie girls versus sea monsters: Children constructing gender'. *Gender & Society* 14 (6): 765–84.

National Mental Health Association. (2002) *National Survey of Teens on Anti-Gay Teasing and Bullying.* Alexandria, VA: National Mental Health Association.

Nayak, A., and Kehily, M.J. (1997) 'Masculinities and schooling: Why are young men so homophobic?' In *Border Patrols: Policing the Boundaries of Heterosexuality*, ed. D.L. Steinberg, D. Epstein, and R. Johnson. London: Cassell.

Pascoe, C.J. (2003) 'Multiple masculinities? Teenage boys talk about jocks and gender'. *American Behavioral Scientist* 46 (10): 1423–38.

———. (2007) *Dude You're a Fag: Masculinity and Sexuality in High School.* Berkeley: University of California Press.

Ross Epp, J. (1996) 'Schools, complicity, and sources of violence'. In *Systemic Violence: How Schools Hurt Children*, ed. J. Ross Epp and A.M. Watkinson. London: The Falmer Press.

Saillant, C., and Griggs, G.W. (2008) 'Oxnard student declared brain dead'. *Los Angeles Times.* Online. Available HTTP: http://www.latimes.com/news/local/la-me-oxnard14feb14,0,7204301.story (accessed 15 February 2008).

Sánchez, L.T., et al. (2009) 'H.R. 2262: Safe schools improvement act of 2009'. Washington, DC: U.S. Library of Congress. Online. Available HTTP: http://thomas.loc.gov/cgi-bin/query/z?c111:H.R.2262: (accessed 29 July 2009).

Simon, M. (2009) 'My bullied son's last day on Earth'. CNN. Online. Available HTTP: http://www.cnn.com/2009/US/04/23/bullying.suicide/ (accessed 29 September 2009).

Sroufe, L.A., et al. (1993) 'The significance of gender boundaries in preadolescence: Contemporary correlates and antecedents of boundary violation and maintenance'. *Child Development* 64 (2): 455–66.

Thorne, B. (1993) *Gender Play: Girls and Boys in School.* New Brunswick, NJ: Rutgers University Press.

Valdes, F. (1995) 'Queers, sissies, dykes, and tomboys: Deconstructing the conflation of "sex," "gender," and "sexual orientation" in Euro-American law and society'. *California Law Review* 83 (1): 3–377.

Valencia, M.J. (2009) 'Constantly bullied, he ends his life at age 11'. Boston Globe. Online. Available HTTP: http://www.boston.com/news/local/massachusetts/articles/2009/04/20/constantly_bullied_he_ends_his_life_at_age_11/ (accessed 29 September 2009).

Watts, I.E., and Erevelles, N. (2004) 'These deadly times: Reconceptualizing school violence by using critical race theory and disability studies'. *American Educational Research Journal* 41 (2): 271–301.

Wilkinson, L., and Pearson, J. (2009) 'School culture and the well-being of same-sex-attracted youth'. *Gender & Society* 23 (4): 542–68.

Yoshino, K. (2006) *Covering: The Hidden Assault on Our Civil Rights*. New York: Random House.

Zemore, S.E., Fiske, S.T., and Kim, H.-J. (2000) 'Gender stereotypes and the dynamics of social interaction'. In *The Developmental Social Psychology of Gender*, ed. T. Eckes and H.M. Trautner. Mahwah, NJ: Lawrence Erlbaum Associates.

9 Administration, Education, and the Question of Trust

Richard Bates

A complete absence of trust would prevent [us] from getting up in the morning.

(Luhmann 1979: 4)

Trust is ubiquitous. Our world is saturated with trust. Our everyday existence exhibits our trust almost every minute. We trust that the alarm clock will go off at the appropriate time; that the light will work; that the shower will be warm; that our breakfast will be safe to eat; that public transport will get our children safely to school; that other drivers will act predictably as we drive to work; that our colleagues will treat us with respect; that the organization we work for will be stable and secure; that the professionals who look after our health and well-being will be skilled and committed; and so on and on. Not that our trust is unconditional or always warranted, but overwhelmingly for most of us most of the time our trust is indeed warranted, which is why we are upset, hurt, angry, and disillusioned when that trust turns out to be misplaced.

Trust, of course, takes many different forms. In the most general sense, we trust the society to which we belong to provide security, prosperity, well-being, and opportunity. Societies that do not or cannot be trusted to provide such assurances are regarded as failed states. At another level, we trust the agencies of government to use their resources efficiently and to our advantage, and to be fair and equitable in their dealings with us. At a third level, we expect private businesses to deliver the goods and services that they say they will deliver in an honest and dependable way. Again, we trust institutions such as hospitals and schools to operate in our best interests. And, of course, we expect to be able to trust the professionals who staff such institutions to have the required skills, motivations, and commitments that will support us. Finally, at the interpersonal level, we expect that our trust in those with whom we deal on a personal level be warranted, respected, and reciprocated. More than this, we also expect there to be mechanisms through which breaches of trust can be redressed, be they the result of political malpractice, organizational incompetence, fraud, misrepresentation, deceit, or, indeed, physical or emotional violence.

There has been, however, over recent years, considerable concern over whether all this trust is indeed warranted. Onora O'Neill, in her 2002 BBC Reith Lectures, asked: 'Is it true that we have stopped trusting? Has untrustworthy action made trust too risky? Is trust obsolete? (2002: vii). Her answer is that the evidence is pretty mixed. While we continue routinely to trust most of the individuals and organizations we come into contact with, there does seem to be poll-based evidence of increasing levels of mistrust in government, business, office-holders, and professionals. Moreover, mass media constantly report cases of misplaced trust where trust is breached by *some* doctors, *some* scientists, *some* companies, *some* politicians, *some* teachers, *some* colleagues. The response, O'Neill suggests, has been to try to eliminate untrustworthy acts by increasing levels of accountability, especially in government, public institutions, and the professions. Such accountability is directed towards the elimination of untrustworthy behaviour through detailed specification of required behaviour coupled with heightened levels of reward and sanction. This is particularly true of the public sector: 'For those of us in the public sector the new accountability takes the form of detailed control. An unending stream of new legislation and regulation, memoranda and instructions, guidance and advice floods public sector institutions' (O'Neill 2002: 46). Moreover:

> The new legislation, regulation and controls are more than fine rhetoric. They require detailed conformity to procedures and protocols, detailed record-keeping and provision of information in specific formats *and* success in reaching targets. Detailed instructions regulate and prescribe the work and performance of health trusts and schools, of universities and research councils, of the police force and of social workers. And beyond the public sector, increasingly detailed and regulatory requirements also bear on companies and the voluntary sector, on self-employed professionals and tradesmen. All institutions face new standards of recommended accounting practice, more detailed health and safety requirements, increasingly complex employment and pensions legislation, more exacting provisions for ensuring non-discrimination and, of course, proliferating complaint procedures. (2002: 46–47)

Along with these specifications comes an explosion of audit procedures where the idea of *audit* has spilled over from its original context of finance into detailed scrutiny of non-financial processes and systems. Indeed, we seem to now be living in what Michael Power (1997) calls 'The Audit Society'. The role of government in particular seems to have changed in its emphasis on increased steering capacity. The idea of an independent public service devoted to the long-term public interest has been replaced by a politicized public service directed towards the delivery of short-term objectives that follow from the 'mandates' of governments despite low turnouts and the relative brevity of electoral cycles. Such demands for increased steering capacity are made clear by the development of strict line management coupled with heavy sanctions such as that instituted by Michael Barber through his imposition of 'deliverology' in education as elsewhere during the Blair government in the UK (Barber 2007: 70ff.).

The result is that in order to control the untrustworthy behaviour of *some* departments, institutions, professionals, businesses, and administrators, and to ensure compliance with government policy, systems are set up that implicitly regard *all* such departments, institutions, professionals, businesses, and administrators as potentially untrustworthy and likely to subvert or ignore government policy through the exercise of independent professional judgment. But such rules, no matter how elaborate, cannot account for all possible occurrences and may result in frequent constraints on the exercise of appropriate professional judgment in particular situations. Again, rules devised by differing agencies with mandates directed towards differing objectives may require inconsistent behaviours or collectively result in overload and what Art Wise (1979) called 'hyper-rationalisation', where individual requirements may be rational but collectively produce huge cognitive dissonance and exhaustion among practitioners and clients alike.

Such demands for 'performativity' (Ball 1990; Marshall 1999) also serve to reorient professional practice away from responding to the needs of clients towards satisfying administrative demands and targets and the reduction of 'risk'. This reorientation is experienced by professionals and clients alike as both 'distorting the proper aims of professional practice' and as 'damaging professional pride and integrity' (O'Neill 2002: 50). Moreover, the imposition of strict targets and indicators coupled with the sticks and carrots of incentive systems may have quite perverse effects:

> Even those who devise the indicators know that they are *at very best* surrogates for the real objectives. Nobody after all seriously thinks that numbers of exam passes are the only evidence of good teaching, or crime clear-up rates are the only evidence of good policing. Some exams are easier, others are harder; some crimes easy to clean up, others are harder. However, the performance indicators have a deep effect on professional and institutional behaviour. If a certain A-level [examination] board offers easier examinations in a subject, schools have reason to choose that syllabus even if it is educationally inferior. If waiting lists can be reduced faster by concentrating on certain medical procedures, hospitals have reason to do so, even if medical priorities differ. *Perverse incentives are real incentives.* (O'Neill 2002: 55)

Such systems, directed as they are towards guarantees of trustworthiness and performance, can become sources of *decreased* trust as professionals redirect their attention to 'incentives to which they have been required to respond rather than pursuing the intrinsic requirements for being good nurses and teachers, good doctors and police officers, good lecturers and social workers' (O'Neill 2002: 56). Much of current mistrust of institutions, systems, organizations, and professionals arises from just such requirements and the concomitant displacement of attention away from individual needs and professional judgment. Indeed, attempts to ensure the administration of trust seem, frequently and perversely, to result in the *diminution* of trust.

EDUCATION AND THE ADMINISTRATION OF TRUST

The humanist tradition in education saw education as the pursuit of ideals such as personal autonomy and emancipation. From Rousseau, Pestalozzi, Montessori, Hume, Mill, Smith, Arnold, Marx, and Dewey onwards, the avowed purpose of education was to be *liberation*: personal, social, economic. While governments justified the expansion of public systems in terms of education's civilizing mission, the moral education of the poor, or the provision of basic functional literacy, the great educational reformers of the eighteenth, nineteenth, and early twentieth centuries proclaimed the purpose of education as the meeting of individual needs. The orientation of schools was, therefore (and despite Mr. Gradgrind), towards concern with the needs of individual pupils and to the extent that they fulfilled this objective, they could be trusted.

Pedagogy developed in ways that served this objective. It mediated the world of knowledge, of science, of art, and of the social virtues in ways that provided access to, or at least a toehold in, the wider world. It provided a more or less trustworthy account of that world and prepared pupils through appropriate knowledge and behaviour to join 'the conversation of mankind' (Oakeshott 1962). This broad pedagogy was administered through the codification of knowledge (curriculum), the rules of engagement (classroom processes), and the assessment of performance (classification). To the extent that such pedagogy was appropriately managed in ways that pupils, parents, and the wider pubic respected, it is possible to regard it as a mechanism for the administration of trust. Such trust inhered in the links between such pedagogy and the everyday experience, social relations, and personal realization that formed what Habermas (1984) called the 'life-world' of individuals.

However, as Lyotard (1984) and Habermas (1975) point out, such an orientation becomes subverted in the modern world by mechanisms that subordinate such ideals to the demands of social efficiency and the 'system'. These demands, demands for 'performativity', require schools to implement an alternative pedagogy directed, not towards individual development and emancipation, or what Nussbaum (2003) and Sen (1999) call 'capabilities', but towards the development of specific skills. These are of two kinds: (a) those that contribute to the ability of a country to compete in competitive world markets; and (b) those that contribute to internal social cohesion and political legitimation.

> Thus, education is not to pursue or to produce ideals, or to provide an elite capable of guiding a society or nation towards emancipation but, instead, to 'supply the system with players capable of acceptably fulfilling their roles at the pragmatic posts required by its institutions' (Lyotard 1984: 5–7). (Marshall 1999: 310)

The issue of trust also becomes transformed from its administration through curricular, classroom, and classification processes directed towards the life-world and individual and collective emancipation into its replacement by an administration of official requirements directed towards market position and political control. Such transformation produces what Habermas (following Luhmann 1979) calls a 'legitimation crisis'. This crisis is essentially one of trust.

In education this currently takes the form of conflict between what Bernstein (2000) calls the *pedagogical* recontextualizing field (PRF) and the *official* recontextualizing field (ORF). The PRF takes knowledge from activities such as physics and, through the *selection* of specialized knowledge, the specification of its *relation* to other forms of knowledge, and the *sequence* and *pace* of its presentation, recontextualizes such knowledge pedagogically. Carpentry becomes woodwork, for instance. For the first half of the twentieth century the PRF was heavily influenced by the humanistic ideals of the Progressive Education movement. Teachers and schools were allowed considerable autonomy in their practices while government was mainly concerned with expanding the provision of education in response to political demands for access to secondary and then tertiary education. From the middle of the century, however, as government expenditures rose, governments of all persuasions took an increasing interest in what James Callaghan in his Ruskin College speech called 'the secret garden of the curriculum' (Lawton 1980). In this speech, Callaghan declared that schools were being run by 'unaccountable teachers, teaching an irrelevant curriculum to young workers who were poorly motivated, illiterate and innumerate' and that 'there is no virtue in producing socially well-adjusted members of society who are unemployed because they do not have the skills' (Carr and Hartnett 1996: 107).

The thesis here is essentially that professionals, specifically teachers, cannot be trusted. The resulting 'discourse of derision' (Wallace 1993) became widespread in political circles during the last three decades of the twentieth century, particularly in Anglo-Saxon countries such as the US (under Reagan and Bush), the United Kingdom (under Thatcher), and Australia (under Howard). But such a discourse not only attacked the trustworthiness of teachers, it also paved the way for the imposition of strict specification and accountability mechanisms designed to reduce the relative autonomy of teachers and replace it with an official pedagogy that demanded compliance with a centrally determined curriculum, high-stakes testing, devolved responsibility for performance, and a quasi-competitive market in educational provision where increased 'private' competition was supported with public funds (Ball 2007; Berliner and Biddle 1995; Bonnor and Caro 2007; Glass 2008).

The educational market created through privatization and competition, coupled with the accountability movement and high-stakes testing, both reduced trust in the capacity of many schools to deliver either a broad education or positional advantage and also 'had a devastating effect on public education . . . destroying the richness of a curriculum that has taken decades to develop . . . obliterating the professional autonomy of teachers and . . . dimming the personal hopes and dreams of hundreds of thousands of children' (Glass 2008: 18).

The new official discourse restructured the functions of school management (Ball 1990; Berliner and Biddle 1995; Grace 1995), turning it away from internal concerns with pedagogy, instructional leadership, and professional development towards external concerns with league tables, reputation, competition, and prestige, that is, with comparative performance on mandated tests. As Bernstein observes:

> The management structure's major focus is upon the school's performance, with regard to attracting and retaining students, their conduct and their attainments . . . The management structure has become the device for creating an entrepreneurial competitive culture. The latter is responsible for criteria informing senior appointments and the engaging or hiring of specialised staff to promote the effectiveness of its culture. Thus there is a dislocation between the culture of the pedagogic discourse and management culture. (2000: 61)

The result is:

> a culture and a context to facilitate the survival of the fittest as judged by market demands. The focus is on the short term rather than the long term, upon the exploration of vocational applications rather than upon exploration of knowledge. The transmission here views knowledge as money. And like money it should flow easily to where demand calls. There must be no impediments to flow. Personal commitment and particular dedication of staff and students are regarded as resistances, as oppositions to the free circulation of knowledge. And so personal commitments, inner dedications, not only are not encouraged, but are also regarded as equivalent to monopolies in the market, and like such monopolies, should be dissolved. The . . . position constructs an outwardly responsive identity rather than one driven by inner dedication. Contract replaces covenant. (2000: 69)

This transformation of curriculum, pedagogy, and assessment, and the concomitant imposition of a managerialism that establishes centralized control over objectives while devolving responsibility for success or failure, has led to a narrowing of both objectives and opportunity and an exclusion of concerns with promoting social justice. As Bernstein suggests, the new official pedagogy is based:

> on a new concept of 'work' and 'life' which might be called 'short-termism'. This is where a skill, task or area of work, undergoes continuous development, disappearance or replacement; where life experience cannot be based on stable expectations of the future and one's location in it. Under these circumstances it is considered that a vital new ability must be developed: 'trainability', the ability to profit from continuous pedagogic re-formations and so cope with the new requirements of 'work' and 'life'. (2000: 58)

Trainability is, however, central to a conception of individuals as workers whose skills are more vital than their identities. Indeed, identity is transitory as successive skill sets are mastered and discarded, leaving no permanent core. As Bernstein suggests, 'There seems to be an emptiness in the concept of trainability, an emptiness which makes the concept self-referential and thus excluding' (2000: 59).

The transitory and 'empty' nature of identity in such circumstances is argued by some to be the result of conditions of modernity. Touraine summarizes this view:

> We are now faced with the task of understanding a society in which change seems to be the primary factor, and in which there seem to be no limits to change. Accelerated technological change, together with the globalization of production, consumption and communications has finally convinced us that nothing is settled anymore. Social life is no longer constructed around any central principle. Social utility, rationalization and even the class struggle are things of the past. If change is everything, how can there be norms, laws or a social definition of good and evil? (2000: 141)

Touraine's answer to this problem is to emphasize the importance of agency within the context of a universal principle of equal respect as a foundation for social justice.

Sen (1999) takes a similar position in response to this situation in his insistence on the intimate connection between individual agency (freedom) and social commitment:

> individual agency is, ultimately, central to addressing . . . deprivations. On the other hand, the freedom of agency that we individually have

is inescapably qualified and constrained by the social, political and economic opportunities that are available to us. There is a deep complementarity between individual agency and social arrangements. It is important to give simultaneous recognition to the centrality of individual freedom *and* to the force of social influences on the extent and reach of individual freedom. To counter the problems that we face, we have to see individual freedom as a social commitment. (xi–xii)

Social justice is, then, in Sen's view, a matter of arranging our social commitments in ways that enhance individual freedom to live a valued life:

in analysing social justice, there is a strong case for judging individual advantage in terms of the capabilities that a person has, that is, the substantive freedoms he or she enjoys to lead the kind of life that he or she has reason to value. (1999: 87)

Capabilities, and the enhancement of individual capabilities through social arrangements, are at the heart of the issue of social justice. Sen offers five 'types of freedom' or capabilities as being fundamental. These include: political freedoms, economic facilities, social opportunities, transparency guarantees, and protective security (1999: 10). It follows that an education directed towards the development of individual agency supported by such capabilities would not be constrained by an official pedagogy solely directed towards the production of transitory skills suitable for particular market conditions. It might also be an education that could be trusted.

LEADERSHIP, CAPABILITIES, AGENCY, AND TRUST

Since the 1980s there has been a growing attempt in the literature to reconnect educational ideals with educational leadership and to recover from the almost complete separation of educational and administrative theory (Bates 1980). Moreover, some of the literature has taken up the challenge to see educational leadership as the management of knowledge and to explore the nature of the power relations that structure the selection of knowledge (curriculum), the means of transmission (pedagogy), and the evaluative systems (examinations) present in schools (Bates 1980). The issue of power, the power to control the message systems of schools and the opportunities that they resent or deny, is central to the exercise of leadership and the issue of trust.

For instance, where management is exercised through manipulation or coercion it is unlikely that teachers will trust the principal or the wider management of the school or school system. Such manipulation may, of course, be visible and systematic in terms of the award of incentives or punishments, praise or blame. Or it may be invisible or exploitative as in the current emphasis on the role of the principal in 'establishing' a school culture that conforms to his or her 'vision' (Hargreaves 1994; Bates 2006, forthcoming). Trust is unlikely in such circumstances.

For trust to be established, it is suggested that two fundamental conditions must be met: 'people must find one another highly predictable and share substantially the same aims' (Nias et al. 1989: 78). This is more likely where schools serve relatively homogeneous communities where there is a consonance of culture, values, and objectives between management, teachers, pupils, and parents. In such circumstances 'schools of virtue' may emerge where there is a 'shared covenant' (Sergiovanni 1992). Such schools are interesting in that while they may well consolidate trust among their members, such trust may well be gained at the price of *distrust* of those who are not members of their virtuous community. As Peshkin remarked in his study of a religious school that clearly met Sergiovanni's definition of a school of virtue with a shared covenant:

> The academy . . . serves an internally integrative or community-main-tenance function. That is, it simultaneously links believers together and separates them from non-believers. In its defensive capacity, the academy shields its students from competitors by promoting dichotomies not only of we and they, but also of right and wrong. *We* follow God's truth in God's preferred institution: *they* are the unfortunates of Satan's dark, unrighteous world. (1986: 282)

Moreover, in the case of many religious schools there is a problematic conflation of trust in exclusive beliefs with an authoritarian insistence on the rightness of those particular beliefs. Such authoritarian approaches are clearly incompatible with a conception of education as emancipation and, in a narrower sense, incompatible with the notion of religious freedom. Ironically, the claim of such schools to pursue their authoritarian and exclusive education freely is based upon a denial of religious freedom, for such religious schools:

> constitute an impediment to student's enjoyment of freedom of religion insofar as they stifle any inclination students have to question the religious beliefs of their parents' community or to discuss or act on beliefs relating to religion that are different from the schools' sponsors. (Dwyer 1998: 163)

The question arises then as to how much trust could be placed in such schools by the wider community or whether such schools might indeed serve to encourage mistrust—particularly mistrust of communities of difference, be they religious, political, cultural, or racial. Moreover, such mistrust might well be encouraged by authoritarian practices that would not be tolerated in other circumstances.

Stephen Law illustrates this point by his imagining of the establishment of 'political' schools that would be open only to children of parents with particular political persuasions (neo-conservative, Trotskyist, socialist, Stalinist, communitarian, etc.). Such schools, he argues, would increase 'choice' for parents and would presumably meet Sergiovanni's criteria for 'schools of virtue' where parents and schools enter into a specific covenant based on shared beliefs. Law describes the practices of such schools:

> Political education at these schools largely takes the form of indoctrination. Portraits of their political leaders beam beatifically down from classroom walls. Each day begins with the collective singing of a political anthem. Pupils are never encouraged to think critically and independently about political questions. They are expected to defer more-or-less unquestioningly to their school's Authority and its revered political texts. Only ideas approved by the school's political Authority are taught. Children are never exposed to alternative political points of view (except, perhaps, in a rather caricatured form, so that they can be all the more sweepingly dismissed). (2006: 169–70)

As Law suggests, were such partisan 'political' schools to be established there would be public outrage and demands that the government ensure that schools expose children to a range of political views and encourage children to think critically and freely about them. Parental 'freedom' to choose would be overridden on the basis that no one could trust those schools to teach more broadly appropriate values that would support both the political freedoms of the broader community and its political cohesion.

Why, asks Law, if this is our attitude to the imaginary 'political' schools, do we not take the same attitude to religious schools? But the issue is surely even broader than this and involves the question of how we can trust schools that seem to incorporate certain interests and exclude others—schools that are partisan and exclusive in their practices rather than democratic and inclusive.

This is a question that is becoming more urgent as the complexity of contemporary societies increases, for 'trust is especially important for organizations that operate in turbulent external environments, that depend heavily on information sharing for success, and whose work processes demand effective decentralized decision-making' (Bryk and Schneider 2002: 33). Such are the conditions of schools and school systems.

One official response to the issue of trust has been to increase accountability and, as indicated earlier, this may well have had results that have diminished trust—especially between teachers and systems. The second key official response has been to endorse and encourage 'choice' in the belief that competition would increase school diversity and performance as well as better match parental values with school character. In England, for instance, the official policy acknowledged that:

We know that not all schools are the same. They have different strengths and serve different communities. We must encourage and celebrate this diversity. All schools need to develop their own ethos and sense of mission. (Department for Education and Skills 2002: 13)

Moreover, in England official policy encouraged this diversity by increased funding for 'faith' schools (Gardner, Cairns, and Lawton 2005) as well as the establishment of Academies (Beckett 2007), despite evidence that parents are less than enthusiastic: fewer than 1 per cent support the idea of faith groups running schools and fewer than 5 per cent private companies and charities ('What Do Parents Want?' 2009: 52).

Here, again there is also a divergence between intention and effect, for:

Despite the grand promises issued by those promoting market-based reform of social institutions—that we will witness increased levels of diversity, participation and equality—what has happened in the *practice* of market reform is a heightening of the inequitable hierarchical relationships that are characteristic of capitalist systems. (Forsey 2007: 158–59)

The result for teachers, pupils, and parents alike is not trust, but alienation from a situation where they are 'being forced to surrender their agency to a reified system that many feel powerless to change' (Forsey 2007: 163).

The issue of power and control is central to the issue of trust. Where education systems and their schools deny agency on the part of teachers, pupils, and parents, trust is likely to be in short supply. This is especially so where such agency is proclaimed through 'local parental control', for instance, but denied by the accountability mechanisms enforced by central agencies through complaisant managers (Forsey 2007). Trust is similarly threatened where promises of 'choice' are made but where significant numbers of parents do not get their first choice or are prohibited by cost or distance from accessing the school of their choice. Again, the promise of the replacement of 'failing schools' under such initiatives as the 'Fresh Start' programme in England, by new schools centred on a 'culture of success' produced through strong leadership may, in reality, both meet the official criteria and fail significant groups of students. Araujo, for instance, in a study of transition from the 'failing' Millhaven High to the 'Fresh Start' Greenfield School, shows how the pursuit of official standards worked against the interests of refugee children:

According to several OFSTED reports, there had been 'very good results' amongst refugee children due to the quality of the work being carried out at Millhaven High, a school committed to raising the aspirations of a community where attainment was traditionally low. This past experience was erased in the transition to the *Fresh Started* school, despite the significant proportion of [such] pupils . . . Greenfield was creating an identity based on 'traditional' approaches, through the policing of teachers' work, strict discipline and increased selection within the school, favouring the 'more able'. (2009: 613)

Similar problems arose in the establishment of the lavishly funded (and privatized) City Academy programme. Such academies were supposed to be beacons of hope built in the most depressed districts of English cities and, through strong leadership and a culture of success, to revolutionize the educational attainments of disadvantaged youth. Despite lavish financial support, cutting-edge design, and specialized recruitment practices, such schools in fact showed little improvement in attainment of their pupils despite their advantages. They did, however, through selective entry and the exclusion of unsatisfactory pupils (for both disciplinary and 'performance' issues—an option not open to public schools), have a significantly depressing effect on adjacent non-selective and inadequately funded public schools (Beckett 2007). Parents find it difficult to trust systems and schools that impose such illusory managerial solutions (Beckett 2007). As Araujo observes, 'managerial solutions are not sufficient to deal with problems that are both educational and social' (2009: 612).

DIVERSITY, A CULTURE OF COMMITMENT, AND SCHOOLS OF HOPE

Educational and social problems are inextricably linked. Moreover, as societies become more complex and differentiated, the social issue of how we live together becomes the most pressing social and educational problem (Bates 2005; Touraine 2000). The 'market' solution to this problem seems likely to hierarchize differences, thereby increasing the economic, cultural, social, and geographical distance between such groups. A competitive marketized education system that hierachizes schools, pupils, teachers, and managers in ways that confer various levels of distinction (or the lack of it) may more or less efficiently allocate its graduates into 'appropriate' locations in various hierarchies, but is unlikely to provide much assistance in reconciling different groups to the task of living together (Bourdieu 1984; Touraine 2000).

Such a system can only be maintained by the exercise of coercive power, through administration by control (Rowan 1990).

Administration by control implies the imposition by a hierarchical structure of authority, of a means-end rationality that not only assumes uniform agreement on goals, but also uniform methodologies to achieve these goals. Administration by control represents a simplistic application of the factory metaphor to schooling. (Starratt 2003: 197–98)

An alternative to administration by control is a more broadly based approach that takes account of difference.

> Rowan (1990) suggested that there may be a more effective strategy for administering a school, which he called *administration through commitment*. In schools that are run by commitment rather than control, there is an entirely different dynamic at work. In these schools there is still a concern with schoolwide goals as well as learning outcomes. However, the assumptions and beliefs behind administration by commitment are quite different. Within the teaching faculty there is a much greater awareness of diversity and difference among the student body. Teachers assume the need for flexibility in teaching protocols, pacing, and the performance of the learning that will be accepted as indicators of mastery. There is the belief that one can teach many things simultaneously, that on any given day students may be more disposed to learn than on others; that cultural pluralism in the classroom requires sensitivity to a variety of meanings generated by classroom activities; and that along with academic learning there are many social lessons to be learned such as how to respect racial, ethnic and sexual differences; how to negotiate disagreements; learning how to control antisocial impulses; learning how to listen to and appreciate another point of view and enrich one's understanding with those other perspectives. (Starratt 2003: 198)

Schools built on such administrative principles would look very different from those demanded by market accountability. Their ideal would be a cosmopolitanism built on the recognition and valuing of difference within the context of a critical pedagogy which opened up differences to examination and negotiation and allowed students the freedom to argue for and adopt a way of life possibly different from that which they inherited but which they can defend as a valuable and valued choice (Touraine 2000). Moreover, as Bottery (2004) argues, the education provided by such schools needs to be framed within the context of a concern with global ecological, social, and cultural issues. Such an education would not only connect individuals and cultural groups, and encourage their reformation in a contemporary context, but would also connect students with the forces shaping their future world and allow them to actively pursue their place within it. Such an education would provide for both respect and agency that could form the foundation for a broader trust in schools, teachers as professionals, and the management of schools and school systems. It would, however, demand that expectations and practices of schools be 'reframed in terms of a cultural struggle for the meaning of school learning and for personal and collective futures' (Wrigley 2003: 183).

Such principles might well provide the foundation for what Wrigley (2003) calls 'Schools of Hope'. The resultant agenda would look markedly different from the administration by control that pervades the current competitive market structures of schooling. It would be an agenda informed by a new sense of leadership through which trust might be renewed:

> We need a sense of leadership as *direction finding*, not just capacity building. We need a fuller sense of the transformative leadership which connects up with dynamic *social transformation*. We need to *turn around* our schools until they engage with the contradictions, hopes and fears of local communities. We need a sense of *achievement* which looks beyond the accumulation of factual knowledge, which links hand, heart and mind and involves moral engagement with the whole of humanity. We need new concepts of intelligence—distributed, emotional, cultural, political—which involves our engagement in shaping the future of our planet . . . We will have to *rethink education*, and not simply 'improve' schools. (Wrigley 2003: 182–83)

An educational leadership based upon such cosmopolitan principles; respectful of equity in diversity; committed to cultural negotiation, to ecological awareness, to fairness in educational and social arrangements, to the development of broadly based capabilities; and conscious of our collective future might well be a leadership that would be deserving of the trust of teachers, parents, pupils, and citizens.

REFERENCES

Araujo, M. (2009) 'A fresh start for a "failing school"? A qualitative study'. *British Educational Research Journal* 35 (4): 599–617.

Ball, S. (1990) *Politics and Policy-Making in Education: Explorations in Policy Sociology*. London: Routledge.

———. (2007) *Education Plc: Private Sector Participation in Public Sector Education*. Abingdon: Routledge.

Barber, M. (2007) *Instruction to Deliver: Fighting to Transform Britain's Public Services*. London: Methuen.

Bates, R.J. (1980) 'Educational administration, the sociology of science and the management of knowledge'. *Educational Administration Quarterly* 16 (2): 1–20.

———. (2005) 'Can we live together? Towards a global curriculum'. *Arts and Humanities in Higher Education* 4 (1): 95–109.

———. (2006) 'Culture and leadership in educational administration: A historical study of what was and what might have been'. *Journal of Educational Administration and History* 38 (2): 155–68.

———. (Forthcoming) 'The history of educational leadership and management'. In *International Encyclopedia of Education*, ed. E. Baker, B. McGaw, and P. Peterson. Dordrecht: Elsevier.

Beckett, F. (2007) *The Great City Academy Fraud*. London: Continuum.

Berliner, D., and Biddle, B. (1995) *The Manufactured Crisis: Myths, Frauds and the Attack on America's Public Schools*. Reading: Addison-Wesley.

Bernstein, B. (2000) *Pedagogy, Symbolic Control and Identity*. New York: Rowman & Littlefield.

Bonnor, C., and Caro, J. (2007) *The Stupid Country.* Sydney: University of New South Wales Press.

Bottery, M. (2004) *The Challenges of Educational Leadership.* London: Paul Chapman.

Bourdieu, P. (1984) *Distinction: A Social Critique of the Judgement of Taste.* Trans. R. Nice. Cambridge, MA: Harvard University Press.

Bryk, A., and Schneider, B. (2002) *Trust in Schools: A Core Resource for Improvement.* New York: Russell Sage.

Carr, W., and Hartnett, A. (1996) *Education and the Struggle of Democracy.* Buckingham: Open University Press.

Department for Education and Skills. (2002) *Investment for Reform.* London: Stationery Office.

Dwyer, J.G. (1998) *Religious Schools v. Children's Rights.* Ithaca, NY: Cornell University Press.

Forsey, M. (2007) *Challenging the System: A Dramatic Tale of Neoliberal Reform in an Australian High School.* Charlotte, NC: Information Age Publishing.

Gardner, R., Cairns, J., and Lawton, D. (eds.) (2005) *Faith Schools: Consensus or Conflict?* London: Routledge.

Glass, G. (2008*) Fertilizers, Pills and Magnetic Strips: The Fate of Public Education in America.* Charlotte, NC: Information Age Publishing.

Grace, G. (1995*) School Leadership: Beyond Educational Management.* London: Falmer.

Habermas, J. (1975) *Legitimation Crisis.* New York: Beacon Press.

———. (1984) *The Theory of Communicative Action.* London: Heinemann.

Hargreaves, A. (1994) *Changing Teachers, Changing Times.* Toronto: OISE Press.

Law, S. (2006) *The War for Children's Minds.* London: Routledge.

Lawton, D. (1980) 'The end of the secret garden? A study in the politics of the curriculum'. In *The Study of Education: A Collection of Inaugural Lectures*, ed. P. Gordon. London: London Institute of Education.

Luhman, N. (1979) *Trust and Power.* Chichester: Wiley.

Lyotard, J. (1984) *The Postmodern Condition: A Report on Knowledge.* Trans. G. Bennington and B. Massumi. Minneapolis: University of Minnesota Press.

Marshall, J. (1999) 'Performativity: Lyotard and Foucault through Searle and Austin'. *Studies in Philosophy and Education* 18 (5): 309–17.

Nias, J., Southworth, G. and Yeomans, R. (1989) *Staff Relationships in the Primary School*, London: Cassell

Nussbaum, M. (2003) 'Capabilities as fundamental entitlements: Sen and social justice'. *Feminist Economics* 9 (2–3): 33–59.

Oakeshott, M. (1962) 'The voice of poetry in the conversation of mankind'. In *Rationalism in Politics and Other Essays*, ed. M. Oakeshott. London: Methuen.

O'Neill, O. (2002) *A Question of Trust, BBC Reith Lectures 2002.* Cambridge: Cambridge University Press.

Peshkin, A. (1986) *God's Choice: The Total World of a Christian Fundamentalist School.* Chicago: Chicago University Press.

Power, M. (1997*) The Audit Society: Rituals of Verification.* Oxford: Oxford University Press.

Rowan, B. (1990) 'Commitment and control: Alternative strategies for the organizational design of schools'. In *Review of Research in Education*, ed. C.B. Cazden. Washington, DC: American Educational Research Association.

Sen, A. (1999) *Development as Freedom.* Oxford: Oxford University Press.

Sergiovanni, T. (1992) *Moral Leadership*, San Francisco: Jossey-Bass

Starratt, R.J. (2003) *Centering Educational Administration.* London: Lawrence Erlbaum.

Touraine, A. (2000) *Can We Live Together? Equality and Difference.* Palo Alto, CA: Stanford University Press.

Wallace, M. (1993) 'Discourse of derision: The role of the mass media within the educational policy process'. *Journal of Education Policy* 8 (4): 321–27.

'What Do Parents Want?' (2009) *Prospect Magazine* 157 (April): 52.

Wise, A. (1979) *Legislated Learning: The Bureaucratization of the American Classroom.* Berkley: University of California Press.

Wrigley, T. (2003) *Schools of Hope: A New Agenda for School Improvement.* Stoke on Trent: Trentham Books.

10 The Politics of Derision, Distrust, and Deficit

The Damaging Consequences for Youth and Communities Put at a Disadvantage

John Smyth

The most crucial ingredient in working with young people is trust—this applies whether in a school context or not (Smyth et al. 2004). Ironically, it seems to be the very ingredient that is in desperately short supply in relation to institutional learning in schools, and even worse, it appears to have been supplanted by distrust, disrespect, and even hatred. These may sound like harsh words, even ones that might be uttered in white rage, but they are not. These are ideas that have their genesis in a long period of frustration around the way in which educational policy has forced educational administration and leadership literally to its knees (Smyth 1989), requiring it to take on a fake mantle (Smyth 2008).

In this chapter I will trace something of the policy relay between contemporary educational policies of disparagement and 'policy hatred' (Hattam 2001) and their associated deficit-driven narratives that have been imposed with such devastating consequences upon young people and communities already ravaged by markets, deindustrialization, and globalization, while also exploring some more respectful and trustworthy alternatives.

The backdrop to my argument is the 'get tough' crackdown policies and populist campaigns on students and young people that commenced in the late 1980s with the emergence of 'zero tolerance' and 'three strikes and you are out' programmes and the variants of these that have been rolled out ever since. Variants of these policy strategies have been directed at discrediting and controlling minorities, students, and young people who come from contexts that *put them at a disadvantage* when it comes to schooling. The chapter will look at the way the moral panic has been constructed, how it has done its damaging work in schools through educational policies, and what an alternative 'rising movement' (Mediratta 2006) around youth, student voice, and the voices of those in poverty might look like as a basis for restoring and reversing the corrosive and corrupting effects of imposed neo-liberal versions of what ought to comprise educational leadership (Smyth et al. 2008, 2009).

In this chapter I want to step back and look at some of the arguments and the evidence to show that over the past three decades in most Western countries there has been a distortion of the social institution of schooling to the point where it is being treated contemptuously and is badly in need of reclamation. I want to conclude by looking at some of the more optimistic grounds upon which this reclamation of trust might occur (for a precursor to this, see Smyth 2005, 2006, 2007; Smyth and Fasoli 2007). But first I need to establish the basis of my argument.

THE 'AUDIT EXPLOSION' AND THE 'CORROSION OF CHARACTER' OF SCHOOLING

In the preceding heading I have invoked in a single phrase two of the most perceptive theoretical categories with which to inform discussion around notions of 'trust and betrayal' in educational administration and leadership. In particular, I borrow the notion of 'audit explosion' and the 'audit society' from Michael Power (1994a, 1994b, 1997), a professor of accounting from the London School of Economics, and the 'corrosion of character' from Richard Sennett (1998), a sociologist, also from the London School of Economics and New York University. Between them these 'big ideas' provide a powerful theoretical lens with which to engage commentary around developing a critical perspective on trust and betrayal as it relates to the contemporary lives of students, teachers, school leaders, and communities, especially those pushed to the margins of society and *put at a disadvantage* through the workings of globalization and neo-liberalism. As I undertake this journey I will also embrace Sennett's (2003) notion of 'respect'.

These ideas are crucial for at least two reasons:

- 'The audit society' is an especially adept shorthand way of depicting one of the seemingly inexorable forces that have been inflicted on public sectors in Western societies.
- As Maltby puts it, the potency of the idea of the audit society does not reside so much in the precision around its definition, so much as 'a particular manner of (re)presenting administrative problems and their solutions . . . [in a way] that is becoming universal' (2008: 3).

I want to push the idea of the effects of the audit explosion as it affects the substance and the integrity of the work of teaching and learning, and the associated aspects of leadership and administration, much further than Power does by arguing that the incursion of this 'uncouth interloper . . . arrogant, alien and improper' (Adorno 1974: 23) discourse into education has radically changed the nature of educational work. What is being seriously impugned is the manner in which schools and educational institutions are being treated in what amount to undeservedly distrustful and disrespectful ways. This is not exclusively the result of the audit mentality, but my claim is that auditing is predisposing the laminating over of a range of other practices onto schools that have such damaging effects. Notwithstanding, I want to be somewhat nuanced in my argument here, by acknowledging cross-cultural and comparative sensitivities. As Power has argued, the audit explosion took root in the UK and coincided with the Thatcher era of the 1980s, even to the point of often being conflated with the 'political program [of] Thatcherism' (2003: 185). Countries like Germany and Japan at that time seemed to have 'values of solidarity, cooperation and trust [that held] greater institutional sway' (Power 2003: 185) and as a consequence were much less affected.

Power finesses how auditing works when he says that 'auditing can be regarded as a technology of mistrust (Armstrong 1991) in which independent "outsiders" must be summoned to restore that trust' (1994b: 300). He argues that the allure of auditing has as much to do with the symbolism of independence as with its technical capacity to make things transparent. Above all, it works through 'the diffusion and generalization of the financial accountability model' (1994b: 302) and the way it infuses a generalized receptivity to the eulogized practices of private sector management. Such has been the reach of auditing as a technology of control that '[i]t has moved to the very centre of administrative discourses as the practical embodiment and enforcement of the values of accountability and transparency of process'. Indeed, what it has become is a pervasive 'all-purpose enabling technology' with such a forceful logic 'that to be against audit appears to be to support non-accountability'. There we have it! In the end, 'submission to audit establishes legitimacy regardless of the operational substance of audit' (1994b: 304).

My argument is that an over-exaggerated emphasis on checking, monitoring, and control of teachers through arbitrarily determined performance indicators, and in the process converting educational leaders into clerks, may not in any way contribute to advancing the real substance of educational work. For example, the current worldwide infatuation with testing students for factual recall is a gross deflection and distraction from the real agenda of schools, which is fundamentally about the formation of intellect and the cultivation of relationships.

Where the notion of the audit explosion has its real impact is through the relay of the social construction of the person (or institution) being audited, that is, the auditee. Power neatly pegs this when he says:

> The auditee is undoubtedly a complex being: simultaneously devious and depressed; she is skilled at games or compliance but exhausted and cynical about them too; she is nervous about the empty certificates of comfort that get produced but she also colludes in amplifying audit mandates in local settings; she fears the mediocrity of the auditors at the same time as she regrets their powerlessness to discipline the

'really bad guys'; she loathes the time wasted rituals of inspection but accepts that this is probably what 'we deserve'; she sees the competent and excellent suffer as they attempt to deal with the demands of quality assurance at the same time as the incompetent and idle manage to escape its worse excesses; she hears the rhetoric of excellence in official documents but lives in a reality of decline; she takes notes after meetings with colleagues 'just in case' and has more filing cabinets now than she did a few years ago; she knows the past was far from a golden age but despairs of the iron cage of auditing; she knows the public accountability and stakeholder dialogue are good things but wonders why, after all her years of training, she is not trusted as an expert anymore. (2003: 199–200)

Here in this single paragraph Power captures many of the fears, contradictions, and tensions that have come to characterize the lives of countless teachers, leaders, and administrators in schools all around the world. Here we see the really insidious way in which auditing does its ugly work of producing fear, loathing, hatred, and feelings of having one's work diminished, at the same time as feeling dirty, implicated, and complicit.

But there is more! The effects of auditing do not stop with the institutions and individuals upon whom the process is perpetrated. Because of the extent of its reach and the way it becomes insinuated into the commonsense logic of the way we think, it reaches deep into the kind of societies we create. Invoking Power again, this time in terms of the deep effects auditing has on societies that become captivated:

When this happens a society tries to tell reaffirming stories, it makes explicit what was implicit and it creates more and more formal accounts that can be checked. An anxious society invests heavily in evaluative practices of self-affirmation and new industries of checkers are created. It is not so much a loss of trust that has occurred but a desperate need to create it through the management of formal appearance.

. . . all this checking makes a certain style of management possible, one that is now firmly established. The problem is not evaluation and assessment as such, but the belief that with ever more of it, real excellence can be conjured into existence. The opposite is almost certainly the case; increasing evaluation and auditing are symptoms of mediocrity rather than its cure. (1996: 18)

What this is saying is that societies that become besotted with auditing become deeply mired in insecurity to the point where they are incapable of allowing professionals to construct and carry accounts of their work on their own terms. In its place, it is claimed, such stories can only be constructed by others—it is only by this means that loss of trust can be reconstituted through image and impression management. Even more worrying than this implicit challenge to organizational legitimacy is Power's preceding claim, and reiterated elsewhere, as to whether audit stories are actually 'a cover for increasing mediocrity?' (1997: 14). If true, this is a serious indictment indeed, especially when the logic being touted is that auditing is really about transparency, accountability, and ensuring value for money.

SCHOOLS AS 'RELATIONAL SPACES'

In recent times I have written extensively about the notion of the 'relational school' (Smyth, Down, and McInerney 2010) and of the 'relational work' (Smyth 2007) that is the defining quality of what ought to go on in schools, but here I want to appropriate and expand on the notion of 'relational spaces' invoked by Gustavson and Cytrynbaum to describe the moments of illumination that go on in their case when undertaking multisited ethnographic research. They use the term 'relational space' to refer to 'those moments when the originally intended purposes of the planned data collection activities get pushed to the periphery and the relational dynamics of the research take center stage' (2003: 253). In essence, they wanted to know 'how the entextualized individuals' in their research accounts understood and were affected by the research and 'how the researchers [in turn] responded to the ways in which participants interpreted the research' (2003: 257). There we have it—relational spaces are the serendipitous venues brought into existence and around which deep, profound, and largely unintended learning occurs.

One of the most grotesque distortions produced by the audit explosion has been the tendency of schools to become configured largely as annexes or handmaidens to the economy. This is something that historically was graphically portrayed by Callahan in his classic *Education and the Cult of Efficiency* (1962), but in recent times in most Western countries it has become our worst living nightmare. Far from being lively places of exploration, passion, and inquiry, mostly speaking, schools have become prison-like places of pedagogical incarceration, characterized by compliance, delivery, accountability, measurement, consumption, and, above all, individualism. The major form this has taken is through what Bingham labels the 'entrenched discourses, entrenched practices, entrenched ontological suppositions, [and the] entrenched philosophies of education' (2004: 23) set in train by the highly individualistic and atomistic ideas of Ralph Tyler (1974) and those who have followed in his wake. As Bingham notes, Tyler's rationale has been especially influential in the US because of the manner in which it 'treats students as disconnected individuals who are to be taught and assessed without regard to their relation to others' (2004: 23).

This situation has been considerably exacerbated in the US with the notion of 'no child left behind', which further entrenches the view of learners as stand-alone individual units, disconnected from others, and who have to be assailed with slogans like 'at-risk' and 'fall[ing] through the cracks' (Bingham 2004: 23) based on so-called high-stakes testing. This approach is used to further solidify images of vulnerable individuals in need of punishment, correctives, or amelioratives, and in respect of whom barriers or obstacles either have to be erected or removed. The centre-piece is the stand-alone disconnected individual learner who is treated in ways that pedagogically reinforce self-responsibility, with forms of assessment, measurement, and testing based on the highly individualistic notion that what is most crucial is demonstrating 'the extent to which one person does or does not measure up to the rest of the lot' (Bingham 2004: 23) according to the arbitrarily normed ability of individuals. The problem, according to Bingham, is that such an ideology may 'not account for the possibility that ability itself may depend on the relational context where such ability is measured' (2004: 23).

Stengel teases this set of connections apart in a most intriguing way. For example, she argues that 'hierarchical relations marked by obedience [serve only to] generate the recitation of "right answers"' (2004: 150), and they are only ever permissive of results that fit preformulated categories developed by others. In other words, such approaches are deeply distrustful of the ability of the learner to generate responses that might be dependent on the context or that are in any way likely to result in ambiguity, complexity, or contradiction. When we start out in highly stipulative ways like this that specify outcomes, then:

> We do not trust that our own wondering and inquiring and communicating with students will result in their knowing, in their developing ability to respond richly in relation to others and the world. (Stengel 2004: 150)

It is this capacity to both embrace existing forms of knowledge and also the preparedness to challenge or jettison them that is the permissive hallmark of an ability to attain 'new understanding and new perspectives' (Stengel 2004: 151). It is not, Stengel argues, that the relational aspects of education are more important than knowledge itself, but rather that 'they are rooted in one another that the very idea of knowledge depends on the presence of relation and vice versa. Every experience that purports to be educational has some quality of relation intertwined at its core'. The tragedy is that in the 'contemporary imagination' knowledge and the relational nature of knowing have been conflated or collapsed down to 'accountability and control' rather than 'response-ability and acceptance' (2004: 151). At its most practical, what this means is that as educators if 'we want our students to develop lively, questioning, and not-always-conventional minds, we must engage them in relations with us that are marked by these qualities' (2004: 150).

HOW NEO-LIBERALISM DAMAGES AND 'CORRODES CHARACTER' IN CONTEXTS OF DISADVANTAGE AND THE EFFECTS ON LEADERSHIP, EDUCATIONAL AND OTHERWISE

If we shift these arguments sideways slightly, it is possible to see how they have some quite profound effects on those sectors of Western societies that have already been dealt a severe blow through globalization and deindustrialization.

The basic policy presumption towards people in contexts of disadvantage is that they are unreliable witnesses of the conditions of their lives and how they came to be in their alleged predicaments in the first place, and furthermore that as a consequence what they need is the assistance of people who are reputedly smarter and wiser than themselves. In other words, there is a heavy presumption of guilt—that people are guilty of not exercising the right amount of self-responsibility and this is the 'cause' of their defects, and, concomitantly, that such irresponsible people cannot be trusted in the analysis of how they came to be this way and certainly cannot possibly have the knowledge by which to extricate themselves from this situation.

There is a quite disturbing, and might I say arrogantly self-serving, logic in this that goes something like this:

- There is a presumption of 'dependence' and an 'inability to cope'.
- As a result, there is a 'problem' to 'be fixed'.
- We need 'experts' suitably qualified to correct these forms of deviance.
- The way to do this is to:
    ○ Undertake 'needs analyses' to expose the nature and extent of defects.
    ○ Develop 'programmes' and 'services' that are to be 'delivered' to 'targeted groups' to address alleged pathological shortcomings.
    ○ Monitor, evaluate, and 'audit' the effects of interventions for their effectiveness in engendering improvements.
- As a consequence, people who have allowed themselves to stray into 'deviant' and unconventional lifestyles as a consequence of not exercising the right amount of self-responsibility will be dutifully rehabilitated and ushered back into the 'mainstream'.
- In the process they will be kept in a situation of deserved 'dependence' lest they become recidivists!

The viewpoint I have just sketched out is somewhat parodied, only just, but it represents what is still the dominant default position with regard to social exclusion, inclusion, disadvantage, and poverty—and it underpins the way in which politicians and policymakers deal with communities and schools they place in the category of 'disadvantaged'. The approach is deeply flawed, paternalistic, patronizing, and, most of all, deeply distrustful of the capacities of the people pigeonholed in these ways. The disparagement that comes with it, it could be argued, is designed to perpetuate situations of dependence, and, as a result, prevent the development of responses that speak more appropriately to real underlying structural complexities—which often have to do with powerlessness.

There are implications here, of course, for educational leadership and administration. If the framing policy agenda within which schools have to operate is one of pathology and deficits, no matter how benevolently informed, then what will be pursued is still a delinquent and rehabilitative view of schools, students, teachers, families, and communities of disadvantage. Versions of leadership will be expected that reflect:

- The need to uphold standards, and people on the fringes of society are seen to contribute to the lowering of standards, therefore needing to be treated in ways that force them to 'lift their game'.
- It follows that schools and teachers need to be treated in performative ways in which they are punished, usually fiscally, if they don't shape up, or alternatively they are named and shamed.

The fundamental problem with educational leadership envisaged in this way is that this 'new logic' (Gunter and Thomson 2009) is based on the notion of 'managing diversity' rather than challenging, questioning, debating, or interrogating the conditions that lead to the creation of social hierarchies of class, disadvantage, inequality, race, and gender in the first place, and indeed how schools have become complicit in reproducing these inequities. As Gunter and Thomson put it, when leaders become managers of standards and test results they become 'tactical implementers and delivers [rather then] strategic decision-makers' (2009: 18).

Where the betrayal of trust becomes most glaringly apparent in all of this is in the erasure of Aristotle's notion of *tekhne* or the art, craft, and skill of the 'reasoned habit of mind' (Cintron 1997: xii) that is crucial to analysing and challenging structures of oppression and exploitation. As Cintron perceptively put it, the controlling question in such situations is: 'How does one create respect under conditions of little or no respect?' (1997: x). Invoking John Locke, Sennett, in his treatise on *Respect in a World of Inequality*, argues that people display trust when they accord to others 'a measure of freedom to act without constant auditing, monitoring, and oversight' (2003: 122). When such autonomy is withheld or not forthcoming, then what exists is a situation of immobility, of not being able to make decisions on the merits of situations, and of outsiders believing they can decide what is best but without the capacity to fully understand the complexities of what is occurring. Alternatively, when autonomy is applied to situations like education and health, what it means is that educators and doctors are accorded autonomy indicative of an acceptance 'that they know what they are doing, even if we don't understand it' (2003: 122). Furthermore, Sennett says, 'the same autonomy ought to be granted to the pupil or patient, because they know things about learning or being sick which the person teaching or treating them might not fathom' (2003: 122).

Given the context from within which this chapter is being written, namely of schools, communities, and young people who have been *put at a disadvantage* by social, economic, and politic forces, then the same line of argument can be applied. If we want to understand the obstacles, impediments, and interferences attached to having a successful and rewarding education, and, by implication, bringing about improvement in life chances, then we need forms of leadership that listen, as Krumer-Nevo (2005) calls it, to 'life knowledge'.

'Life knowledge' amounts to the largely ignored personal stories of people who are labeled and positioned as being merely 'anecdotal' by the wider official social policy discourses of statistical, academic, objective knowledge. 'Life knowledge is knowledge that comes from "the street" by "natural" everyday means . . . acquired through seemingly endless experiences and encounters shaping opinions and points of view towards the self and others' (Krumer-Nevo 2005: 99, 100). It is a form of knowledge largely dismissed and distrusted by policymakers because the people who possess it have little formal education and, 'moreover, their way of life is perceived as corroboration of this lack of knowledge as well as ostensible evidence of poor learning and abstraction skills' (Krumer-Nevo 2005: 100). From an official point of view, this knowledge is not to be trusted despite the fact that the people who posses it might just happen to have 'a better view of the shortcomings [of the] social institutions' (Krumer-Nevo 2005: 100) that supposedly exist to serve them.

It is interesting that one of the reasons we seem not to have been able to do anything about the so-called hard core, concentrated, protracted, intergenerational pockets of disadvantage and poverty that continue to be so persistently prevalent in Western countries is that we fail dismally to understand the point made by Hills et al. that 'we have come to the end of the line for traditional models of poverty research' and we need approaches that 'are more dynamic, differentiated and democratic' (2000: 294, 296).

The kind of 'learning for life knowledge' that Krumer-Nevo is alluding to, and that needs to be front and centre in leadership approaches in schools *put at a disadvantage*, 'requires involving participants as active partners in the process of learning' (2005: 104). This will involve jettisoning a whole lot of prejudices, myths, misconceptions, and stereotypes, such as:

> people in poverty do not want to work . . . people living in poverty have no opinions or thoughts on abstract ideas like knowledge, time or citizenship, or that they are not interested in articulating them . . . [and that as a consequence, since] . . . 'the poor' cannot achieve any

significant transformation in their lives, there is no point in offering them sophisticated treatment or rehabilitation services. (2005: 103–4)

Most disturbingly, what these presumptions of betrayal do is enable social institutions to 'ignore and deny, in fact fail to recognise the knowledge possessed by those who live [on] the margins' (2005: 104). In short, they license forms of intellectual laziness that provide policymakers with the excuse they need to get off the hook of having to engage with the real complexities of these people's lives.

LEADERSHIP THAT IS INFORMED BY FOSTERING 'A CAPACITY TO ASPIRE'

Bringing about a turnaround in the circumstances of schools, students, and communities who have been damaged by neo-liberalism and the associated workings of the audit explosion will require starting the reclamation from 'the capacity to aspire' (Appadurai 2004). Appadurai argues that the more powerful in society 'have a more fully developed capacity to aspire' (2004: 68)—meaning that because they have more resources, they have had richer experiences and they experience more complex sets of relations. They have a more sophisticated understanding of the connection between educational means and ends. In other words, the already advantaged 'are in a better position to explore and harvest diverse experiences of exploration and trial, because of their many opportunities to link material goods and immediate opportunities to more general and generic possibilities and options'. That is, the capacity to aspire is thus 'a navigational capacity' (2004: 68, 69):

> The more privileged in any society simply have used the map of its norms to explore the future more frequently and more realistically and to share this knowledge with one another more routinely than their poorer and weaker neighbors. (2004: 69)

Because they have fewer opportunities, the disadvantaged have had a relative 'lack of opportunities to practice the use of this navigational capacity . . . [and consequently] have a more brittle horizon of aspirations' (2004: 69).

Developing the opportunity structures within which the capacity to aspire can flourish must surely be the *sine qua non* of educational leadership rather than continuing to perpetuate a flawed muscular or macho view that people who have been excluded must be forced to shape up to some top-down, externally driven, and arbitrarily determined meritocratic ideals or standards. The crucial issue seems to be how to go about replacing these heroic ideas of leadership with a set of understandings that are located in a more robust view of what constitutes 'deep democracy' (Appadurai 2002).

These ideas have direct relevance to the reform of schools, and, by implication, a view of educational leadership that is embedded in 'grassroots globalization' or networks of community activists who have 'an eye to building their own capacity to set goals, achieve expertise, share knowledge, and generate commitment' (Appadurai 2006: 131, 134). This is a form of capacity building that is rooted in 'local imaginings of power' that involves making these people 'architects of their local political worlds' (2006: 137, 135).

As Anyon has demonstrated in her book *Radical Possibilities*, in the US there is an emerging 'new wave' of social movements that are adopting quite a different approach to previous classical social movements that have tended in the past to act as catalysts for 'the enactment of social justice legislation, progressive court decisions, and other equity policy' (2005: 127). What is different on this occasion, Anyon argues, is that personal agency features much more prominently in the way 'individuals actually get into contentious politics' (2005: 130). Drawing from McAdam, Tarrow, and Tilly's *Dynamics of Contention* (2001), Anyon argues that what is required is a much greater focus on contentious episodes that provide opportunities for new 'movement-building spaces' that move 'from self-blame or angry rebellion to well-informed political engagement' (2005: 188). Anyon provides examples of five already existing but not well-known movements in the US—community organizing, for example, the Association for Community Organizations Now (ACORN) (Delgado 1986) and the Industrial Areas Foundation (IAF) (Shirley 1997; Warren 2001, 2005); educational organizing (Gold, Simon, and Brown 2002; Mediratta et al. 2001; Zachary and olatoye 2001), for example, the Logan Square Neighborhood Association (LSNA) in Chicago (Mediratta, Fruchter, and Lewis 2002); progressive labour unions; the living wage movement; and youth organizing, for example, the Boston Area Youth Organizing Project (BYOP), Schools Not Jails, and the Student Labor Action Project (SLAP). What all of these have in common is that while they may be relatively small movements that are in need of drawing together, their intent is to 'identify personal and social processes that assist people in producing sustained public contention' and the starting point lies in people regarding development 'as presenting opportunities for waging struggle' (Anyon 2005: 131). What is beyond denial is that 'education policy cannot remain closeted in schools, classrooms, and educational bureaucracies. It must join the world of communities, families, and students; it must advocate for them and emerge from their urgent realities' (Anyon 2005: 199).

At the heart of Appadurai's notion of the capacity to aspire, the beginnings of which we can see in some of the new social movements just described that impact on the most marginalized schools, students, and communities, is a fundamental redefinition of the 'politics of recognition' (Taylor 1994) from below. People who have historically been excluded need to 'change the terms of recognition' (Appadurai 2004: 77) in ways so that what is normally considered as material deprivation and exclusion are reconfigured as sets of positive attributes and possibilities that congregate around a number of general principles, such as:

- the rituals through which consensus is produced within disadvantaged communities and how these are negotiated with the more powerful in society
- forms of learning that 'increase the ability of poor people to navigate the cultural map in which aspirations are located' and to make explicit connections between 'wants or goals and more inclusive scenarios, contexts and norms' (Appadurai 2004: 83)
- encouraging the cultivation and extension of 'voice' and dissent rather than 'loyalty' and compliance; in other words, asking critical questions like: *how come things are this way? how did they come to be like this? who benefits and who loses from this state of affairs? and who can we connect with around what strategy to change this?*

What these principles comprise, in effect, is a set of technologies or a toolkit with which to redefine the cultural map of aspirations from below. To have the desired effect they need to be accompanied by narratives of how these more satisfying aspirations are experienced, how they are understood, and what they mean to the changed life chances of those whose lives are most directly transformed as a consequence. Rather than allowing educational leadership and administration to continue to remain captured by the diminished notions of blame that accompany the neo-liberal agenda of accountability, what is required instead is that we vociferously and insistently demand that educational leadership from outside as well as from within educational institutions be overtly and quite explicitly framed around what Rao and Walton (2004) aptly refer to as 'culture and public action'.

CLOSING COMMENTS

What I have been at pains to argue in this chapter is that the effects of lack of trust and disrespect, as embodied in neo-liberal approaches to educational administration and leadership, have significant consequences, especially for schools and communities of disadvantage. I have traced the way in which auditing works to both construct school people in particular ways while actively denying the relational nature of the work of schools. This disparagement and denial of the 'life knowledge' of disadvantaged people sits very uneasily with an audit mentality. An alternative, and more respectful, form of educational leadership was seen as needing to start from the quite novel point that what is missing from contexts of disadvantage are opportunities. Such alternative grassroots approaches need to be carefully cultivated and nurtured in ways that enable the dislodging and supplanting of the dominant distrustful views of leadership and administration. Until and unless this happens, we can expect little to occur in the way of reducing the learning and achievement gap, and its palpable absence may even exacerbate the gap.

NOTE

The ideas for this chapter come from an Australian Research Council Discovery project entitled *Individual, Institutional and Community 'Capacity Building' in a Cluster of Disadvantaged Schools and their Community*. I express my appreciation to the ARC for its funding support and to my co-investigator Lawrence Angus.

REFERENCES

Adorno, T. (1974) *Minima Moralia: Reflections from Damaged Life*. London: Verso.

Anyon, J. (2005) *Radical Possibilities: Public Policy, Urban Education and a New Social Movement*. New York: Routledge.

Appadurai, A. (2002) 'Deep democracy: urban governmentality and the horizon of politics'. *Public Culture* 14 (1): 21–47.

———. (2004) 'The capacity to aspire: Culture and the terms of recognition'. In *Culture and Public Action*, ed. V. Rao and M. Walton. Palo Alto, CA: Stanford University Press with the World Bank.

———. (2006) *Fear of Small Numbers: An Essay on the Geography of Anger*. Durham, NC: Duke University Press.

Armstrong, P. (1991) 'Contradiction and social dynamics in the capitalist agency relationship'. *Accounting, Organisations and Society* 16 (1): 1–25.

Bingham, C. (2004) 'Let's treat authority relationally'. In *No Education Without Relation*, ed. C. Bingham and M. Sidorkin. New York: Peter Lang.

Callahan, R. (1962) *Education and the Cult of Efficiency*. Chicago: University of Chicago Press.

Cintron, R. (1997) *Angels' Town: Chero Ways, Gang Life, and Rhetorics of the Everyday*. Boston: Beacon Press.

Delgado, G. (1986) *Organizing the Movement: the Roots and Growth of ACORN*. Philadelphia: Temple University Press.

Gold, E., and Simon, E., with Brown, C. (2002) *Successful Community Organizing for School Reform: Strong Neighbourhoods Strong Schools: The Indicators Project on Education Organizing*. Chicago: Cross City Campaign for Urban School Reform.

Gunter, H., and Thomson, P. (2009) 'The makeover: A new logic in leadership development in England'. Unpublished manuscript, University of Manchester and University of Nottingham.

Gustavson, L., and Cytrynbaum, J. (2003) 'Illuminating spaces: Relational spaces, complicity and multi-sited ethnography'. *Field Methods* 15 (3): 252–70.

Hattam, R. (2001) 'Nurturing democratic relationships in schools against policy "hatred"'. Paper presented at the annual meeting of the American Educational Research Association, Seattle.

Hills, J., et al. (2000) 'The future of poverty research: Panel session'. In *Experiencing Poverty*, ed. D. Bradshaw and R. Sainsbury. Aldershot: Ashgate.

Krumer-Nevo, M. (2005) '"Listening to life knowledge": A new research direction in poverty studies'. *International Journal of Social Welfare* 14 (2): 99–106.

Maltby, J. (2008) 'There is no such thing as audit society: A reading of M. Power (1994) "The Audit Society"'. Paper presented at the Practical Criticism in the Managerialist Social Services conference, Leicester University Management School, January.

McAdam, D., Tarrow, S., and Tilly, C. (2001) *Dynamics of Contention*. New York: Cambridge University Press.

Mediratta, K. (2006) 'A rising movement'. *National Civic Review* 95 (1): 15–22.

Mediratta, K., Fruchter, N., and Lewis, A. (2002) *Organizing for School Reform: How Communities are Finding their Voices and Reclaiming their Public Schools. A Report.* New York: Institute for Education and Social Policy, New York University.

Mediratta, K., et al. (2001) *Mapping the Field or Organizing for School Improvement: A Report on Education Organizing.* New York: Institute for Education and Social Policy, New York University.

Power, M. (1994a) *The Audit Explosion*. London: Demos.

———. (1994b) 'The audit society'. In *Accounting as Social Institutional Practice*, ed. A. Hopwood and P. Miller. Cambridge: Cambridge University Press.

———. (1996) 'I audit, therefore I am'. *Times Higher Education Supplement* 18 (October): 18.

———. (1997) *The Audit Society: Ritual of Verification*. Oxford: Oxford University Press.

———. (2003) 'Evaluating the audit explosion'. Special issue on Auditing in Regulatory Perspective, *Law and Policy* 25 (3): 185–202.

Rao, V., and Walton, M. (eds.) (2004) *Culture and Public Action*. Palo Alto, CA: Stanford University Press with the World Bank.

Sennett, R. (1998) *The Corrosion of Character: The Personal Consequences of Work in the New Capitalism*. New York: W.W. Norton.

———. (2003) *Respect in a World of Inequality*. New York: W.W. Norton.

Shirley, D. (1997) *Community Organizing for Urban Reform*. Austin: University of Texas Press.

Smyth, J. (ed.) (1989) *Critical Perspectives on Educational Leadership*. London: Falmer Press.

———. (2005) 'An argument for new understandings and explanations of early school leaving that go beyond the conventional'. *London Review of Education* 3 (2): 117–30.

———. (2006) 'Researching teachers working with young adolescents: Implications for ethnographic research'. *Ethnography and Education* 1 (1): 31–51.

———. (2007) 'Teacher development against the policy reform grain: An argument for recapturing relationships in teaching and learning'. *Teacher Development* 11 (2): 221–36.

———. (2008) 'Australia's great disengagement with public education and social justice in educational leadership'. *Journal of Educational Administration and History* 40 (3): 221–33.

Smyth, J., Down, B., and McInerney, P. (2010) *'Hanging in with Kids' in Tough Times: Engagement in Contexts of Educational Disadvantage in the Relational School.* New York: Peter Lang.

Smyth, J., and Fasoli, L. (2007) 'Climbing over the rocks in the road to student engagement and learning in a challenging high school in Australia'. *Educational Research* 49 (3): 273–95.

Smyth, J., et al. (2004) *'Dropping Out', Drifting Off, Being Excluded: Becoming Somebody without School.* New York: Peter Lang.

Smyth, J., et al. (2008) *Critically Engaged Learning: Connecting to Young Lives.* New York: Peter Lang.

Smyth, J., et al. (2009) *Activist and Socially Critical School and Community Renewal: Social Justice in Exploitative Times.* Rotterdam: Sense.

Stengel, B. (2004) 'Knowing is respons-able relation'. In *No Education without Relation,* ed. C. Bingham and A. Sidorkin. New York: Peter Lang.

Taylor, C. (1994) *Multiculturalism: Examining the Politics of Recognition.* Princeton, NJ: Princeton University Press.

Tyler, R. (1974) *Basic Principles of Curriculum and Instruction.* Chicago: University of Chicago Press.

Warren, M. (2001) *Dry Bones Rattling: Community Building to Revitalize American Democracy.* Princeton, NJ: Princeton University Press.

———. (2005) 'Communities and schools: A new view of urban school reform'. *Harvard Educational Review* 75 (2): 133–73.

Zachary, E., and olatoye, s. (2001) *A Case Study: Community Organizing for School Improvement in the South Bronx.* New York: Institute for Education and Social Policy, New York University.

11 (Non)-Legal Requirements for Trust in Slovenian Higher Education

Uroš Pinterič

In the last few years, European Union member states and applicant countries have been facing significant higher education reform that should unify higher education systems in the area into something that can be called a European higher education space. This should lead to more comparable levels of education and consequently, according to the Lisbon strategy, increase individuals' competitiveness in labour markets. In reality, there are two basic effects of this reform that are already showing results, especially in Central and Eastern European member states and some applicant countries. In general, states that have no tradition of private education are facing increasing numbers of different high schools, faculties, and universities with questionable quality, and the level of knowledge in the general population is falling despite an increasing number of university degrees awarded. However, this chapter is mostly concerned with what is going on with relations in certain policy arenas in the aforementioned framework. Even though one can argue that observations are valid for all Central and Eastern European countries, as well as South-West European countries, that is, all transitional countries with a communist past that are trying to adapt to the EU context, all basic information for this chapter is mainly gathered on the case of Slovenia.

These changes in the higher education sphere were not only structural but also in some cases reflected changes in social/policy networks. Even though many authors understand networks as relations among actors (see Kickert, Kljin, and Koppenjan 1997), they simultaneously ignore that any relation is, in fact, (im)possible and managed on different levels of trust among the involved actors. However, different levels and forms of trust can be basic obstacles or accelerators of interpersonal relations as well as of different outputs/outcomes of their activities. This chapter approaches an understanding of the background of Slovenian higher education reform through changes in trust patterns in the higher education policy network. In the literature on social relations we can find different descriptions or definitions of the concept of trust; however, it is widely accepted that trust is not a unitary concept (Cvetkovich and Löfstedt 1999; Eisenstadt and Roniger 1984) and has different forms, each with different influences on trust-based activities.

INSTITUTIONAL AND PERSONAL TRUST

If trust is the belief that something will be as it was proclaimed, or promised in general, we can hardly argue that there are different types of trust. Levels of trust can differ based on an assessment in previous experience and on the basis of relationship type. To better understand processes in the higher education policy arena (mostly in Slovenia but also in other Central and Eastern European countries) we can distinguish between two basic types of trust: institutional/legal and personal. Institutional trust excludes human factors as relevant, instead recognizing only legal procedures and consequences. It is based on the rule of law that applies in practice as well as the expectation that the legal framework will not be changed arbitrarily from one formulation to its opposite overnight. Institutional trust is so realistic an expectation that institutional relations in the policy network cannot be changed without the acceptance of all or a majority of involved actors. Personal trust, on the other hand, relies on interpersonal relations, where the human factor has a strong impact and where individuals (who can and usually do) play the role of institutional representatives who shape policy solutions and where agreements and deals are expected to be respected and, if necessary, implemented into policies.

In both cases we can find elements of what Cvetkovich and Löfstedt (1999: 4–5) define as 'social trust': the expectation that certain behavioural patterns in relationships of trusted individuals in their relation to the interests of one who is trusting them can be relied upon. Cvetkovich and Löfstedt warn that trusting does not guarantee that a violation of trust will not happen since trust can be influenced by many factors, such as individual perception, the general structure of the system, and activities of certain institutions (1999: 7).

It is more than evident that there can also be tensions between institutional and personal trust, especially when representatives personalize institutional trust, in other words, when they not only represent the institution but they internalize representation to the level that they identify themselves with the institution and its welfare.

If one combines differing aspects of personal trust and institutional trust with (Cvetkovich and Löfstedt 1999: 7) elements that influence them, we can create a model of trust rationales that help determine what happened with the trust in higher education in Slovenia (see Table 11.1).

Table 11.1   Trust Rationales

Factors of influence	Personal trust	Institutional trust
Individual processes	Friendship	Not important
System structure	Not important	Rule of law
Institutional activities	Legitimacy	Legality

Personal trust depends on individual behaviour that can result in bonding through friendship or a similar relationship, based on mutual trust that is at least not initially institutionalized. Structures of political, economic, cultural, or social systems seem not to be relevant to personal trust. Activities of different institutions in relation to individuals can produce legitimacy. In the case of creating legitimacy bonds, trust is connected to the aforementioned success in serving individuals' interests.

Institutional trust is, on the other hand, not usually affected by individual behaviour. System structures create trust on an institutional level through rule of law, especially in the sense of the legal predictability of activities and actors respecting basic legal principles such as legal equality of all subjects and differentiation of cases by relevant differences among them. Activities of different institutions in relation to institutional trust produce (il)legality.

Both types of trust are interconnected and cannot simply be separated in reality—individuals follow their own interests and the interests of institutions at the same time, especially in cases where they are in 'power positions'. Long-time institutionalized contacts can also cause relational change between the institutional and the personal that will necessary also change trust patterns, most commonly from legality to legitimacy and from rule of law to friendship.

SOCIAL/POLICY NETWORKS AND TRUST

Higher education is not only about education on a higher level, but it also involves the state perception of certain values and knowledge needs as well as interpretations of reality. From this point of view, higher education has strong political connotations and is also one of the policy fields covered by specific policy networks where actors enter in various relations that cause higher education policy. Policy networks can be relatively closed, with a limited number of actors who enter the arena and try to stay in as long as possible. On the other hand, arenas can be relatively open to anyone, the number of actors growing much bigger, but they will stay in only as long as necessary to fulfill their own interest. The state can invite certain actors and exclude others and, at the same time, can play an important role in deciding who to invite (and legitimize as representatives) and who to exclude. However, according to van Waarden (1992), in certain types of policy networks the state can be a captured actor, surrounded by more powerful actors who are trying to fulfill their interests through the state support that can be gained or forced. Despite van Waarden's characterization, only some combinations of these elements commonly occur in the flexibility of today's world.

Even though the institutional approach to policy networks is most common, van Waarden (1992) warns that one has to be aware that relations in policy networks (as well as other networks) can be based on interpersonal relations among the individual representatives of institutions. This element introduces a psychological dimension where interpersonal relations based on character or personality affect the mutual thrust and negotiation capabilities of crucial importance for the composition and work of policy networks as well as for public policies as a result of processes within the network. Or, more simply, we can talk about the human factor in policy networks. Here it is necessary to stress that institutionalized or operationalized processes and activities are far from sufficient to understand policy output and outcomes. It is necessary to include those 'soft' factors shaping the process built from the personal characteristics or psychological profiles of individuals: daily mood, their individual knowledge and experience, personal prejudices, and their personal relations with other members of network. This also includes their mutual trust, which is based on individuals' character, knowledge, prejudices, and relationships with other individuals.

Higher education policy networks should be understood in formal and informal ways. The black box model is far from sufficient to understand results of higher education policy—it does not even try to include all processes that take place. On one hand, formal structures of policy networks are generally defined by European and national legislation that defines legally acceptable input and outcomes. In this sense, the source of trust is the belief that all involved actors will play within the legal framework: it is trust in institutions and institutionalized processes. However, involved actors, despite institutional socialization, can also be motivated by their individual interests or those of their individual institution, which are not always in keeping with legislation.

Policy reality usually allows for different outputs and has certain and necessary different outcomes due to factors in the implementation process. Outcomes are understood in this context as direct consequences of policy implementation and can be represented by governmental legislation establishing new faculties or universities, and in this sense can produce better access or a higher level of knowledge produced by newly established institutions. Searching for policy solutions, their adoption, and implementation is strongly burdened by informal relations that can take different forms of policy advocacy, such as lobbying, expertise, information filtration, et cetera. Through these means, representatives are able to influence the normative frame of policy, but also can interpret legislation if interpretation is possible. In such informal relations trust in legislation is relatively weak, and all the participants in policy networks mostly count on personal connections and attempts to adjust institutional frameworks to their particular interests.

SOCIAL AND POLITICAL ARENAS
IN HIGHER EDUCATION POLICY

Depending on the country, but still common to all European post-communist countries, was a strong system of public universities that had established levels of quality and which produced competent (but more or less indoctrinated) experts. After 1990, a slow liberalization of higher education began with the introduction first of private higher education institutions. These private institutions lacked appropriate faculty and researchers and were usually not recognized by public universities. In some cases, faculty from public universities also worked for these private institutions as additional sources of income to what was generally a meagre salary. It was not rare that they worked for more than one private institution. The state financially supported private higher education institutions from the public budget, which lowered monies available for the public system. Not only members of public universities sat on committees of related public agencies; later, members of private higher education institutions did, as well as government representatives and civil servants. Generally, the public was excluded as incompetent. Many civil servants and government representatives were previously students from (logically) public universities, and some professors were also strongly politically active (as members of parliaments or government officials).

According to van Waarden's (1992) typology of policy networks, we see evidence of something that can be called a combination of captured statism and clientelism (for an in-depth exploration of clientele relations, see Eisenstadt and Roniger 1984). In all cases we can talk about strong relationships among recognized relevant actors in each policy area and state actors. However, it is hard to recognize what actual pattern of relations is prevailing and most influencing the results of higher education policy. Captured statism and clientelism are present in combination when, on one hand, the state as a relevant partner in higher education policy recognizes only public higher education institutions, and, on the other, at the same time is more or less dependent on public higher education institutions due to the fact that they represent about 80 to 90 per cent of the higher education sphere.

Such stable interlocking relations between public higher education and state actors in Slovenia was partly destabilized after national higher education reforms, when the state, under a right-wing government, tolerated and supported the first private higher education institutions. It consequently cut part of the finances to public higher education directly or by changing the rules of higher education financing. The most common method was to change from a financing by study programme or number of employees system to one based on the number of registered students, causing the emergence of intense campaigning for students.

THE HISTORICAL PERSPECTIVE

All former communist or socialist countries had state-run educational systems, not only for welfare society reasons but also with a strong interest in systematic indoctrination of children and youth into a 'right values system'.

No private schools at any level were allowed. After the fall of communist regimes in Central and Eastern Europe, with greater or smaller support by the international community, the first private schools were established. This support was mainly conducted through different demands by international organizations 'to democratize' and to 'liberate' all spheres of life. They were generally more successful in transitional countries with higher debts to the International Monetary Fund (IMF) and the World Bank (like Slovakia), while countries with lower levels of foreign debt, like Slovenia, could afford to remain more independent in their transitional paths. In 2004, the majority of Central and Eastern European Countries entered the European Union. At the same time, the European Union introduced the Bologna reforms, which shattered higher education systems, especially in countries with long traditions of strong national educational systems based on 'hard core' theoretical knowledge redistributed generally with an 'ex cathedra' approach and lack of practical work. Bologna reforms demanded the unification of educational systems on the basis of European Credit Transfer and Accumulation System (ECTS) credits and higher mobility of students among institutions, with mutual recognition of knowledge and skills gained at other institutions.

The main time-frame for the implementation of these reforms of national practices was a target date in 2010, and states quickly started to prepare the necessary legal foundations. However, one is not allowed to forget that Central and Eastern European Countries were at that time, and still are today, transitional countries or at least not consolidated democracies in terms of a needed time-span to gain traditions in democratic procedures and principles. In order to change one of the most important structures of the state ideological apparatus (see Althusser 2008), the transitional period was inappropriately short. This can be especially true for ideologically divided states such as Slovenia, where cleavages concerning the Second World War and communist past are still very lively. However, in a context of ideologically divided politics, a relatively small number of private higher education institutions, and a fresh EU membership, the Bologna reforms started.

In the pre-transition era, trust was mostly mirrored in political compatibility between political actors and non-political actors. In this situation we can hardly speak about trust at all. A more appropriate term would be 'political loyalty'. Division of the politically loyal and their opponents was the basis for mutual trust, and can be understood in this manner as personal trust, due to constant monitoring of relationships and the possibility that trust could be lost due to indirect reasons such as criticism of the political regime. Despite change in the political regime after the fall of socialism/communism, there was no significant change in trust patterns: the old personal trust and system of personal networks still prevailed. Only the importance of political loyalty was diminished. This is evident in the ability of many individuals who 'changed' their political views yet still kept or gained important positions in higher education networks as members of different expert committees for national agencies in the field of higher education, research, and culture. It seems that the first important element in trust relations in Slovenian higher education sphere was the introduction of the Bologna reform.

CHANGES AFTER THE BOLOGNA REFORM

The Bologna reform caused a new, or in some cases like Slovenia the first, wave of privatization and liberalization of the higher education space. New higher education institutions were established, mostly as private faculties, with only one public exception so far in Slovenia. Before 2004, few faculties were established or developed from colleges (post-secondary level between public school and university faculties) and later on amalgamated into a third public university. By 2004 in Slovenia, a few circumstances were created that changed this picture. First, Slovenia entered the European Union, requiring it to reform the higher education system. Second, the autumn national elections changed the political profile of government from a 12-year left-wing coalition to a right-wing coalition. This caused serious changes in public administration and government agencies and ministries. Even though higher education legislation was not substantially changed, these developments changed the reading of the legal framework by the new government and higher civil servants, most of whom were educated on public universities but their political ties to a left-wing majority in academia were much weaker. They were much more open to new ideas and attempts to decentralize higher education by establishing institutions fulfilling minimal legal demands. Decentralization was rather intense.

Two new universities were established, next to the three state and one private from the pre-2004 period, and about 20 different post-secondary academies (mostly arts) and colleges. With one exception, all newly established institutions are private and spread all over the country, while previously they were mainly present in the four major urban centres of Ljubljana, Maribor, Koper, and Nova Gorica. Ljubljana University, as the oldest and biggest, has 26 faculties and almost 60,000 students, with an annual national population of students around 114,000 in the time-period between 2004 and 2008. The second largest is the University of Maribor with 18 faculties and approximately 23,000 students. Together these universities have more than 70 per cent of the nation's students and about 80 to 90 per cent of the study programmes (Statistični urad Republika Slovenije 2009). Because of their size they have a strong negotiating position, and with a third state university contributing some additional percentage, one can see the extent of higher education centralization in Slovenia, supported by a continuity of political elite and a system of personal bonds with people in governmental agencies.

TRUST AT STAKE?

The reforms mentioned earlier caused changes in expected activities. If previously, different attempts to create new, usually private, faculties were relatively successfully blocked or postponed by governmental agencies due to pressure from public universities and faculties (usually from scientific fields), the change of governing coalitions and senior civil servants brought substantial transformation to policy implementation. (Here we are not referring in one way or another about the quality of 'old' and 'new' higher education institutions.) Where before a public faculty was able to prevent or postpone the upgrading of a public college to faculty status (even if formal conditions were fulfilled) and both organizations were members of the same public university, after the Bologna reform such practices were increasingly less effective. Or better, if such practices were possible within the public university, they were not possible for organizations that acted as independent public/private institutions. This increased the possibilities for potentially new higher education institutions to become recognized by the state without effective political suppression carried out by institutions with a longer tradition.

We can analyse these activities through the trust model in Table 11.1. Previously (pre-reform), relationships on the institutional level also became ones of personal trust through friendship, due to long-term contact between individuals representing their respective organizations, where institutional activities gained mutual legitimacy by serving each others' institutional and personal interests. After the Bologna reform began, new forms of behaviour, sometimes as the result of a change in institutional representatives (mainly on the government side), caused a lowering of personal trust on the individual level, causing a reformalization of relations back to institutional behaviour, where individuals are not important in any manner other than as representatives of their organizations. At the same time, in the sphere of personal trust connected to institutional behaviour, the legitimacy of some organizations dropped due to a change in the interests of previously important actors. However, the same situation also meant a return to the rule of law, where situations are managed equally, causing institutions (especially government agencies) to perform activities according to legal principle rather than by recognizing legitimacies claimed by long-present actors in the policy network.

In 2008, the ruling coalition turned back to a left-wing government, causing the higher education policy network to change yet again, this time in the direction of pre-2004 relationships where public universities had a higher level of influence on policy implementation. Due to the relatively short period of the intervening political coalition, the old dominance of public universities was re-established, blocking one of the previously mentioned private universities and accreditation of new higher education institutions and programmes that were not developed in the framework of public universities.

The last case demonstrating the influence of public universities is the draft university legislation that was submitted to public debate only a few weeks after the national election in 2008. If we concentrate on trust/power relations only in analysing this document, prepared by the informal rectors' conference of Ljubljana, Maribor, Primorska, and Nova Gorica universities, we can find indications of the predominance of public universities (Delovna Skupina rektorske konference 2008).

The first element in the framework was an attack on the higher education act with the intent of splitting universities and other higher education organizations into two separate systems on the basis of programme differentiation. According to the draft, all higher education organizations not included as universities would not be able to teach 'university' but only 'college' programmes. This would impose a strong limiting factor on private faculties, causing them to abandon university programmes (which are more demanding than college ones). In addition, existing public universities demand their exclusion from the public sector system but simultaneously insist on retaining public financing for themselves.[1] The same draft proposes that existing universities be required to give consent to newly established ones. At the same time, a newly established agency for higher education quality would control the new organizations to ensure that they meet a number of criteria: appropriate infrastructure (classrooms, laboratories, libraries with 50,000 titles, etc.); conduct research in at least five major OECD recognized FRASCATI disciplines; have at least 100 professors and other teaching staff; and at least 1,500 students (1,000 being full time). Other criteria are connected to the quality of work and are not important for our purposes here because there is no significant difference in the quality of employees.

Conducting research in five out of six major FRASCATI fields automatically eliminates the possibility of being recognized for small universities oriented in one or a few fields. Only Ljubljana, Maribor, and Primorska universities have the capacity to fulfill this criterion, effectively blocking the formal chances of any others because most of the newly established institutions systematically concentrate on social sciences and natural sciences while more or less leaving other areas aside. In addition, providing such infrastructure can be an additional burden for private institutions because they rent rather than own their buildings, in contrast to established universities that have their own buildings constructed under the communist regime, setting an additional unfair condition for new universities.

A third difference is that the majority of teaching staff at new universities are on contract for lecturing and co-operating in research projects, making it difficult for them to employ at least 100 professors and other teaching staff due to the employment expenses On the other hand, public universities have guaranteed payment for teaching staff from the state budget.

Finally, 1,500 students, with 1,000 of them regularly enrolled[2] is another barrier making it impossible for newly established institutions to structurally create universities rather than existing as loosely connected independent faculties and colleges. Even Nova Gorica University is only halfway towards fulfilling this criterion with about 800 students in 2008–2009. These targets would not be reached for decades.

There are also some quality criteria that are less problematic, due to the need to provide an appropriate level of quality that really should be the main criterion for establishing any new university. While the draft act describes these features in more detail, the description here is sufficient to see what the rectors' conference initial idea was in blocking any attempt to establish new universities that would remain focused in one or a few particular areas, with no intent of becoming so-called 'higher education mastodons' (a relatively common Slovenian description for oversized and inflexible systems blocked in development by their own characteristics) with a few thousand employees, more than tens of thousands of students, and no flexibility in organizational management.

This draft act did create panic among many independent faculties and colleges, not only because of the proposed conditions for university establishment, but also because three to four major actors in the policy network tried to degrade their efforts through simply prohibiting the use of common programme names like 'university'. Consequently, the intent seems to be to degrade the educational level achieved at such institutions, and it opens the possibility of disputing the right to conduct master's and doctoral-level studies. Under such circumstances, no development of Slovenian higher education is possible, due to the possible greed of the three institutions holding 90 per cent of students and their fear that more flexible and smaller institutions will take over their students (and also part of their funding), due to smaller study groups and more applicable knowledge.

Under such circumstances there is no possibility for institutional co-operation, or institutional trust, due to the fear from particular interests involved in redefining the public interest for better higher education in order to protect existing study programmes. This is done even in cases where it has been proven that students with such degrees hardly ever find jobs (and almost never in the field of their study). Such conditions in the policy network are leading to a polarization of the higher education sphere in line with a left/right political cleavage and, in the case of Slovenia, to ideological differences inherited from the communist past. This kind of politicization, despite originating in a lack of support for higher education decentralization, can certainly affect possibilities for co-operation required for quality research and the overall quality of knowledge. They will become burdened with political views and affected negatively by a redistribution of public money available for national research grants. Policy and research arenas can become, from this perspective, in part political arenas that will cause a drop in Slovenian knowledge quality in world rankings.

In order to prevent this, there is a strong need to reshape the higher education system by splitting big state universities into normal size and carrying out power decentralization in order to open policy networks to become modern issue networks, instead of remaining at the level of captured statism. For example, Ljubljana University could be divided into three universities, one each for social sciences, natural sciences, and humanities. Such ideas emerge every few years, but so far there has been no significant effort to apply them. After the mid-term period of the government in power, one can expect that old personal trust–based relationships will be transformed into institutional trust–based relationships, where power of any particular interest group will be weak enough to be blocked by others if they do not serve the broader interest.

REASONS FOR POLICY NETWORK CHANGES

When talking about changes in higher education networks and consequent changes in policy trust, we have to answer questions about why the trust was at stake and what the real reasons for all changes in relationships are. Roughly about 5 per cent of the Slovenian population is enrolled in higher education. In other words, the enrolment is consistently more than 110,000 students at any one time in the last decade (Statistični urad Republika Slovenije 2009). Previously, students had no real opportunity to choose: they could only go to Ljubljana or Maribor universities. Since 2003 they could enrol at Primorska University, and in 2006 University of Gorica was established (they have a few years longer tradition as independent faculties that were merged together). During this period, 70 to 80 per cent of the student population was enrolled at major universities (Statistični urad Republika Slovenije 2009), publicly financed for conducting studies and research via research grants.

However, faculties from overlapping educational programme and research areas have been competing for the same monies. The argument that competition occurs between research groups even within individual faculties is valid—it is not unusual for a faculty in Ljubljana University to have more than 3,000 students, 200 employees, and more than 20 different research groups (University of Ljubljana 2009). With no understanding of such internal competition or even rivalry, project documentation is signed by the university rector, research group leader, and leading researcher of the project. Such bureaucratization is a strong obstacle to effective project work. On the other hand, *ex cathedra* lectures, usually attended by over 400 students, do not provide an individual approach or manage knowledge acquisition in forms most suitable for students. Since the Bologna reform, the number of students registered influences the size of budget made available. The state is setting limits to enrolment quotas, but 20 students instead of 40 students provide much less money.

In such conditions, the state, under the pressure of political change, liberalizes access to the higher education arena. A number of small and relatively flexible faculties have been established with a clear vision of decentralizing higher education opportunities and providing a high level of qualitative knowledge based on research (although such liberalization is also producing free riders who are trying to make additional money making the process ambivalent).

These institutions have the legal ability to apply for the same research grants as main public universities. However, their administrative flexibility and dependence on non-grant money is adding an additional motivation to systematically apply for grants previously belonging only to the four major research institutions. From an institutional point of view, grant funds were not so decentralized because research groups were still only part of the older universities. The emergence of new institutions has caused significant decentralization and a net loss of money for major organizations. Due to the inability to rearrange the institutional framework of public universities without losing key positions in networks and money, the only possibility that was available was to use trusted peers in state agencies in order to keep established patterns of work. However, politically caused changes in government agencies resulted in less effectiveness of such lobbying.

Recognition of this situation caused a lowering of the personal trust level in established informal networks. It also initiated additional efforts to block the decentralization of the higher education system, usually under the masque of claimed lower quality of newly established organizations, despite national measures of research quality demonstrating that their research groups can compete equally (see Table 11.2).

Table 11.2 describes points awarded to selected research groups active in main social science areas (as is evident, some institutions have more, some only one, not all research groups for FSS are included). Additionally, another 100 similar research groups could be included but the results would not differ significantly. Among 12 different research groups from higher education organizations, we see that four were established after 2005, each of which has one active research group. There are, however, eight research groups from two major universities and one private college established prior to 2005.

No matter which indicator we select, we can see that the output of newly established research groups is not systematically worse than those that have been operating much longer. It is obvious that scientific output per group member is even better in newly established research groups—75 per cent of new research groups are in the first half among chosen research groups. If we use as a measure quality and recognition of research work (measured by cited articles in the Web of Science index), we can see that the first and last three research groups belong to the group of pre-2005 established organizations while younger research groups are located in the middle ranking. And if we try to rearrange research groups by individual researcher with greatest output we can see again that 75 per cent of new research groups are in the first half of the rankings, with both longer active and newer researchers participating. If one were to analyse all 797 research institutions in

Table 11.2   Major Research Groups by Main National Quality Indicators (as of 2 August 2009)

Institution/Research Group	Number of Researchers	Points	Points/ Researcher	Leading Researcher Points	Citiations	Citations/ Researcher	Period of Establishment
Faculty of Organizational Studies	3	1332	444,00	692	1	0,33	2008
University & Research centre Novo Mesto	4	1763	440,75	941	9	2,25	2006
UL FSS* Centre for Political Research	16	7006	437,88	927	4	0,25	Pre-2005
UL FSS Centre Theoretical Sociology	2	711	355,50	501	14	7,00	Pre-2005
UL FSS-Centre Critical Political Science	8	1847	230,88	580	1	0,13	Pre-2005
Faculty of Applied Social Studies	19	3351	176,37	941	23	1,21	2006
UL Faculty of Economics	154	24278	157,65	970	242	1,57	Pre-2005
Umb* Faculty of Organization	53	8164	154,04	548	323	6,09	Pre-2005
UL Faculty of Public Administration	40	5780	144,50	789	124	3,10	Pre-2005
School of Business & Management Novo Mesto	14	1940	138,57	410	0	0,00	Pre-2005
International Faculty for Business and Social Studies	17	2173	127,82	388	25	1,47	2006
UL FSS Centre for Evaluation & Strategic Research	3	320	106,67	135	4	1,33	Pre-2005

From <http://sicris.izum.si/default.aspx?lang=eng> (Izum 2009).
* UL FSS—University of Ljubljana, Faculty of Social Sciences; UMb—University of Maribor.
** Points are automatically awarded to all bibliographic units, added to research group if author is member of research group. They are defined by the Research Agency, Republic of Slovenia, and cannot be changed by any other institution. Different types have a different number of points awarded. Citations: number of citations in Web of Sciences without autocitations. All data is for 2004–2009. Decimal points are not taken into account.

Slovenia, with approximately 1,500 research groups, one would find the newly established groups and/or institutions ranked even higher (in relative terms) by national indicators. Using this qualitative picture of research grant criteria, it is obvious that the older groups are under pressure, contributing to the attempts of the policy network to limit the participation of independent higher education organizations.

CONCLUDING REMARKS

Trust in the higher education policy arena is, like all relationships, one of the most important factors in making the whole system operate in a predictable way. Trust can be institutionalized via legal requirements, or can be based on predictable co-operative interpersonal relations. Even though difficult to measure, trust is an element that influences policy output and outcomes. If there is no appropriate mutual trust in policy networks, networks can become closed through minor actors opting out or effectively being marginalized from policy influence. However, changes can be made in the policy environment that can lead to a transformation of network characteristics, supportive of establishing better trusting relationships.

The Slovenian case shows that in the case of higher education there were strong connections between governmental and non-governmental actors that had been stable for a long period of time, creating a relatively closed network that excluded new actors or even had not allowed them to form. This created strong trust relationships based primarily on personal relationships among organizational representatives rather than formal legal relations. With the recent change in the political arena, the old policy network was deconstructed, causing a decrease in trust among the old policy actors while new ones were able to rely mostly on institutionally conditioned legal trust.

When analysing the role of trust in the development of a higher education system, we should first determine the kind of trust, and desirable forms, one is using. As demonstrated earlier, in the development of policy, in this case of higher education, not all kinds of trust are equally valuable and they certainly have different characteristics. The form of trust is related to the previous level of policy issue development and of socio-demographic factors of the environment in which the policy will be implemented. In an environment where the population is relatively small, and all relevant actors know each other, there is much more space for personal trust based on friendship to develop that results in reciprocating favours, especially if the network is relatively closed to new actors. On the other hand, barriers can reduce intense personal relationships of trust that can allow for the network to be opened to new actors under the conditions for participation established in new legislation.

NOTES

1. In Slovenia, private faculties cannot teach university programmes, only at the college level. 'University programme' refers to the undergraduate level delivered by a faculty (which can be a member of any university or a public or private independent one), and such programmes are usually more theoretical and demanding. On the other hand, college programmes can be delivered by public or private faculties whether a university member or not, or by colleges. College programmes are usually more practically oriented and understood to be less demanding. As well, 'university' or 'college programme' refers to the level of education and the basic payment coefficients. There are coefficients dictating the rate of hourly wage based on level of education attained. Public universities are part of the public sector, and, as such, have their salaries regulated by law, where private higher education organizations can pay their teachers as they want, more or less. Public universities are trying to opt out of the public sector in order to operate more independently financially (as long as they are part of the public sector they are responsible to Audit Court and other financial institutions supervising the national budget). Private organizations are responsible only when using public monies for projects, et cetera. Public universities want greater financial freedom, but still demand the privilege of complete public financing.
2. There are two regimes. Regular enrolment is full-time study, while the other is most comparable to part-time study, where students have shorter extensions of lectures and other study activities. This latter type is generally designed for those who want to study while employed, but is widely misused by those who are not able to enrol regularly but are willing to pay tuition fees.

REFERENCES

Althusser, L. (2008) *On Ideology*. London: Verso.
Cvetkovich, G., and Löfstedt, R.E. (1999) 'Introduction'. In *Social Trust and the Management of Risk*, ed. G. Cvetkovich and R.E. Löfstedt. London: Earthscan Publications.
Delovna skupina rektorske konference RS. (2008) *Delovni osnutek zakona o univerzi*. Online. Available HTTP: http://www.uni-mb.si/dokument.aspx?id=13628 (accessed 2 August 2009).
Eisenstadt, S.N., and Roniger, L. (1984) *Patrons, Clients and Friends: Interpersonal Relations and the Structure of Trust in Society*. Cambridge: Cambridge University Press.
IZUM. (2009) SICRIS. Online. Available HTTP: http://sicris.izum.si/default.aspx?lang=eng (accessed 2 August 2009).
Kickert, W.J.M., Kljin E.-H., and Koppenjan J.F.M. (eds.) (1997) *Managing Complex Networks: Strategies for the Public Sector*. London: Sage.
Statistični urad Republika Slovenije (Statistical Office of Republic of Slovenia). (2009) 'Izobraževanje'. Online. Available HTTP: http://www.stat.si (accessed 2 August 2009).
University of Ljubljana. (2009) 'Univerza v številkah'. Online. Available HTTP: http://www.uni-lj.si/o_univerzi_v_ljubljani/univerza_v_stevilkah.aspx (accessed 2 August 2009).
Van Waarden, F. (1992) 'Dimensions and types of policy networks'. *European Journal of Political Research* 21:29–52.

12 Personalization
The Individual, Trust, and Education in a Neo-Liberal World

Helen M. Gunter, Stephen Rogers, and Charlotte Woods

'Trust' is presented by Tilly as a relational process through which agency and structure interplay:

> Trust consists of placing valued outcomes at risk to others' malfeasance, mistakes or failures. Trust relationships include those in which people regularly take such risks. Although some trust relationships remain purely dyadic, for the most part they operate within larger networks of similar relationships. Trust networks, then, consist of *ramified interpersonal connections, consisting mainly of strong ties, within which people set valued, consequential, long-term resources and enterprises at risk to the malfeasance, mistakes, failures of others.* (2005: 12; author emphasis)

This focus on the interconnections between people who may not be genetically or legally bound to each other is at the core of how people have sought to develop ways in which to live together. As O'Neill (2002) argues, we 'place our trust' in individuals and institutions, and even if opinion polls continue to show that we do not trust politicians and big business as much these days, we continue to act as if we do through the use of public and purchasing private services. This interrelationship between the individual and the state is central to matters of trust. Tilly identifies a continuum between 'indirect integration,' where trust networks such as religious organizations and trade unions engage in bargaining with the state regarding the borderline between private and public interests, and 'direct integration' (2005: 7), where trust networks are formally connected with government, for example, welfare systems that assimilate everyone. It is the location of trust within the relationship between the private interests of the individual and the public interests of the collective that this chapter will focus on, with a particular emphasis on radical reforms to public sector education over the past 30 years in England. In particular, we examine the shift from a social democratic settlement towards the adoption of neo-liberal ideas that have underpinned recent radical reforms that are based on different assumptions of trust.

England has experienced the breakdown of a post-war social democratic settlement where integration of the private with the public through social welfare, public education, health and key services (e.g. transport), and industries (e.g. coal) was strong and based on notions of the public good and equity of access. We call this the 'social democratic trust network'. Risk was pooled through the common good, with agreed areas of public life that were treated as non-negotiable through a social and socializing contract that all would fund and could access. However, this 'settlement' was not settled, leaving it open to ongoing questions regarding concerns over national economic decline and how state services could respond to an increasingly diverse society. The solutions promoted by and pragmatically implemented by successive Thatcher governments from 1979 was through markets and consumerism entering into the provision of public services. This included the sale of public assets, outsourcing of services, and cultural changes to eradicate dependency through the promotion of the active consumer. We call this the 'neo-liberal trust network'. Here risk is about reliance on the self in relation with others. It is a question of 'buyer beware' where all is open for individual negotiation through negotiated contracts. In education, this neo-liberal trust network has manifested itself in a range of changes to structures and cultures where practice as a taxpayer, a parent, a student, and a professional has seen a shift towards marketized norms and expectations variously as funders, contractors, choosers, and deliverers.

We intend to examine the emergence of this neo-liberal trust network by focusing on New Labour from 1997 which has launched a 'modernization' of the state and public services. Notably, New Labour both continued the neo-liberal project through the privatization of education (Ball 2007) and sought to rework the sediments and deeply embedded Labour Party values from the social democratic trust network through reworking citizenship. As Ozga states, 'the development of active citizens is dependent on raising their levels of capacity to be receptive to information, to engage with evidence and to participate in networks, particularly among groups excluded by the inequitable operation of the market' (2002: 322). Consequently, New Labour has promoted 'personalization' as a means by which the relationship between trust networks (e.g. families, communities, professional groups, and networks of organizations) and the state have been reworked. Through an examination of this development in relation to education and schools we intend to examine the impact of personalization on those who are located in pivotal positions in education (e.g. head teachers) and the issues involved in handling contradictions and tensions that arise through conflicting policies. We are interested in uncovering what it means to be trusted and not trusted in the reform process. We begin by focusing on the construction of the personalization agenda and then examine what this means for governance and the school.

PERSONALIZATION AS A POLICY STRATEGY

The reform of public services over the past 30 years has been premised on an end to the idea of 'big government' through the ascendancy of private interests. This has generated tensions and contradictions in connection with the degree and type of centralization and decentralization. Where under the Thatcher regimes of the 1980s and early 1990s the emphasis was on putting public services out to marketized and efficient delivery, New Labour continued this but with stronger regulation regarding the control of performance and outcomes. Whilst New Labour continued the market discourses of previous conservative government 'managerialism' (Clarke, Gewirtz, and McLaughlin 2000), it nevertheless attempted in its policy texts to defend public services, introducing a language of modernization that incorporated notions of social justice, accountability, democratic control, and partnerships (Newman 2001). For New Labour, the three key challenges facing public service reform are 'equity and excellence', 'flexibility and accountability', and 'universality and personalization' (Blair 2003; Miliband 2006). Thinking and literature from the business community have been very important in their discourse with secretary of state, David Blunkett, using Bobbitt's (2002) market state to support his thinking (Tomlinson 2005), and education minister, David Miliband (2006), quoting Hirschman (1970) and Prahalad and Ramaswamy's (2000) use of the term 'personalization' to argue for a much more radical notion of individual involvement in the organization and creation of business than customization would suggest. Therefore, in a 2006 discussion paper on public service reform, New Labour put emphasis on how public investment had to secure tangible results, with a combination of top-down performance management through targets and a 'self-improving' system through bottom-up choice and demand from 'users shaping the service from below' (Prime Minister's Strategy Unit 2006). Children as users should therefore have a direct role in shaping education through what the government called 'personalization'.

Following David Miliband's (2004) North of England speech, the Department for Education and Skills (DfES) published a pamphlet that launched a 'conversation' with education professionals about an 'idea' the department claimed is 'capturing the imagination of teacher children and young people across the country' (DfES 2004b: 3). Personalized learning is defined as: 'building the organisation of schooling around the needs, interests and aptitudes of individual pupils; it means shaping teaching around the way different youngsters learn; it means taking the care to nurture the unique talents of every pupil' (Miliband 2004: 3). Miliband goes on to say that what this means is: first, the use of data within assessment for learning so that progress and planning go hand-in-hand for each student; second, teaching and learning strategies are focused on and respond to individual learning needs; third, curriculum choice with pathways made clear for the learner; fourth, the organization of the school around learner needs with the deployment of staff to support opportunities for children to have a voice in school improvement; and fifth, strong partnerships beyond the school with parents and the community. Emphasis was put on what it is not. So personalization is not, for instance, 'individualised learning', 'sitting alone at a computer', 'pupils left to their own devices' (Miliband 2004: 3). One senior official, David Hopkins, argued that personalization is not a move away from the standards agenda, and 'neither is it a return to child-centred theories or letting pupils coast along at their own pace or an abandonment of the national curriculum' (National College for School Leadership [NCSL] 2004: 8).

The importance of personalization in bringing about change is clear in the *Five Year Strategy for Children and Learners* where the then secretary of state for education, Charles Clarke, wrote that 'personalization' would be a 'central characteristic' of a 'new system' in education (DfES 2004a: foreword). The central position of personalized learning has been reinforced by subsequent documents:

> The distinctive feature of the pedagogy of personalisation is the way it expects all pupils to reach or exceed expectations, fulfil early promise and develop latent potential. Personalised lessons are stretching for everyone. At the heart of personalisation is the expectation of participation, fulfilment and success. The hallmarks are ambitious objectives, challenging personal targets, rapid intervention to keep pupils on trajectory, and vigorous assessment to check and maintain progress. There are clear plans to support those who do not or cannot maintain trajectory.
> (Department for Children, Schools and Families [DCSF] 2007: 64)

Here the emphasis is on the student as active learner, where the government presents itself as being tough on the expectations and delivery of learning outcomes. Professionals are the local deliverers, and the risk-taking of trusting teachers is managed by central government taking a lead role in both establishing and controlling the process and measurement of impact. There is a consistency in the message, where personalized learning remains a feature of ministerial speeches (e.g. Knight 2007a, 2007b) and in the restructured DfES (currently DCSF) personalized teaching and learning is seen not as 'something that will be nice to have, rather it is an essential component of modern education—what every parent wants and what every child deserves' (Knight 2007a: 2). By 2009, the secretary of state for education, Ed Balls, declared that: 'Many schools already offer a genuinely personalised learning experience for their pupils and succeed both in improving standards and in supporting their children's development in the round' (DCSF 2008: foreword). For the department the 'task' is to bring all schools up to the level of these 'great schools'.

Personalization has not just remained a feature of political rhetoric but an explosion of interest was generated with an international seminar in May 2004 (reported in Organization for Economic Co-operation and Development [OECD] 2006). This drew in Non-Departmental Public Bodies (NDPBs) and 'licensed thinkers' such as The Innovation Unit,[1] DEMOS,[2] the NCSL (NCSL 2005),[3] the Specialist Schools Trust,[4] and the Teaching and Learning Research Programme[5] to debate the issues of personalized learning and new directions for public services. Through the NCSL, personalization was heralded as 'the big idea for our time' (Fink 2005: 21) and by David Hopkins (then head of the DfES Standards and Effectiveness Unit) as a 'tremendously powerful concept' (Hopkins 2004: 7). The Institute for Public Policy Research,[6] many of whose researchers are or have been connected to New Labour ministerial teams, has also been very active in producing research and proposals for the future of public services that use the themes of personalization (Brooks 2007; Johnson 2004; Lewis 2007). The interplay of think-tanks, NDPBs, and consultants has brought ideas from business into the discourse (e.g. Leadbeater 2004, 2005). Dramatic techniques were used to demonstrate how change could and should happen (e.g. Leadbeater 2004), and drew on notions of the market and choice in the production of solutions. Often research into the brain (e.g. Bransford, Brown, and Cocking 2000) was used in order to justify the individualization of education (see DEMOS Learning Working Group 2004; Gilbert 2006). A 'thriving industry' (Guildberg 2004) emerged offering advice and guidance on 'how to do it' (e.g. Smith 2005; West-Burnham and Coates 2005). They have helped to translate and broker what to practitioners remained a vague, 'rather grand and possibly over-reaching' (Rudduck, Brown, and Hendy 2006: 35) if not 'incoherent and inchoate' (Hartley 2007: 529) policy drive.

The years 2004 and 2005 witnessed a flourishing of conversations to develop the concept of personalized learning within schools. Personalization was exhorted as central to reform, with policy declarations littered with references to it being 'nothing new', just something 'good teachers and good schools have always done' (DCSF 2007; DfES 2004a, 2004b, 2005, 2006; Gilbert 2006; Knight 2007a, 2007b; Miliband 2003). A series of initiative and keynote publications have been important in drawing together and making the message both coherent and achievable. First, David Miliband commissioned a Learning Working Group, co-ordinated by DEMOS, to consider the issue of learning, where they argued that while there is an abundance of ideas with 'a teaching profession actively engaged in innovation', the personalization 'will not flourish as it should unless everybody is clear about what it is that is being personalised' (DEMOS Learning Working Group 2004: 6). Second, during 2004 to 2005 Professor David Hargreaves (2004, 2006) held a series of conversations with about 250 school leaders in schools affiliated with the Specialist Schools Trust. He produced *Next Steps* guidance with nine 'gateways' to personalized learning, focusing on curriculum change and enhanced student voice. The 'gateways' are described as the content of personalization; however, Hargreaves argued that formal definition of personalization at this point should be avoided because 'we shall discover what personalisation is during the journey itself' (2004: 10). The gateways became clustered into four deeps: 'deep learning', 'deep-experience', 'deep leadership', and 'deep support' (Hargreaves 2007). Third, in addition to the practical professional support for teachers and school leaders, the government also wanted to move the debate forward, and the idea of personalization became associated with the notions of equity, and as such is proposed as a lever to raise standards for *all* pupils. The 2020 Review Group report explicitly stated this principle as: 'personalisation is a matter of moral purpose and social justice' (Gilbert 2006: 7). This review places 'personalising learning and teaching' at the heart of transforming secondary education. They again reiterate the need for innovation, knowledge creation, capture, and transfer across the system and refer to 'the journey'. At its most fundamental the review report believes personalizing learning (to which they add 'and teaching') 'means taking a highly structured approach to each child's and young person's learning, in order that all are able to progress, achieve and participate' (Gilbert 2006: 6). In this way, personal dispositions can change into the required attitudes, behaviours, and practices necessary to identify and articulate needs in order to be an active consumer of educational services. This can be secured in two ways. First, for children in school it means that the Children's Plan (DCSF 2007) will turn the Gilbert Review recommendation of 'learning guides' into academic coaches and personal tutors along with the advocacy of setting and group coaching. Therefore, the individual can demonstrate their choice orientation through individual relationships, and their needs can be met through the direct link between provision and demand. So, instead of children attending lessons based on a common timetable, there can be choices in addition to a core of literacy and numeracy about what is learned. Second, for children outside the system (such as non-attenders) services can be organized around their particular needs. This may involve multiagency work between educationalists with health and welfare services. Through the radical shake-up of existing educational structures implied in this understanding of personalization, Leadbeater argues that the 'scripts' of universal public service production and delivery can be changed so that the child can actively participate in control of their own learning. On one level users can improve their access but on a deeper level students would be 'co-producers and co-designers' of services, and so 'at the core there would still be a common script—the basic curriculum—but that script could branch out in many different ways, to have many different styles and endings' (2004: 12, 15).

PERSONALIZATION AS A POLICY EXPERIENCE

Our reading of this rapid and frenzied introduction of personalization in English education is that it is an example of a neo-liberal trust network where desegregated and fragmented relationships are based on permanent individualized negotiation in order to manage risk. While there are claims for social justice and equity, the emphasis is less on the collective as a means of securing this, and more on the individual as a brain, a consumer, and a self who has needs. The implications of this for schools is where we turn to next and we do this through relating the personalization agenda to the bigger picture of governance and interplay this with the localized situation of what it means for the education process.

We begin with the bigger picture of governance and we base this on Newman's four models as illustrated in Table 12.1:

We argue that the social democratic trust network that dominated the orientation and power processes in public services in England during the post–World War II period is illuminated by Models 1 and 4. In many ways, the state integrated people into a system of government based on shared risks with a trust in the system to provide in ways that are very Model 1 through top-down, legalistic mechanisms where stability and continuity were respected and required. Those within the system had goals of democratic development, where Model 4 based on opportunities for localized involvement and participation was seen as desirable. However, it was Model 1 that was the focus of attack from promoters of the neo-liberal trust network since such a model was regarded as too risky because power was in the hands of producers (such as educational professionals) who ran the system in their own interests (they could not be trusted with the education of the nation's children). The emphasis on procedures meant that children and parents did not get the education system they wanted. However, the strong regulatory demands of both the Thatcherite governments from 1979 (e.g. national curriculum, OfSTED inspections) and New Labour governments from 1997 (e.g. national standards, target setting, performance management) has meant that Model 1 has remained a powerful form of governance.

Models 2 and 3 were more attractive to neo-liberals because the emphasis was on the individual rather than the collective consensus-making integral to Model 4. In Model 2, the market could flourish with the opportunity

Table 12.1 Models of Governance

	Model 1	Model 2	Model 3	Model 4
Label	Hierarchy	Open Systems	Rational Goal	Self-Government
Orientation	Predictability Control Accountability	Networks Interaction Iterative	Maximization of Outputs Short-Term	Sustainability Civil Society Partnerships
Power	Top-Down Bureaucratic Legalistic	Fluid Interdependence Reciprocity	Managerial Contractual Delivery	Democracy Co-Production Responsibility
Change	Continuity Change Is Slow	Action Experimentation Responsiveness	Targets Incentives Measurement	Citizens and Communities as Agents of Change

Source: adapted from Newman (2001: 33–37).

for power brokers to control production and delivery, and so trust is based on the commercial exchange of capital and contracts. Concerns over basic morality, that is, core values and basic skills that are human capital requirements for the economy, meant that Model 3 was also attractive to some neo-liberals as it enabled formalized systems to be put in place to ensure that those who may not normally be trusted could, and would, comply or face contractual termination. Overall, Bobbitt presents arguments that the nation-state, based on Model 1 and potentially on Model 4, is no longer relevant for the world and indeed is dysfunctional in creating the problems that the state is seeking to resolve. Hence, the integration of the individual into the social democratic trust network is a mistake because the state cannot be trusted to deliver, not least because the options are limited—if one breaks the law one is coerced. The market state is more akin to Model 2 because it 'exists to maximise the opportunities enjoyed by all members of society' and it engages with Model 3 because 'the market state pursues its objectives by incentive structures and sometimes draconian penalties . . . to prevent the social instability that threatens material well-being' (Bobbitt 2002: 229). Here the state needs to enable economic production through safe money but does not actually do the production. However, the endurance and indeed strengthening of Model 1 forms of governance along with the emergence and overlaying of Models 2 and 3 have produced contradictions and tensions within the system.

Newman argues that governments tend to operate across all four models, and certainly New Labour has done this in ways that create incoherence and systemic stress:

> The initiatives linked to Labour's modernisation programme tend to draw on a mix of approaches—delegation *and* central control, long-term capacity building *and* short-term targets—producing tensions in the process of institutional change. The most significant lines of tension arise between . . . maximising outputs (rational goal model) on the one hand and building sustainability (self-governance model) on the other since rational practices tend not to generate the inclusive and flexible approaches required to engage citizens and communities in the long term. For example, the enhancement of managerial power is not readily compatible with the devolution of power to associations and communities. A second major line of tension operates between the consolidation and continuity associated with hierarchy on the one hand, and the adaptive, dynamic and outward-orientated focus of the open systems approach. In the former, rules and procedures—how things are done—matter a great deal, while in the latter, fluidity, flexibility and experimentation are valued. The hierarchy model stresses proper procedures in order to ensure accountability, while the open system model works through fluid networks where accountability is hard to pin down. (2001: 37)

This complex interplay between different forms of governance is the context in which personalization was introduced into professional discourse and practice. This has had implications for the way schools are run and professionals both understand their work and go about their work. In approaching this we draw on Fielding's development of a fourfold typology of schools and link it with Newman's models of governance, as illustrated in Table 12.2:

We have extended Fielding's framework so that the ways emotional expression and trust might be experienced within human relations are made explicit. The personal aspect to being a member of a school community is variously conceptualized. At one extreme, it can be subjugated to the demands of a hierarchical system of governance which produces organizational bureaucracy (Type 1), while at the other it dominates purposes and practices where in order to operate in networks personal relationships are essential to making and sustaining interdependence (Type 2). The *impersonal* state (Model 1) or school (Type 1) is typical of the modernist construction of organization: one where rules and logic are the guiding principles. Here emotion is seen as inimical to reason and therefore counter to efficient progress towards organizational goals (Fineman 2000b; Soloman 2000); outward displays of emotion and personal connection are discouraged. Whereas the network (Model 2) and school (Type 2) as *affective community* is in Fielding's terms 'restorative', emphasizing personal relations above all else, even at the expense of the effective functional arrangements needed to adequately support learning.

Table 12.2 Trust and Schooling

	Type 1	Type 2	Type 3	Type 4
Newman's Models	Hierarchy	Open Systems	Rational Goal	Self-Governance
School Orientation	Impersonal Organization	Affective community	High Performing Learning Organization	Person-Centred Learning Community
Functional-Personal	The Functional Marginalizes the Personal	The Personal Marginalizes the Functional	Personal Used for the Sake of the Functional	Functional Used for the Sake of the Personal
Characteristic Mode	Efficient	Restorative	Effective	Morally and Instrumentally Successful
Emotional relations	Emotion under Control	Emotion given Free Rein	Emotion in Use	Emotion as Enabling
Trust	Trustless	Trusting	Trustworthy	Trusted
Personalization	Impersonal	Personal	Personalized	Participant

Source: adapted from Fielding (2006).

Where in Type 1 the person is a not-to-be-trusted cog in a machine, a scenario that the New Labour promoters of personalization have argued against for children in school, the other three types give recognition to various degrees of the relationship between agency and structure. In Type 2, children as agents in their own learning are those enabled to be trusting of others and to seek recognition for the personal aspects and emotional impacts of life through networking within and outside school. To be trustworthy means that others, normally elite adults both inside and outside school, inculcate a culture wherein they operate as rational agents by using incentives to build trust in children to produce the right type of learning outcomes in a high-performing school in Type 3. In Type 4, consensus-building is based on all who trust and are to be trusted with education of the self and the school community as they share a genuine, emotional commitment to it.

A key difference between human relations in school Types 3 and 4 is in terms of *authenticity*, for example, as glimpsed in a caring demeanour adopted as part of a professional role versus genuine caring. The theme of authenticity is one that resonates strongly with critical work on emotion in organizations via notions of 'emotional labour' and 'emotional intelligence'. The term 'emotional labour' refers to the dissonance that can be experienced in donning a professional mask in order to present an appropriate emotional face at work (Hochschild 1983). The concept of 'emotional intelligence' has become pervasive in business and education practice but has been roundly criticized as a covert means of manipulating individual emotion in the organizational interest (Fineman 2000a).

In a Type 3 school, in line with guidance on effective organizational practice, it might be imagined that pupils and staff would be encouraged to voice their opinions and feelings in respectful and emotionally mature ways, be consulted on important matters of policy, and be invited to discuss their learning and development frankly. School policies would be likely to emphasize the importance of establishing trust in creating an environment where organizational members feel secure enough to take the necessary risks involved in effective learning. This school would be experienced as a happy, harmonious, and inclusive school for most members most of the time, and the term *trustworthy* could be adopted to describe human relations. The commitment to trust and having open communication would be apt to be put under strain, however, where the needs of the individual student or staff member were at odds with those of the organization. Therefore, people would experience being personalized where their needs are identified in relation to an external policy agenda. The realization that feelings and opinions are to be tolerated only insofar as they coincide with the organizational interest might give rise to a reduction in trust and feelings of isolation or even betrayal. In the Type 4 school the more genuine nature of relations means that high levels of trust exist. In this context, emotions are viewed as natural and inevitable and as a means of signalling what organizational members care deeply about in order that these matters can be attended to in a purposive and enabling manner. To reflect this, in Table 12.2, people are described as *trusted*. The emphasis is not on doing personalization through systemic functional design, such as student councils or personal mentors, but on participating within a collective enterprise of learning.

While these four types of school are important ways to enable thinking, not least through generating different perspectives, we would argue that all four are potentially in play within a school at any one time. Head teachers and senior leaders will be simultaneously told and trained to do personalization and face the consequences of non-compliance (Model 1/Type 1), they will be drawn into networks to develop the ideas (Model 2/Type 2), they will be required to operate target setting and national standard performance management (Model 3/Type 3), and they may have a vision of the purposes of education that is about develop learning communities (Model 4/Type 4). Consequently, heads and school leadership teams are critical pivots within delivery of personalization as they have to juggle between, and reconcile, ever-increasing poles of tension (Newman 2001) such as audit and accountability, centralized strategy and local improvement, new localisms and extended services, the needs of service users, their own professional beliefs and credos, their staffs' well-being, and capacity to deliver. For the head, trust has to be negotiated with an increasing range of users and deliverers spread across imperatives and initiatives whose longevity is uncertain whilst maintaining a core trust in his/her professional vision. This brokering role is consistent with the remodelling of the school work-force where teachers and assistants teach and heads no longer have to be trained teachers (Butt and Gunter 2007), and with other parts of public services where, for example, social workers may be replaced by brokers who link people with needs to social care products (Beresford 2008).

Drawing on Raffo and Gunter (2008), we would argue that coherence for the professional has come through a common thread of functionalism within the New Labour reform strategy. The approach has been functional with the purposes of personalization being efficiency and effectiveness with narratives about access and the structuring of teaching to meet identified and measured needs. Consequently, the Gilbert Review provides the following definition: 'personalised learning and teaching means taking a highly structured and responsive approach to each child's and young person's learning, in order that all are able to progress, achieve and participate. It means strengthening the link between learning and teaching by engaging pupils—and their parents—as partners in learning' (2006: 6). So, the approach is to use technical data to describe and measure a child and then use this to predict outcomes and hence determine remedial action or developmental priorities. When a school is declared to be failing, then the response can be to move to Type 1, at least for the initial move out of special measures, and once things begin to improve, according to official measures and inspection, then the restorative qualities of Type 2 can be evidenced (see, for example, the stories of heads who have turned schools around, e.g. Stubbs 2003). While New Labour texts focus on citizenship, student voice, and equity, functionality takes over through performance targets with labels of people and organizations. The claims made about standards, human capital, and a flexible work-force often remain unproblematized and so the opportunities to develop schools like Model 4/Type 4 are lost. Consequently, the possibilities for a modernized social democratic trust network are marginalized, not least through how rights and responsibilities are not used as rationales for change. Again, following Raffo and Gunter (2008), this means that social critical awareness and activism are left underdeveloped. The notion of learning collectively, through and with others, forms no part of the neoliberal agenda, and while there are targeted projects that focus on emotional intelligence and the well-being of the child, the personal is an unexamined prism for service reform. While the language of social justice and equity is used in pro-personalization texts, it is not delivered in the reality of what is proposed, because what is outlined is a learner who is treated as an individual who has needs without conceptualizing others, and how in meeting those needs others might be advantaged or disadvantaged. Whereas in Type 3 schools the decision to pursue the government's personalization agenda might be underpinned by largely instrumental reasons such as improving test scores and league table position, in a Type 4 school the same agenda might be embraced in the belief that it is an effective means of meeting the individual and collective needs of children and in developing opportunities to extend rights and responsibilities.

SUMMARY

Recent reforms in Western-style democracies have been based on neo-liberal ideas located in arguments about the individual in control of their lives and work. For example, in England, attempts to locate trust in the collective and social practice of post-war public education failed, and the response to the demand for the state to recognize diversity and needs is through 'personalization', where the individual is able to exercise choice through the structures, cultures, and customer experience of services. Instead of membership in a school community, the student is conceptualized as a selector of options. Trust is located in negotiations about the personal and gambles over choices regarding the risk that the individual carries alone. The relationship between governance and policy as experienced at school level is complex and full of tensions and contradictions for those who are simultaneously trusted and not trusted to deliver changes in teaching and learning.

As we write, New Labour texts continue to present personalization; however, the energy and appetite for it amongst its promoters seems to have waned. Indeed, following David Miliband's departure from the education portfolio it is interesting to note that one of his successors, Ruth Kelly, thought the phrase to be 'jargon' (Slater 2005). David Hargreaves (Hansard 2008) went as far as to declare personalization 'well intentioned waffle'. In undertaking a scoping exercise for research, one of the authors of this chapter (Rogers 2009) reports that a head teacher who has lived through the reform programme states that the lack of conceptual clarity 'from the centre' represented a real lost opportunity to do some radical and far-reaching reform of schooling. After all, as Paludan states, there 'is something inherently redundant about the concept of personalised learning' (2006: 83) as it would be unlikely to find anyone disagreeing with it. It is seductive and difficult to argue against.

Our concluding comments are that much energy and political capital have been invested in personalization in education but our analysis demonstrates an irony in the relationship between trust and policy change: first, children as users of education have been spoken of and about in the reform texts and by the marketized industry that has rapidly grown, but there is little evidence of children actually being involved personally in devising the personalization agenda. They are expected to be trusted to operate in and to put their trust in a new personalized education system but they have not been trusted to co-produce it. Secondly, personalization is about enabling a more productive relationship between the active citizen and the enabling government, but the grounds on which change is based are highly problematic. It seems as if the state is giving the person as service user the right to have personalized services, yet the person as citizen has the right to be involved in life decisions that are *a priori* state jurisdiction under a democratic system. It seems as if the English state is trusting people with newly empowered lives—only if they learn and demonstrate the necessary responsibility and accountability—and yet democratic change should be based on how people have the right to make decisions, full stop. Third, and finally, marketization experts are involved in creating personalization as a way of restructuring and reculturing the relationship between the state and the public. Much is being claimed, not least how negotiating with brokers and being coached about our choices means that our 'self-esteem' can be boosted while simultaneously being used to revitalize a failing public sector. However, it is in the interests of the neo-liberal trust network to promote forms of economized personalization because it enables the deep market penetration of public services. As Hartley (2007) and Beresford (2008) have argued, personalization could be the means by which basic services for human capital is the residual public provision for all, and personalization is what is customized and purchased by the individual. People are being asked to trust a policy strategy that is in effect removing collective and universal services that as a society they have learned to trust. As we have argued, there is a need to examine the nature of governance, and how different ways of organizing the polity can have an impact on a public service such as a school. The contradictions and tensions experienced by educational professionals in handling the personalization agenda variously delivered through Models 1 to 3 are not in our view the means by which trust can be usefully and meaningfully debated and restored. We are arguing for a different type of public space, one that Fielding (2006) presents as Model 4 and regards as 'person centred', rooted in a humanistic dialogue and social respect.

NOTES

1. The Innovation Unit formed by the DfES in 2002 to promote innovation and spread 'good practice' is now an independent company, now working in partnership to commissions from government and third-sector organizations.
2. DEMOS is an independent think-tank describing themselves as the think-tank for 'everyday democracy'. Their aim is to put this idea into practice by working with organizations in ways that make them more effective and legitimate. One of their six policy areas is public services.
3. The NCSL was set up by New Labour in 2000 to commission and deliver leadership training for aspiring and serving leaders at middle, senior, and head teacher levels.
4. Specialist Schools Trust (since 2005 the Specialist Schools and Academies Trust) had its roots in the City Technology Colleges Trust founded 1987. Describes itself as the largest school network of its kind in the world and uses the motto 'by schools, for schools'.
5. Teaching and Learning Research Programme based at the Institute of Education, London. Teaching and Learning Programme is the UK Economic and Social Research Council's largest research programme and provides co-ordination for 700 researchers in some 70 project teams and almost 20 initiatives of cross-programme thematic analysis across the UK. Aims to promote high-quality research and evidence-based practice.
6. The Institute for Public Policy Research, formed in 1986, describes themselves as: the UK's leading progressive think tank, producing cutting edge research and innovative policy ideas for a just, democratic and sustainable world'.

REFERENCES

Ball, S.J. (2007) *Education Plc: Understanding Private Sector Participation in Public Sector Education*. London: Routledge.
Beresford, P. (2008) 'Whose personalisation?' *Soundings* 40 (1): 8–17.
Bobbitt, P. (2002) *The Shield of Achilles*. London: Penguin.
Blair, T. (2003) 'Prime Minister's speech to the Labour Party Conference'. Bournemouth, 30 September. Online. Available HTTP: http://www.guardian. co.uk/politics/2003/sep/30/labourconference.labour2 (accessed 17 August 2009).
Bransford, J.D., Brown, A.L., and Cocking, R.R. (eds.) (2000) *How People Learn: Brain, Mind, Experience, and School*. Washington, DC: National Academy Press.
Brooks, R. (ed.) (2007) *Public Services at the Crossroads*. London: Institute for Public Policy Research.
Butt, G., and Gunter, H.M. (eds.) (2007) *Modernizing Schools: People, Learning and Organizations*. London: Continuum.
Clarke, J., Gewirtz, S., and McLaughlin, E. (2000) *New Managerialism, New Welfare?* London: Sage.

DEMOS Learning Working Group. (2004) *About Learning. Report of the Learning Working Group*. London: DEMOS.
Department for Children, Schools and Families. (2007) *The Children's Plan: Building Brighter Futures*. Norwich: TSO.
——. (2008) *Personalised Learning*. Online. Available HTTP: http://www.standards.dfes.gov.uk/personalisedlearning/ (accessed 5 January 2008).
Department for Education and Skills. (2004a) *Five Year Strategy for Children and Learners*. Norwich: TSO.
——. (2004b) *A National Conversation about Personalised Learning*. Nottingham: DfES Publications.
——. (2005) *Higher Standards, Better Schools for All: More Choice for Parents and Pupils*. Norwich: TSO.
——. (2006) *The Five Year Strategy for Children and Learners: Maintaining the Excellent Progress*. Norwich: TSO.
Fielding, M. (2006) 'Leadership, radical student engagement and the necessity of person-centred education'. *International Journal of Leadership in Education* 9 (4): 299–313.
Fineman, S. (2000a) 'Commodifying the emotionally intelligent'. In *Emotion in Organizations*, ed. S. Fineman. London: Sage.
——. (2000b) 'Emotional areas revisited'. In *Emotion in Organizations*, ed. S. Fineman. London: Sage.
Fink, D. (2005) 'Growing into it'. In *Leading Personalised Learning in Schools: Helping Individuals Grow*, ed. National College for School Leadership. Nottingham: NCSL.
Gilbert, C. (2006) 'A vision for teaching and learning in 2020'. In *Report of the Teaching and Learning in 2020 Review Group*. Nottingham: DfES.
Guildberg, H. (2004) *Class Division: Who Benefits from the 'Personalised Learning' Strategy of Dividing School Pupils into Subsets?* Online. Available HTTP: http://www.spiked-online.co.uk/printable/0000000AGOE.htm (accessed 18 October 2007).
Hansard. (2008) *Uncorrected Transcript of Oral Evidence; Children Schools and Families Committee House of Commons*. Online. Available HTTP: http//www.publications.parliament.uk/pa/cm200708/cmselect/cmchilsch/uc651-vii/uc65102.htm (accessed 19 January 2009).
Hargreaves, D.H. (2004) *Personalising Learning: Next Steps in Working Laterally*. London: Specialist Schools and Academies Trust.
——. (2006) 'Personalising learning'. In *Booklets 1–6*. London: Specialist Schools and Academies Trust.
——. (2007) *System Redesign-1: The Road to Transformation in Education*. London: Specialist Schools and Academies Trust.
Hartley, D. (2007) 'Personalisation: The emerging "revised" code of education?' *Oxford Review of Education* 33 (5): 629–42.
Hirschman, A. (1970) *Exit, Voice and Loyalty: Responses to Decline in Firms, Organisations and States*. Cambridge, MA: Harvard University Press.
Hochschild, A.R. (1983) *The Managed Heart: The Commercialization of Human Feeling*. Berkeley: University of California Press.
Hopkins, D. (2004) 'Press for action'. In *Personalised Learning: Tailoring Learning Solutions for Every Pupil*, ed. National College for School Leadership. Nottingham: NCSL.
Johnson, M. (2004) *Personalised Learning: An Emperor's Outfit?* London: Institute for Public Policy Research.
Knight, J. (2007a) 'Launching resourcing personalised learning'. The Innovation Unit, London, 26 February. Online. Available HTTP: http://www.dfes.gov.uk/speeches/speech.cfm?speech ID=528 (accessed 29 August 2007).

————. (2007b) 'Personalised learning'. North of England speech by Jim Knight, Minister of Schools and Learners, Preston, 4 January. Online. Available HTTP: http://www.dfes.gov.uk/speeches/seach-detail.cfm?ID=469 (accessed 29 August 2007).

Leadbeater, C. (2004) *Learning about Personalisation? How Can We Put the Learner at the Heart of the Education System?* Nottingham: Department for Education and Skills and National College for School Leadership/Innovations Unit/DEMOS.

————. (2005) *The Shape of Things to Come: Personalised Learning through Collaboration.* Nottingham: Department for Education and Skills and National College for School Leadership.

Lewis, M. (2007) *States of Reason: Freedom, Responsibility and the Governing of Behaviour Change.* London: Institute for Public Policy Research.

Miliband, D. (2003) 'Teaching in the 21st century'. Speech delivered at North of England Education Conference, Warrington, January. Online. Available HTTP: http://www.dcsf.gov.uk/speeches/search_detail.cfm?ID=57 (accessed 17 August 2009).

————. (2004) 'Personalised learning: Building a new relationship with schools'. Speech delivered at North of England Education Conference, Belfast, January. Online. Available HTTP: http://www.dfes.gov.uk/speeches (accessed 10 May 2004).

————. (2006) 'Choice and voice in personalised learning'. In *Schooling for Tomorrow: Personalising Education*, ed. OECD. Paris: OECD.

National College for School Leadership. (2004) *Personalised Learning: Tailoring Learning Solutions for Every Pupil.* Nottingham: NCSL.

————. (2005) *Leading Personalised Learning in Schools: Helping Individuals Grow.* Nottingham: NCSL.

Newman, J. (2001) *Modernising Governance.* London: Sage.

O'Neill, O. (2002) 'Spreading suspicion'. Lecture 1 of the Reith Lectures, BBC Radio 4. Online. Available HTTP: http://www.bbc.co.uk/radio4/reith2002/lecture1.shtml (accessed 10 June 2009).

Organization for Economic Co-operation and Development. (2006) *Schooling for Tomorrow: Personalising Education.* Paris: OECD.

Ozga, J. (2002) 'Education governance in the United Kingdom: The modernization project'. *European Educational Research Journal* 1 (2): 331–41.

Paludan, J.P. (2006) 'Personalised learning 2025'. In *Schooling for Tomorrow: Personalising Education*, ed. OECD. Paris: OECD.

Prahalad, C.K., and Ramaswamy, V. (2000) 'Co-opting customer competence'. *Harvard Business Review* 78 (1): 79–87.

Prime Minister's Strategy Unit. (2006) *The UK Government's Approach to Public Service Reform: A Discussion Paper.* London: United Kingdom Cabinet Office.

Raffo, C., and Gunter, H.M. (2008) 'Leading schools to promote social inclusion: Developing a conceptual framework for analysing research, policy and practice'. *Journal of Education Policy* 23 (4): 363–80.

Rogers, S. (2009) 'Personalisation in education'. Paper presented to the Educational Policy and Leadership Network seminar, School of Education, University of Manchester.

Rudduck, J., Brown, N., and Hendy, L. (2006) *Personalised Learning and Pupil Voice: The East Sussex Project.* Nottingham: DfES/Innovation Unit.

Slater, J. (2005) 'Whither that old personal touch?' *Times Educational Supplement*, 1 April. Online. Available HTTP: http://www.tes.co.uk/article.aspx?storycode=2086461 (accessed 30 December 2007).

Smith, A. (2005) *The Future of Learning to Learn: Personalised Learning in Practice*. Bourne End: Alite.

Soloman, R.C. (2000) 'The philosophy of emotions'. In *Handbook of Emotions*, ed. M. Lewis and J.M. Haviland-Jones. New York: Guilford Press.

Stubbs, M. (2003) *Ahead of the Class*. London: John Murray.

Tilly, C. (2005) *Trust and Rule*. New York: Cambridge University Press.

Tomlinson, S. (2005) *Education in a Post Welfare Society*. Maidenhead: Open University Press.

West-Burnham, J., and Coates, M. (2005) *Personalizing Learning: Transforming Education for Every Child*. Stafford: Network Education Press.

Contributors

Richard Bates is Professor of Social and Administrative Studies in the Faculty of Education, Deakin University, Australia. His international reputation rests primarily on his contributions to the debate over the New Sociology of Education, on his work in developing an alternative 'cultural' tradition in Educational Administration, and on his contributions to Teacher Education. He has published some 70 papers and books as well as being on the editorial boards of numerous journals. Some of his recent publications are: 'Public Education, Social Justice and Teacher Education' (*Asia-Pacific Journal of Teacher Education* 2006), *Handbook of Teacher Education* (with Tony Townsend, Springer 2006), *Aesthetic Dimensions of Educational Administration and Leadership* (with E.A. Samier, Routledge 2006), 'Educational Administration and Social Justice' (*Education, Citizenship and Social Justice* 2006), 'Culture and Leadership in Educational Administration' (*Journal of Educational Administration and History* 2006), 'An Anarchy of Cultures' (*Asia-Pacific Journal of Teacher Education* 2005), 'On the Future of Teacher Education' (*Journal of Education for Teaching* 2005), 'Can We Live Together: Towards a Global Curriculum' (*Arts and Humanities in Higher Education* 2005), *The Bird that Sets Itself on Fire: Thom Greenfield and the Renewal of Educational Administration* (Althouse Press 2003), and 'Morals and Markets: Adam Smith's Moral Philosophy as a Foundation for Administrative Ethics', in *Ethical Foundations for Educational Administration*, ed. E.A. Samier (Routledge 2003). He is past president of the Australian Association for Educational Research, The Australian Council of Deans of Education and The Australian Teacher Education Association, and is a Fellow of the Australian Council for Educational Leaders and the Australian College of Educators.

Cheryl L. Bolton is a Senior Lecturer in education for the Institute for Education Policy Research at Staffordshire University, UK, where she manages and develops programmes in post-compulsory education. She has been an active principal co-investigator and researcher on decision heuristics with Fenwick W. English, which has led to papers at BELMAS and Division A of the American Education Research Association, as well as 'My Head and My Heart: De-Constructing the Historical/Hysterical Binary that Conceals and Reveals Emotion in Educational Leadership', in *Emotional Dimensions of Educational Administration and Leadership*, ed. E.A. Samier and M. Schmidt (Routledge 2009). Her current research interests include decision-making variables of leaders in educational institutions and agencies and altering aspects of the role of further education lecturers in the United Kingdom.

Fenwick W. English is currently the R. Wendell Eaves Senior Distinguished Professor of Educational Leadership in the School of Education at the University of North Carolina at Chapel Hill. As co-principal investigator with Cheryl L. Bolton, he served as senior author with her of 'An Exploration of Administrative Heuristics in the United States and the United Kingdom' (*Journal of School Leadership* 2008). His most recent publications include General Editor of the SAGE International Library of Educational Thought and Practice (2009) (4 volumes), *The Art of Educational Leadership* (Sage 2008) ,and the *Anatomy of Professional Practice: Promising Research Perspectives on Educational Leadership* (Rowman and Littlefield 2008). He is the former President of the University Council for Educational Administration, 2006–2007.

Marybeth Gasman is an Associate Professor of higher education at the University of Pennsylvania. In 2006, Dr. Gasman was awarded the Association for the Study of Higher Education's Promising Scholar/ Early Career Award for her scholarship. She was recently awarded the Penn Graduate School of Education Excellence in Teaching Award. Dr. Gasman is an historian of higher education. Her work explores issues pertaining to philanthropy and historically Black colleges, Black leadership, contemporary fund-raising issues at Black colleges, and African American giving. Dr. Gasman's most recent book is *Envisioning Black Colleges: A History of the United Negro College Fund*. She has published several other books, including *Charles S. Johnson: Leadership beyond the Veil in the Age of Jim Crow* (with Patrick J. Gilpin), *Supporting Alma Mater: Successful Strategies for Securing Funds from Black College Alumni* (with Sibby Anderson-Thompkins), *Uplifting a People: African American Philanthropy and Education* (with Kate Sedgwick), *Gender and Philanthropy: New Perspectives on Funding, Collaboration, and Assessment* (with Alice Ginsberg), *Understanding Minority Serving Institutions* (with Benjamin Baez and Caroline Turner), and *Philanthropy, Fundraising, and Volunteerism in Higher Education* (with Andrea Walton).

Cynthia Gerstl-Pepin is an Associate Professor and Chairperson of the Department of Education at the University of Vermont. Her scholarly research agenda seeks to expose submerged social justice issues in education via praxis, the intertwining of theory and practice. She is an interdisciplinary scholar who explores the social justice and epistemological implications concerning how social and cultural inequities have an impact on the research process and media representations of educational politics. Her work ranges from examining individual classroom practice to national school reform such as the No Child Left Behind Act. Her research reflects an interdisciplinary focus and involves studying communities external to the university as well as turning a critical eye to her own practice as a researcher, scholar, mentor, teacher, and colleague. Some of her recent publications include: 'Learning from Dumbledore's Pensieve: Metaphor as an Aid in Teaching Reflexivity in Qualitative Research', in the *Journal of Qualitative Research* (2009), 'Special Issue on the Media, Democracy, and the Politics of Education' (co-edited with V. Darleen Opfer), in the *Peabody Journal of Education* (2007), and 'The Paradox of Poverty Narratives: Educators Struggling with Children Left Behind', in *Educational Policy* (2006). She has also authored a book (with Catherine Marshall) entitled *Re-Framing Educational Politics for Social Justice* (2005) and published in such journals as *Teachers College Record*, *Equity & Excellence in Education*, *Review of Higher Education*, *Journal of Educational Administration*, and *Educational Foundations*.

Helen M. Gunter is Professor of Educational Policy, Leadership and Management in the School of Education, University of Manchester. Her main area of research is in knowledge production and New Labour education policy-making, with a particular emphasis on leadership. She has recently completed an ESRC funded project (RES-000–23–1192): Knowledge Production and Educational Leadership, which examined the relationship between the state, public policy, and knowledge. This was based on interviews with knowledge producers and users in government, private sector consultancies, universities, and schools. She has written on theory and leadership as a social and political practice, and her most recent books include: *Leading Teachers* (Continuum 2005) and, with Graham Butt, *Modernising Schools* (Continuum 2007).

Dominique E. Johnson is Assistant Professor of Law and Society in the School of Social Science and Human Services at Ramapo College, New Jersey. Her work has appeared in the *Journal of Curriculum and Pedagogy*, *Handbook of Social Foundations in Education* (with Catherine Lugg), *Children, Youth, and Environments*, and *Inclusion in Urban Educational Environments: Addressing Issues of Diversity, Equity, and Social Justice*. She previously received an American Educational Research Association Spencer Research Fellowship in Education and Adolescent Health and is currently an Associate Editor of the *Journal of LGBT Youth*.

Sheri R. Klein is a Professor of Art Education at the University of Wisconsin-Stout, Menomonie, WI, where she teaches undergraduate and graduate education courses. She earned a BFA and MFA in Painting from the School of the Art Institute of Chicago and a PhD in Curriculum and Instruction from Indiana University, Bloomington. She has published numerous articles in national and international education, curriculum, art education, and leadership journals (*Art Education, International Journal of Leadership in Education, Reflective Practice, Studies in Art Education*), and serves on the editorial boards for several journals. Her areas of scholarship cover aspects of art and design, teacher education, holistic education, and higher education issues that include leadership. She is a co-author of 'Aesthetic Leadership: Leaders as Architects' (with R. Diket), in *Aesthetic Dimensions of Educational Administration and Leadership*, ed. E.A. Samier and R. Bates (Routledge 2006). She is the editor of *Teaching Art in Context: Case Studies for Preservice Art Education* published in 2003 by the National Art Education Association. Her book *Art and Laughter* was published by I.B. Tauris in 2007. She has presented papers at National Art Education Association (NAEA), British Educational Leadership Management Administration Society (BELMAS), Southeastern College Art Association (SECAC), and International Society for Education in Art (INSEA). In addition to other scholarly work, she is also working on 'zines' about academia.

Stephanie Mackler is Assistant Professor of Education at Ursinus College. She is the author of *Learning for Meaning's Sake: Toward the Hermeneutic University* (Sense 2009). She has also published in *Educational Theory, Teachers College Record, Education Review, Philosophy of Education, Policy Futures in Education, Encyclopedia of Education and Human Development* (M.E. Sharpe 2005), and contributed 'Hermeneutic Leadership: Hannah Arendt and the Importance of Thinking What We are Doing', in *Political Approaches to Educational Administration and Leadership*, ed. E.A. Samier (Routledge 2008). She received her BA summa cum laude from Mount Holyoke College, and her PhD in Philosophy and Education from Teachers College of Columbia University where she was awarded a Spencer Dissertation Fellowship for her research. Her current scholarly work involves research in philosophical hermeneutics, liberal arts and teacher preparation, the philosophy of higher education, and philosophy as a way of living.

Séamus Mulryan is a doctoral candidate in Philosophy of Education at the University of Illinois at Urbana-Champaign and earned his MA in Philosophy and Education from Teachers College of Columbia University in 2005. His current studies are on the meaning, role, and cultivation of courage in dialogue and interpretation. He was the recipient of the 2008 Graduate Student Award by the Society for the Philosophical Study of

Education, a 2008 Love of Learning Award by the Honor Society of Phi Kappa Phi, and a 2008 William Chandler Bagley Doctoral Scholarship by the University of Illinois, College of Education. He has presented his work at the Philosophy of Education Society of Great Britain, the International Conference of Philosophy (Greece), the Society for the Philosophical Study of Education (US), the Philosophy of Education Society (Canada), and the American Educational Studies Association (US). His previous scholarship can be found in *Paideia: Education in the Global Era* (Ionia Publications), *Philosophy of Education 2009* (Philosophy of Education Society, forthcoming), *The Encyclopedia of Curriculum Studies* (Sage, forthcoming), and *Policy Futures in Education*.

Uroš Pinterič is Assistant Professor in political science, teaching courses on political systems, policy analysis, and public finances in the Faculty of Applied Social Studies in Nova Gorica, Slovenia. His major research interests are in public administration, local self-government, and e-governance. He earned his PhD in political science at the University of Ljubljana. Next to his academic work, he was heavily involved in the implementation of the Bologna reform by preparing new educational programmes at the BA, MA, and PhD levels. He has written several books (in Slovenian) about e-governance and municipal administration. His articles have been published in *Central European Political Science Review*, *The Public Manager*, *Lex Localis*, *Društvena iztraživanja*, and other national and international journals.

Stephen Rogers is National Director of the University of the Age, a national education charity founded by Professor Tim Brighouse in 1996 that aims to raise aspiration and achievement for young people through innovative learning practices. Stephen is currently undertaking part-time PhD research into the policy area of personalization, under the supervision of Professor Helen Gunter. Prior to his work with the UFA, Stephen was teaching in special education and primary schools in inner-city Birmingham for 20 years, which included spells as a deputy and a head teacher.

Eugenie A. Samier is Senior Lecturer at the British University in Dubai. Her research concentrates on administrative philosophy and theory, interdisciplinary foundations of administration, theories and models of educational leadership, and comparative educational administration. She has frequently been a Guest Researcher at the Humboldt University of Berlin, was Visiting Professor in the Department of Administrative Studies at the University of Tartu, Estonia (2003), and has been a guest lecturer at universities and institutes in Germany, Estonia, Russia, Norway, Lithuania, and Finland. Her publications include 'Demandarinisation in the New Public Management: Examining Changing Administrative Authority from a Weberian Perspective', in *Max Webers Herrschaftssoziologie*.

Studien zu Entstehung und Wirkung, ed. E. Hanke and W. Mommsen (Mohr/Siebeck 2001), 'The Capitalist Ethic and the Spirit of Intellectualism: The Rationalized Administration of Education', in *L'éthique Protestante de Max Weber et L'esprit de la Modernité* (Editions de la Maison des Sciences de l'Homme 1997), and several articles on organizational culture and values, the New Public Management, the role of history and biography in educational administration, the role of humanities, aesthetics, and literary analysis in administration, and Weberian foundations of administrative theory and ethics in *Educational Management & Administration, Journal of Educational Administration, Educational Administration Quarterly, Journal of Educational Administration and History,* and *Halduskultuur.* She is a founding board member of *Halduskultuur* and is editor of *Ethical Foundations for Educational Administration* (Routledge 2003), principal editor (with R. Bates) of *Aesthetic Dimensions of Educational Administration and Leadership* (Routledge 2006), editor of *Political Approaches to Educational Administration and Leadership* (Routledge 2008), and principal editor (with M. Schmidt) of *Emotional Dimensions of Educational Administration and Leadership* (Routledge 2009), with contributions on a broad range of philosophical and theoretical foundations. She is also an associate editor of the four-volume Master Works *Educational Leadership and Administration* (Sage 2009), and contributor (on authority, bureaucracy, and critical theory) to *Encyclopedia of Education Law* (Sage 2008). Her most recent publications include 'The Problem of Passive Evil in Educational Administration: Moral Implications of Doing Nothing' and 'On the Kitschification of Educational Administration: An Aesthetic Critique of Theory and Practice in the Field' (*International Studies in Educational Administration* 2008, 2009).

Michèle Schmidt is Assistant Professor in the Faculty of Education at Simon Fraser University. Her research interests and publications are in the areas of the emotions of teaching and leading, leadership within a context of accountability and classroom assessment, and socio-cultural perspectives of education that focus on the implications of capital on children's school experiences. She received her PhD at OISE/University of Toronto and completed postdoctoral studies at Johns Hopkins University. Previously she was a department head and high school teacher in Ontario. Her most recent publications include 'Portfolio Assessment as a Tool for Promoting Professional Development of School Principals: A South African Perspective' (*Education & Urban Society* 2009); 'Risky Policy Processes: Accountability and School Leadership' in *Political Approaches to Educational Administration and Leadership,* ed. E.A. Samier (Routledge 2008); 'Accountability and the Educational Leader: Where Does Fear Fit In?' in *The Emotional Dimensions of Educational Administration and Leadership,* ed. E.A. Samier and M. Schmidt (Routledge 2009); co-editor of (with E. Samier) *Emotional Dimensions of Educational Administration and Leadership* (Routledge 2009); 'Exit Exams and Organizational Change in a Vocational High School', in *Strong States, Weak Schools: The Dilemmas of Centralized Accountability*, ed. B. Fuller and E. Hannum (Oxford University Press 2008); and is co-editor of an upcoming special issue of the *Journal of Educational Administration* on emotions in professional graduate programmes.

John Smyth is currently Research Professor, School of Education, University of Ballarat, Australia. John is the research leader for a cross-university interdisciplinary research theme around *Addressing Disadvantaged and Inequality in Education and Health*. He is also Emeritus Professor, Flinders University, Australia, Senior Research Fellow Wilf Malcolm Institute of Educational Research, University of Waikato, New Zealand, and Graduate Adjunct Faculty Professor, College of Education, Texas State University-San Marcos. Formerly, he held the Roy F. and Joann Cole Mitte Endowed Chair in School Improvement at Texas State University-San Marcos, Research Professor at Edith Cowan University, and Foundation Chair of Teacher Education and Founding Director of the Flinders Institute for the Study of Teaching, Flinders University. For six years he was the Associate Dean of Research, School of Education, Flinders University. His scholarship has been recognized through a Senior Fulbright Research Scholar Award (1991), one of the rare ones awarded to Education in Australia, and was the first non-American to receive the Palmer O. Johnson Award from the American Educational Research Association (1993) for outstanding published educational research. He is the author and editor of 20 books with international publishers, and has authored over 200 articles and book chapters. Recent books include: *Activist and Socially Critical School and Community Renewal: Social Justice in Exploitative Times* (with L. Angus, B. Down, and P. McInerney, Sense 2009); *Critically Engaged Learning: Connecting to Young Lives* (with L. Angus, B. Down, and P. McInerney, Peter Lang 2008); *Teachers in the Middle: Reclaiming the Wasteland of the Adolescent Years of Schooling* (with P. McInerney, Peter Lang 2007); *'Dropping Out', Drifting Off, Being Excluded: Becoming Somebody Without School* (with R. Hattam et al., Peter Lang 2004); *Critical Politics of Teachers' Work: An Australian Perspective* (Peter Lang 2001); *Teachers' Work in a Globalizing Economy* (with A. Dow et al., Falmer 2000); *Schooling for a Fair Go* (with R. Hattam and M. Lawson, Federation Press 1998); *Remaking Teaching: Ideology, Policy and Practice* (with G. Shacklock, Routledge 1998); and *Being Reflexive: Critical Approaches to Social and Educational Research* (with G. Shacklock, Falmer 1998). His book currently in press (with Down and McInerney, Peter Lang) is *Hanging in with Kids in Tough Times: Engagement in Contexts of Educational Disadvantage in the Relational School*. He is currently a member of the following editorial boards: *British Journal of Sociology of Education, International Journal of Leadership in Education, Teacher Development, London Review of Education,* and *Journal of Learning Communities.* His research interests are in the areas of policy sociology of teachers' work, critical policy analysis, social justice and educational disadvantage, and the policy impact of educational reform on teachers and students.

Charlotte Woods has experience over many years as an educator and educational manager, both in the UK and overseas (Italy, Portugal, and Morocco). Her doctoral research was on emotion in the higher education work-place. The findings underscored the significance of trust in shaping working life and in impacting on mental and physical health. It further highlighted the importance of leadership in establishing and maintaining a positive affective work-place climate. In her current role as Lecturer in Education at the University of Manchester, Charlotte has been exploring leadership in school settings and, since 2002, has acted as researcher and consultant on various projects for the National College for School Leadership. Her principal focus has been the College's nationwide programme of professional development for School Business Managers, investigating its impact on the day-to-day experience of the school work-force in a period of reform.

Index